OXFORD WORLD'S CLASSICS

THREE MAJOR PLAYS

LOPE DE VEGA (1562–1635) was one of the three great dramatists of the most vital political and cultural period in Spanish history, the Golden Age, when Spain ruled much of the western world. Born in Madrid, where he spent most of his life, Lope's passionate and impulsive nature led to his involvement in numerous sexual relationships, even after he took holy orders at the age of 51, and often landed him in serious trouble with the law.

Lope's sexual appetites were equalled only by his energy as a writer. During a literary career of some fifty-five years, he wrote both poetry and prose and, it was claimed, more than 2,000 plays. At a time when the theatre was beginning to flourish in Spain, Lope largely shaped the three-act play, with its exciting action, vivid characterization, and mixture of serious and comic elements, which would be adopted by his contemporaries and successors.

Drawing for his material on history, the Bible, and contemporary life, Lope's theatre had a vitality which thrilled contemporary audiences and made him the most popular dramatist of his day. *Fuente Ovejuna*, *The Knight from Olmedo*, and *Punishment Without Revenge* are three of Lope's greatest plays and exemplify not only the characteristic themes of his drama—love, honour, revenge—but also his consummate artistry.

GWYNNE EDWARDS is Professor of Spanish at the University of Wales, Aberystwyth. He has written critical studies of Lorca and Buñuel, as well as of Spanish theatre and cinema in general. He has also translated more than forty Spanish plays, of which more than twenty have been published and performed professionally.

OXFORD WORLD'S CLASSICS

*For almost 100 years Oxford World's Classics have brought
readers closer to the world's great literature. Now with over 700
titles—from the 4,000-year-old myths of Mesopotamia to the
twentieth century's greatest novels—the series makes available
lesser-known as well as celebrated writing.*

*The pocket-sized hardbacks of the early years contained
introductions by Virginia Woolf, T. S. Eliot, Graham Greene,
and other literary figures which enriched the experience of reading.
Today the series is recognized for its fine scholarship and
reliability in texts that span world literature, drama and poetry,
religion, philosophy and politics. Each edition includes perceptive
commentary and essential background information to meet the
changing needs of readers.*

OXFORD WORLD'S CLASSICS

LOPE DE VEGA

Fuente Ovejuna
The Knight from Olmedo
Punishment Without Revenge

Translated with an Introduction and Notes by
GWYNNE EDWARDS

Oxford   New York
OXFORD UNIVERSITY PRESS
1999

Oxford University Press, Great Clarendon Street, Oxford OX2 6DP

Oxford New York

Athens Auckland Bangkok Bogotá Buenos Aires Calcutta
Cape Town Chennai Dar es Salaam Delhi Florence Hong Kong Istanbul
Karachi Kuala Lumpur Madrid Melbourne Mexico City Mumbai
Nairobi Paris São Paulo Singapore Taipei Tokyo Toronto Warsaw
and associated companies in Berlin Ibadan

Oxford is a registered trade mark of Oxford University Press

British Library Cataloguing in Publication Data

Data available

Library of Congress Cataloging in Publication Data

Vega, Lope de, 1562–1635.
[Plays. English. Selections]
Three major plays / Lope de Vega; translated with an introduction
and notes by Gwynne Edwards.
(Oxford world's classics)
I. Edwards, Gwynne.   II. Vega, Lope de, 1562–1635. Fuente
Ovejuna. English.   III. Vega, Lope de, 1562–1635. Caballero de
Olmedo. English.   IV. Vega, Lope de, 1562–1635. Castigo sin
venganza. English.   V. Title.   VI. Series: Oxford world's classics
(Oxford University Press)
PQ6459.A2   1999   862'.3—dc21   98–26991
ISBN 0-19-283337-5

1 3 5 7 9 10 8 6 4 2

Typeset by Ace Filmsetting Ltd, Frome, Somerset
Printed in Great Britain by
Cox & Wyman Ltd,
Reading, Berkshire

CONTENTS

INTRODUCTION

The Golden Age

The Spanish Golden Age, in which Lope de Vega was one of the brightest jewels, embraced, broadly speaking, the sixteenth and seventeenth centuries, when Spain was, in territorial terms, the most powerful nation in the world. In 1492, with the conquest of Granada, the Catholic Kings, Ferdinand and Isabella, had succeeded in ending the Muslim domination of Spain which had lasted for eight centuries, and in unifying, both in a political and a religious sense, a country which had long been divided. The same year also witnessed, significantly, Columbus's discovery of the Indies, a momentous event which would lead in the years which followed to Spain's conquest and exploitation of the New World. Under Charles I, the grandson of the Catholic Kings who succeeded to the Spanish throne in 1516, Spain's influence in Europe also increased significantly, for in 1519 he was elected Holy Roman Emperor (as Charles V of Austria), which meant that large areas of northern Europe were effectively under Spanish control. He was, in short, the most powerful ruler in Europe, with an empire in the New World which grew larger by the year.[1]

In 1556 Charles, exhausted by his efforts, abdicated in favour of his son Philip II, who ruled Spain almost until the end of the sixteenth century. Less imperialist in outlook than his father, Philip's dream, nevertheless, was to be the sole ruler of a Catholic Europe, as well as to spread the Catholic faith in the New World, regardless of the cruelty and suffering which this might involve. By the end of the sixteenth century, however, the image of a powerful and successful country scarcely concealed the underlying reality of serious and rapid decline, due in no small measure to the economic demands of maintaining a large empire. The wealth imported from the New World, though vast, proved insufficient, and led to inflation in Spain itself. High taxation became crippling, Spanish industry gradually declined,

---

[1] Authoritative studies of the history of the Golden Age include J. H. Elliot, *Imperial Spain, 1469–1716* (London, 1963) and J. Lynch, *Spain under the Hapsburgs*, 2 vols. (Oxford, 1964 and 1969).

and agriculture was seriously affected as countrypeople abandoned the land in the hope of a better life in the towns and cities. When Philip II died in 1598, his prophecy that God had given him many kingdoms but no son fit to rule over them was uncannily accurate.

Philip III (1598–1619) and his successor Philip IV (1619–65) lost little time in handing over power to a succession of powerful royal favourites in order to spend their leisure in often facile amusements. During their reigns Spanish influence in Europe was slowly whittled away, while at home the economic situation reached a stage where devaluation became common, the cost of collecting taxes became greater than the value of the taxes themselves, and neither soldiers serving overseas nor the palace guards at home received their wages. When Philip IV died in 1665 he was replaced by his wife Mariana of Austria, acting as regent until their son, Charles II, came of age. The result of constant inbreeding, he was, however, a sickly individual whose poor health in a way mirrored that of his country. His death in 1700 at the age of 40 marked not only the end of Spain's Golden Age but also the end of the Spanish Habsburg dynasty.

In cultural terms Spain's achievements during the two centuries in question reflect her political and territorial supremacy, though, paradoxically, the greatest triumphs in the arts occurred during the years of Spanish decline. Lope de Vega, born six years after the accession of Philip II, achieved his greatest theatrical successes during the reigns of Philip III and Philip IV, a period which also witnessed the flowering of many other dramatists, and which in that respect was the equal of its English counterpart. These were years which saw too the publication of Cervantes's *Don Quijote*, as well as a string of picaresque novels which would eventually influence English writers such as Fielding, Smollett, and even Dickens. Velázquez (1599–1660), arguably the greatest Spanish painter, was Court painter to Philip IV. It was the age, too, of the greatest works of the Spanish poets Francisco de Quevedo (1580–1645) and Luis de Góngora (1561–1627). In short, at a time when Spain's political and economic fortunes were increasingly shaky, there occurred in the arts an outburst of creative energy the like of which Spain would never experience subsequently.[2]

---

[2] On the cultural achievements of Spain during the sixteenth and seventeenth centuries, see P. E. Russell (ed.), *Spain: A Companion to Spanish Studies* (London, 1973).

Lope de Vega's Life and Work

Lope Félix de Vega Carpio was born in Madrid on 25 November 1562, the son of Felices de Vega Carpio and his wife, Francisca, both from the area around Santander. From his father Lope seems to have inherited an impulsive nature, a combination of erotic and religious tendencies, and a capacity for writing verse, for it is said that he dictated verses before the age of 5 and was writing plays at the age of 12. He received his early education at a Jesuit school in Madrid and later at the University of Alcalá de Henares, near Madrid, where he was a student until about 1582. His impulsive nature is revealed by the fact that at the age of 12 or 13 he ran away from school with a friend, but was eventually caught and sent home. His early twenties also saw the beginning of his involvement in amorous affairs which would greatly complicate his life.[3]

Around 1583 Lope fell passionately in love with Elena Osorio, the daughter of an actor-manager for whom he had agreed to write plays. The relationship lasted until 1587, when Elena began to show her affections for someone else, a betrayal which Lope attempted to avenge by publishing libellous attacks against her and her family. Tried for libel in 1588, he was banished from Madrid for eight years and from Castile for two. Defying the sentence, despite the threat of execution, Lope returned to Madrid in order to elope with Isabel de Urbina Alderete y Cortinas, daughter of the King at Arms, whom he married without her parents' permission before joining his brother on the *San Juan*, a ship which was part of the Spanish Armada bound for England. After his return he lived in Valencia until 1590 when, his banishment from Castile over, he moved to Toledo and then to Alba de Torres, near Salamanca, where he entered the service of the Duke of Alba. After the death of his wife in 1595 he began a series of relationships with various women: an involvement with Antonia Trillo de Armento in 1596 led to his appearance before the courts; in 1598 he married Juana de Guarda, the daughter of a wealthy Madrid butcher; and shortly afterwards he embarked on

---

[3] One of the most detailed accounts of Lope's life and work is that by Karl Vossler, *Lope de Vega y su tiempo* (Madrid, 1940). See too Gerald Brenan, *The Literature of the Spanish People* (Cambridge, 1953), in particular ch. 9.

an extramarital affair with Micaela de Luján, a beautiful and well-known actress whose husband was out of the country. The relationship lasted for some eight years and produced a large number of children.

During these years Lope worked in the service of various noblemen and, when his second wife died in 1613, he became a priest. Despite this, his amorous exploits continued, for two years later he began an affair with Marta de Nevares Santoyo, a married woman living with her husband in Madrid. Lope took her to live with him but she later became blind and insane, dying in 1632. It was one of several tragedies which clouded Lope's last years. In 1634 his 16-year-old daughter, Antonia, ran off with an influential courtier, and in the same year his son Lope was drowned in the Caribbean. Lope himself died one year later, on 27 August 1935.

Lope de Vega's amorous drive was surpassed only by his energy as a writer, for his literary works embraced prose and poetry, as well as drama. A pastoral novel, *Arcadia*, appeared in 1598, while his last work was a prose piece in dialogue form—*La Dorotea*—which drew on his early love affair with Elena Osorio. He also wrote several epic poems and various volumes of shorter poems. But it was, of course, as a dramatist that he was most prolific, the phrase used by Cervantes to describe him—*monstruo de naturaleza* (monster of Nature)—suggesting his amazing productivity. Lope boasted of writing a play a day, and one of his contemporaries, Juan Pérez de Montalbán, claimed after Lope's death that 1,800 secular plays and 400 religious plays had been performed. Modern scholarship points to around 340 extant plays—many have disappeared—which are definitely by Lope. These alone are ten times as many plays as Shakespeare wrote, and as many as all the works of the other Elizabethan and Jacobean dramatists put together.

More than any other dramatist, Lope gave the theatre of the Golden Age its definitive form, paving the way for younger dramatists such as Tirso de Molina and Calderón. Its principal characteristics, demonstrated in the plays and set out in his poetic essay, *The New Art of Writing Plays* (*Arte nuevo de hacer comedias*), consisted of: mixing the comic and the serious; breaking the classical unities of action, time, and place; making the characters speak in an appropriate style; and combining entertainment with a moral purpose. As far as subject matter is concerned, Lope's range was very great indeed.[4] Many of his plays belong to the tradition of the *comedia de capa y espada* (cloak-and-dagger plays): light comedies of love and jealousy in which the characters belong to the lower nobility. Many other amorous comedies, however, fall outside this category, for their characters come from a higher social class, one of the best-known being *The Dog in the Manger* (*El perro del hortelano*) (1613–15), its characters well drawn and its plot cleverly managed. Another fertile source for Lope's imagination was the Bible, which provided him with material for two kinds of play extremely popular at the time: *comedias a lo divino* (religious plays) and *comedias de santo* (plays about saints). An example of the former is *The Beautiful Esther* (*La hermosa Ester*) (1610). History also yielded many powerful stories. From ancient history came *Against Bravery there is no Misfortune* (*Contra valor no hay desdicha*) (1625–30), which dramatizes the rise of Cyrus of Persia, while from more recent Spanish history Lope fashioned plays which had lessons for the present. Such is *The Duke of Viseo* (*El Duque de Viseo*) (1608–9), in which the innocent Duke becomes the victim of a suspicious king, of envy, and of circumstances, the play serving as a warning for those who rule and administer justice. Lope's most famous 'historical' play is, though, *Fuente Ovejuna* (1612–14), its action set in the fifteenth century during the reign of Ferdinand and Isabella. Within this historical context, Lope focuses on the abuses perpetrated upon the inhabitants of the village of Fuente Ovejuna by Fernán Gómez de Guzmán, their overlord and Commander of the Order of Calatrava.

Lope also wrote a number of powerful tragedies, some inspired by historical stories, others based on popular or literary sources. Two of the very best of these—justifying their inclusion here—are *The Knight from Olmedo* (*El caballero de Olmedo*) (1620–5) and *Punishment Without Revenge* (*El castigo sin venganza*) (1631). The former is the story of two young lovers, Inés and Alonso, who foolishly conduct their love affair through the machinations of a cunning go-between, Fabia. *Punishment Without Revenge* is a still darker piece, its action centred on the womanizing Duke of Ferrara, his illegitimate son Federico,

---

[4] For a more detailed survey of the plays, see E. M. Wilson and Duncan Moir, *A Literary History of Spain, the Golden Age: Drama 1492–1700* (London, 1971), Margaret Wilson, *Spanish Drama of the Golden Age* (Oxford and London, 1969), and Melveena McKendrick, *Theatre in Spain 1490–1700* (Cambridge, 1989).

and the Duke's young bride Casandra, who, abandoned by her husband, engages in a fatal affair with her stepson.

Fuente Ovejuna

Fuente Ovejuna was first published in Madrid in 1619 in the *Docena parte de las comedias de Lope de Vega* (volume 12 of his collected plays). As far as the date of composition is concerned, S. Griswold Morley and C. Bruerton have suggested, on the basis of their study of Lope's metres and rhyme schemes, that it was written between 1611 and 1618, and probably between 1612 and 1614.[5]

The action of *Fuente Ovejuna* is set in 1476, roughly 150 years before its composition, and is based to a large extent on historical events. In 1469 Princess Isabella of Castile had married Ferdinand of Aragon, joining the destinies of the two great kingdoms and paving the way for Spain's great achievements in the years ahead, in particular the completion of the Reconquest of Spain from the Muslims and the discovery and conquest of the New World. Although Isabella did not succeed to the throne of Castile until the death of her half-brother, Enrique IV, in 1479, 1476 proved to be an important year in several ways. First, in March of that year the forces of Isabella and Ferdinand defeated in the Battle of Toro the troops of Juana la Beltraneja and her husband, Alfonso of Portugal, claimants to the throne of Castile, and thus consolidated Isabella's position. Secondly, in support of the claims of Juana and Alfonso to the crown of Castile, the 17-year-old Rodrigo Téllez Girón, Grand Master of the Military Order of Calatrava, attacked and seized the town of Ciudad Real, important for its strategic position near the border of Castile. And thirdly, 1476 was the year in which the citizens of Fuente Ovejuna, a town in the province of Cordoba, rebelled against their overlord, Fernán Gómez de Guzmán, a Commander of the Order of Calatrava under the authority of Rodrigo Téllez Girón, killing him in revenge for his cruel and brutal behaviour towards them. When the incident was subsequently investigated by an emissary of the royal authorities, and the villagers were interrogated and even tortured in an attempt to discover the guilty

---

[5] S. Griswold Morley and C. Bruerton, *Cronología de las Comedias de Lope de Vega* (Madrid, 1968), 330–1.

parties, the only response proved to be a communal one: 'Fuente Ovejuna killed him'. Consequently, no individual guilt could be established and no one was punished.

Various sources have been suggested for the play: in particular, Francisco de Rades y Andrada's *Chrónica de las tres Ordenes y Cavallerías de Santiago, Calatrava y Alcántara*, published in Toledo in 1572, and two works by Sebastián de Covarrubias Horozco: the *Emblemas morales* of 1610, and the *Tesoro de la lengua castellana* of 1611. In the *Emblemas morales* Covarrubias described the confusion of the judge sent to investigate the incident at Fuente Ovejuna when he is confronted by the solidarity of the inhabitants. In the *Tesoro de la lengua castellana* he provided a more detailed account of the villagers' rebellion against their overlord, drew attention to the latter's alleged offences against his vassals, and explained the origin of the subsequently popular phrase 'Fuente Ovejuna lo hizo' ('Fuente Ovejuna did it'). Nevertheless, the information provided by Covarrubias is relatively limited in comparison with the detailed account presented by Francisco de Rades y Andrada in the *Chrónica*, and there can be no doubt that this became the principal source of Lope's play.[6]

In general, Lope followed Rades's *Chrónica* quite closely, but also introduced significant changes. One of the most important concerns the attack on Ciudad Real by Rodrigo Téllez Girón. In the *Chrónica* he is persuaded to seize the town by his cousin and his brother, but in the play it is Fernán Gómez who urges him to do so. Fernán Gómez is thus presented as an even greater villain, for he is responsible both for the atrocities against the citizens of Fuente Ovejuna and for an act of treachery against the Catholic Kings. The play's main plot—the events of Fuente Ovejuna—has a local significance which, through the events of the sub-plot—the attack on Ciudad Real—acquires a much more national, political dimension, underlining the fact that it is in part a play about the abuse of political power. Writing it between 1612 and 1614, when Spain was ruled by Philip III, Lope knew that power was effectively in the hands of a royal favourite, the Duke of Lerma. Lope's play is thus a comment

---

[6] On the sources, see J. B. Hall, *Lope de Vega, Fuente Ovejuna, Critical Guides to Spanish Texts* (London, 1985), 11–19, and Victor Dixon, *Lope de Vega, Fuente Ovejuna* (Warminster, 1989), 2–4, 218–23.

on contemporary events, a lesson both for kings and their ministers. In contrast to the essentially weak Philip III, the Catholic Kings are presented as model rulers, eager to bring peace and justice to a previously unruly Castile. When they are informed of wrongs and injustices, they send their representatives to investigate and seek the truth, and, in consequence of the findings, act fairly and justly. Moreover, they inspire a loyalty in most of their subjects which is emphasized throughout the play. In this respect Lope's idealization of the Catholic Kings is little different from his presentation of royal figures in other plays in which the stability of society is an important theme, nor indeed is it very different from the treatment of kings in some of the plays of Shakespeare. In order to draw attention to his political theme, Lope had no reservations about distorting historical truth, in accordance with the Aristotelian doctrine that fiction is superior to history. The fact that *Fuente Ovejuna* depicts the triumph of the oppressed over an evil overlord should not, however, be taken to signal Lope's approval of revolution. Rather, he shared the desire of his contemporaries for the continuity of established social structures, ending the play, therefore, not with the victory of the citizens but with the restitution of order by the Catholic Kings.[7]

The moral dimension embodied in the evil behaviour of Fernán Gómez towards essentially good peasants lies too at the heart of another of the play's principal themes: the contrast between court and country. Praise of the countryside and condemnation of city life—a preoccupation of Classical authors such as Horace—later found expression in European writers of the Renaissance, and in Spain, for example, in Antonio de Guevara's influential *Menosprecio de corte y alabanza de aldea* (*Contempt for the Court and Praise of the Village*) of 1539. Praise of country life was based in part on aspects of the countryside—freedom, fresh air, cheap and wholesome food and drink—which were not to be found in the city or at Court. But equal, if not more, importance was attached to the moral superiority of country people, who were thought to lack the cunning and deviousness of those who lived in cities. As presented by Guevara and others, such a view was clearly both an idealization and an over-

---

[7] See R. D. F. Pring-Mill's introduction to *Lope de Vega, Five Plays*, translated by Jill Booty (New York, 1961), pp. xxiii–xxvi.

simplification of country life, and so it is, to some extent, in many of
Lope de Vega's plays. On the other hand, there are in *Fuente Ovejuna*
village girls who are far less virtuous than Laurencia, the principal
female character, and who are persuaded by the Commander's promises.[8] Again, even if the traditional immorality of the city and the
Court is embodied in Fernán Gómez, Lope's presentation of the
Catholic Kings suggests that the Court is also a place where virtue
and justice may be found. Lope's treatment of the court–country
theme is, therefore, rather more complex than was the case with
many other writers of his time.

Another theme, central to *Fuente Ovejuna* and extremely popular in
the drama of the Golden Age, is that of honour.[9] In the strictest sense,
honour meant the respect and esteem accorded to a man who was
virtuous, worthy, or of noble standing, and had been an important
concept in Spain from Visigothic times. An individual could lose the
respect and esteem of others, and thus be dishonoured, in a variety of
ways: by being called a liar; by having his face slapped; by having his
beard pulled; or by the sexual misdemeanours or the violation of his
wife or daughter. The dishonoured man, according to medieval law,
was socially dead until his honour was restored, and this could be
achieved either by legal means, thus avoiding bloodshed, or by killing
the offender of one's honour. Indeed, the obligation to avenge a dishonour done to another member of one's family was fully recognized
by the law. Similarly, the law allowed for the killing of one's unfaith-
ful wife and her lover, even in cases where adultery was suspected
rather than proven. If the dishonour was a public one it required a
public vengeance, if private, the vengeance should be concealed. Furthermore, there existed from medieval times the belief that honour
was the prerogative of the nobility, and that commoners therefore
were without honour, a prejudice which survived into the Golden Age
but which by the late sixteenth century began to change somewhat as
the more sensitive Spanish intellectuals began to recognize that all
men merit respect. Honour, therefore, began to be associated more
with nobility of spirit than with noble birth.

---

[8] See Hall, *Fuente Ovejuna*, 81.

[9] On the question of honour, see Margaret Wilson, *Spanish Drama of the Golden
Age*, 43–8; and Julian Pitt-Rivers, 'Honour and Social Status', in J. G. Peristiany (ed.),
Honour and Shame: The Values of Mediterranean Society (London, 1965).

In *Fuente Ovejuna* the concept of honour as something which stems from noble birth, and which has little to do with virtue, is exemplified above all in Fernán Gómez, for he believes that his social position allows him to indulge his every whim at the expense of others, and fails to acknowledge that it carries with it certain obligations to those in his charge. He does not, of course, consider that the peasants possess honour and that his violation of the village women and his abduction of Laurencia therefore dishonours them. The play suggests, too, that those who have prospered in life and put behind them their lowly origins are also entitled to respect and esteem, as in the case of Laurencia's father, Esteban, who has risen to a position of authority and power in the village. But above all, Lope advances in many of the characters the concept of honour as moral virtue. It is embodied in the Catholic Kings, as well as in many of the villagers. Frondoso shows great respect for Laurencia and her father, his honest love a complete contrast to Fernán Gómez's lust. And Laurencia herself, abducted by the latter's men, reveals herself to be a woman of principle and integrity, not least in her efforts to inspire the villagers to take revenge upon their unscrupulous overlord.

A fourth theme, closely linked to some of the play's other concerns, is that of love, which in turn leads to harmony.[10] The relationship between Laurencia and Frondoso is one form of it, but love exists too in the respect and loyalty of the villagers towards each other, as well as in their feelings towards their country and its rulers, the Catholic Kings. The love of the people is in turn reciprocated by Fernando and Isabel (Ferdinand and Isabella), for they feel a strong obligation to the subjects they rule and to the general well-being of the country. The harmony which exists between Laurencia and Frondoso is thus seen to exist on a broader front in consequence of people's love and mutual respect, and this in turn reflects a divinely created universe distinguished by the love of God.

Fernán Gómez is the very opposite of selflessness, for he is always motivated by self-love and, far from creating harmony, his influence is constantly disruptive of the lives of Laurencia and Frondoso, as well as of the villagers' lives in general. His treachery towards the Catholic Kings, embodied in the Ciudad Real episode

[10] See Hall, *Fuente Ovejuna*, 91–3.

and stemming from his own self-interest, also threatens national and political harmony, for it disrupts the attempts of Fernando and Isabel to bring peace, justice, and order to Castile. In the sense that man and his world is a microcosm of a divinely ordered universe, Fernán Gómez is also an embodiment of the evil which constantly threatens to disrupt that order. Only with the death of the Commander and the final judgement of the Catholic Kings are order and harmony restored on every level.

A particularly striking feature of the play is the diversity and liveliness of its characters.[11] From the outset Fernán Gómez is portrayed as a man who, in order to satisfy his desires, rides roughshod over everyone. The ruthlessness of his political ambitions is seen to be paralleled by his lust for the young women of Fuente Ovejuna which, when frustrated, turns to violence. He does not hesitate to take revenge on those who thwart his attempts to take advantage of their women or to have them abducted, as in Laurencia's case. In his relationships with noblemen, servants, and villagers alike, Fernán Gómez is seen to be the very embodiment of arrogance, impatience, and cruelty: in short, a monster who has no redeeming virtues but who, in his excesses, is the very stuff of drama.

Of the villagers, Laurencia is particularly striking. Spirited in her relationship with Frondoso, her true integrity and independence of spirit emerge after her escape from the Commander, when she confronts the men of the village and urges them to take action against him. Her great speech is one in which, however outraged she may feel, her arguments are carefully marshalled for maximum effect, revealing her to be a woman of intelligence as well as courage. She is indeed a true match for the villainous Commander, and in every respect one of the most memorable and heroic female characters in Golden Age theatre.

Frondoso is in some ways a kindred spirit: like her an opponent of Fernán Gómez and, in his selfless love for Laurencia, his complete opposite. Indeed, it is this selfless love which underpins his defiance of the Commander, for, despite the risks involved, he is less concerned with his own safety than with Laurencia's. Nevertheless, unlike Fernán Gómez he is always in control of his passions, and his behaviour, whether in relation to Laurencia's father, the

---

[11] See Dixon, *Fuente Ovejuna*, 13.

Commander, or the Catholic Kings, is invariably governed by a sense of what is correct.

The other villagers are also vividly drawn. Mengo is the *gracioso*, the typical comic character in Golden Age plays who has his origins in the quick-witted servants of Roman and, later, Italian comedy, but his moments of bravery make him more than just the village funny-man. Pascuala, resisting Fernán Gómez, defending Frondoso, and joining in the rebellion, is Laurencia in a minor key. Barrildo, arguing that ideal love is entirely spiritual, is an unusually intelligent peasant. Esteban, Laurencia's father, is a man to be admired: a loving father and, as a magistrate, a defender of his fellow citizens against Fernán Gómez's abuses. In short, although Lope places great emphasis on Fuente Ovejuna as a community—'Fuente Ovejuna did it'—the peasant characters are sharply differentiated from one another and presented as individuals in their own right.

Apart from Fernán Gómez, the nobility is represented by Rodrigo Téllez Girón. Because he is young and inexperienced, he is easily manipulated by the much more worldly Commander, notably in relation to the attack on Ciudad Real. His impulsive youthfulness is revealed too when, on learning of Fernán Gómez's murder, he vows to raze Fuente Ovejuna to the ground. But he also has good qualities: brave in battle and ultimately loyal to the Catholic Kings, towards whom he has acted treacherously and misguidedly. The latter are, of course, idealized figures, but they too have their touches of individuality, especially in their love and respect for each other.

The Knight from Olmedo

The Knight from Olmedo was written sometime between 1620 and 1625, probably around 1620, but the first edition did not appear until some twenty years later, when it was included in Volume 24 of Lope's plays, published in 1641 in Zaragoza.[12] At the time of composition Lope was almost 60, and the play was therefore the work of a man who had enjoyed considerable experience of life, as well as of writing for the theatre.

One possible source was a real event which occurred in 1521, involving the murder of a certain Don Juan de Vivero on the road

---

[12] See Francisco Rico (ed.), *Lope de Vega, El caballero de Olmedo* (Madrid, 1981), 84–7.

between the towns of Medina and Olmedo by Don Miguel Ruiz, also from Olmedo, and three of his men. This event may have given rise to a popular ballad which described the murder of 'the knight from Olmedo', and this in turn became the inspiration for the various forms of the story which followed.[13] Against this, it has been suggested that the song which in Act Three of Lope's play is sung by a peasant ('For at night they killed | That noble soul, | The jewel of Medina, | The flower of Olmedo'), appeared for the first time in print in an anonymous play called *The Knight from Olmedo*, published in 1606.[14] An even more likely source for Lope's play was, however, another anonymous play, the *Dance of the Knight from Olmedo* (*Baile del Caballero de Olmedo*), which appeared in print in 1617 in Volume 7 of Lope's plays and was attributed to him, though there is no clear evidence that he wrote it. The 'dance' (*baile*) was in fact a kind of interlude, consisting of a mixture of dance, song, and spoken word which, in the early seventeenth century, was introduced between the acts of full-length plays in order to provide the audience with additional entertainment. The play in question contains many details which find an echo in Lope's third Act.[15] And finally, he was undoubtedly influenced, in particular in Acts One and Two, by Fernando de Rojas's *La Celestina*, first published in 1499 and one of the truly great and influential works in the whole of Spanish literature. The story of the young couple, Calisto and Melibea, whose love-affair is placed in the hands of the cunning go-between Celestina, and which ends tragically, has many clear points of contact with Lope's play.

Lope called *The Knight from Olmedo* a *tragicomedia*, yet from beginning to end, and despite its many comic moments, the play is characterized by an underlying darkness, as well as by a deep tragic irony.[16] In the popular ballad which the peasant sings in Act Three, there is, for example, an ambiguity—the brightest jewel of Olmedo meets his end in darkest night—which exists throughout the play in the form of the love–death contrast. This was, of course, a common-

---

[13] The historical background is discussed in detail by Rico, ibid. 36–42.

[14] See J. W. Sage, *Lope de Vega, El caballero de Olmedo, Critical Guides to Spanish Texts* (London, 1974), 16.

[15] On the *Dance of the Knight from Olmedo*, see ibid. 20–1, and Rico, *El caballero de Olmedo*, 45–51.

[16] Ibid. 18–35.

place in the poetry of the Golden Age, as it was indeed in European poetry in general, but in *The Knight from Olmedo* Lope develops the theme in a way which makes it central to the play's meaning. When, for example, Alonso first describes the beauty of Inés (1.63–150), he observes, in relation to some of her admirers, that her eyes 'spared many lives' but, in the case of others, inflicted 'the mortal wound'. As far as he is concerned, her love for him gives him life, notably when he is with her, while his absences from her deprive him of true life and constitute a living death. What is more, there is a very strong suggestion from the very beginning that the love of Alonso and Inés is inevitable, predestined, determined by the stars. In his opening speech Alonso wonders if between him and Inés there is a 'correspondence which is mutual' (1.16), while at the end of Act Two Tello has no doubts on the matter: 'We all | Know love is written in one's star!' (2.699–700). In short, the themes of love and death are also linked to the theme of fate, and what on one level may seem to be a commonplace in the literature of the period, begins to take on a deeper meaning as the action of the play unfolds.

The fateful outcome is, of course, already announced in the play's title, *The Knight from Olmedo*, which, for Lope and his contemporaries—as well as for anyone familiar with Spanish literature—is inevitably associated with the murder of the hero by his enemies on the road to his home town. References in the text to *La Celestina* would also have indicated to an audience of the time that Alonso's fate would be that of the tragic Calisto. And if this were not enough, Alonso compares himself at the beginning of Act Two to Leander, who each day swam the Hellespont to see his beloved Hero (2.25–30), and who, as any educated audience would know, drowned while doing so. Similarly, Alonso is described by Fabia in terms of Hector, Achilles, and Adonis, classical heroes who all suffered a premature death. And so, in this context, the love–death–fate triangle, prominent already in the early part of the play, gradually assumes a deeper and darker significance, as well as a grim irony, as the action unfolds. In Act Three, prior to his murder, Alonso comes to Inés's window as if he 'had no life' (3.263). In the poem which he recites to Inés before his departure, he observes: 'I am convinced I am to die' (3.305); 'I go, then, to my death . . .' (3.331); 'How can I not be dead when I arrive?' (3.335). Furthermore, the irony in Alonso's words is to be found too in the comments of his deadly rival, Rodrigo.

In Act One he complains to Inés of her coldness towards him: 'I pray that either Love|Or Death provide me with a remedy|For your disdain' (1.377–80), adding, a few lines later: 'If you'll not be|My life, then be my death!' (1.391–2). He is, of course, oblivious to the fact that in the end his feelings of rejection and his hatred of Alonso will, in fact, bring about his death. The love-triangle of Inés, Alonso, and Rodrigo is thus imbued with a linguistic irony whose tragic resonance becomes increasingly clear as the three characters are engulfed by events.

It is also worth noting that, although *The Knight from Olmedo* lacks the grim and horrific character of the final act of *Punishment Without Revenge*, it nevertheless satisfies many of the requirements of tragedy set out by Aristotle and inherited by the Renaissance. Spanish Golden Age theorists, such as Alonso López Pinciano in his *Philosophía antigua poética* (*Ancient Poetic Philosophy*) of 1596, and Francisco Cascales in his *Tablas poéticas* (*Poetic Manual*) of 1617, favoured *tragedia patética*, the kind of tragedy which moves the spectator through the spectacle of human suffering, and in this context considered that the tragic hero should be neither wholly good nor wholly bad but a mixture of the two, a rounded character whose good qualities will arouse admiration and whose downfall will therefore awaken a sense of pity.[17] Moreover, that downfall should come about not as the result of a deliberate error on his or her part, but as the consequence of some involuntary act or acts, which will in turn deepen feelings of pity and compassion and in which such outside influences as fortune or chance may play their part. In *The Knight from Olmedo*, Alonso is clearly such a character.

As far as good qualities are concerned, Alonso is a young man distinguished by his good looks, nobility of character, honest love for Inés, filial concerns, and, in particular, his bravery—the latter most evident in the bullfight. Indeed, he is acclaimed by everyone, including the King, and is fully worthy of our admiration. Against this, his attraction to Inés seems to blind him to the imprudence of conducting his relationship with her in secret, and equally to the folly of employing a go-between, who has a reputation for witch-craft, to further that relationship—though this mistake on his part

---

[17] See Gwynne Edwards, *The Prison and the Labyrinth, Studies in Calderonian Tragedy* (Cardiff, 1978), pp. xvii–xviii.

seems attributable less to a dishonest intention than to the force of his passion and a certain lack of foresight. Again, though brave, he seems to be over-conscious of his good name and reputation, and it is a fear of possibly being branded a coward which leads him to ignore all the warnings against venturing forth on the road to Olmedo, and which therefore leads to his death. In short, the spectacle of an essentially good man destroyed by flaws in his character which are in no way evil and a combination of circumstances—his falling in love with Inés, which in turn fires the hatred of Rodrigo—allows us to feel for him that deep sense of pity demanded by tragedy. The same is largely true of Inés, for she is an essentially good and beautiful young woman, yet such is the strength of her feelings for Alonso and her dislike of Rodrigo, that she engages in a duplicity which, though understandable in the circumstances, ultimately contributes to Alonso's death and her own empty future. Lope concluded the play with the words: 'So ends the tragic history of | *The Knight from Olmedo*' (3.759–60), a clear enough indication of how he intended his play to be regarded.

Another much-discussed aspect of the play concerns the time in which it is set: the reign of Juan II of Castile in the first half of the fifteenth century. As far as history is concerned, the period from 1420 to 1445 was one in which Juan II constantly faced the threat of attack from the Infante Enrique of Aragon and King Juan II of Navarre, and in which Castilian nobles began to support either Juan II of Castile or his enemies. Throughout this period Medina, one of the two focal points of the play, was often visited by the Castilian King and became a centre of support for him, while Olmedo became associated with support for the Infante of Aragon and the King of Navarre. The outcome of this rivalry proved to be the first Battle of Olmedo, which took place in 1445 on the plains between Olmedo and Medina.

In *The Knight from Olmedo* Lope emphasizes the fact that Alonso's presence distinguished the marriage celebrations of Juan II of Castile (1.688–700), which points, perhaps, to the fact that Alonso, unlike most people from Olmedo, was a supporter of the Castilian King. Indeed, in the course of the play Alonso travels from Olmedo to Medina specifically in order to pay homage to him, as the Constable indicates: 'He comes to | The fiesta, I believe, intent | On serving you' (2.604–6). And the King, in turn, thinks highly of Alonso's

loyalty, bravery, and sense of honour. It has been suggested, therefore, that Lope clearly wished to establish a link between Alonso
and the King in terms of those particular qualities.[18] The argument
has also been advanced that the envy and jealousy of Rodrigo towards Alonso, the principal source of which is the latter's love for
Inés, are further fanned by the very fact that Alonso comes from
Olmedo, which was traditionally hostile to Juan II of Castile. In
these circumstances it would be particularly galling for Rodrigo to
discover that Alonso has not only stolen the affections of Inés, but
has also been favoured and honoured by the King. In short, Lope
has placed the traditional story of a knight from Olmedo murdered
by an enemy from Medina in the context of the historical rivalry
between the two towns, accounts of which he would have found in
various chronicles of the time. Although the historical background
to the play is neither as extensive nor as crucially important as that
of *Fuente Ovejuna*, it nevertheless serves to link the various elements
of the plot, as well as to highlight particular themes—honour, loyalty to the King, political divisions—which were just as relevant to
the Spain in which Lope lived.

As far as characterization is concerned, Alonso is to some extent
a stereotype—the traditional lover, noble, dashing, good-looking,
and courageous. On the other hand, Lope constantly fills out the
stereotype with touches which make him a truly interesting character. He is, despite the attributes outlined above, somewhat unworldly:
an aspect of his character which explains why he employs Fabia, a
woman of the world, to conduct his love-affair, and which also, in a
sense, leads him to ignore the warnings he receives about proceed-
ing on the journey to Olmedo, for he rather naively believes that
Rodrigo will do him no harm. Again, it seems quite possible that the
shadowy figure who appears to him as he sets out for Olmedo, as
well as the Peasant who later sings the ominous song, are not so
much figures of flesh and blood as projections of his own fearful
imagination, already evident in the dream which he has at the end of
Act Two. In this context, his refusal to listen to the warning could
be seen to be an attempt to still the voice of his own fears, and
therefore a pointer to the complexity of his character.

Of the other major characters, Fabia is the most memorable. In

---

[18] J. W. Sage, *El caballero de Olmedo*, 35–40, 90–105.

many ways she is like Fernando de Rojas's Celestina: a go-between delivering messages for lovers and arranging their meetings; a sharp and cunning individual, well-known for her activities; an old woman who, no longer active herself in matters of love, takes delight in the relationships of others. On the other hand, although there are in the play various references to Fabia's spells and belief in her magical powers, she is a far less sinister character than Celestina. She is 'mischievous rather than devilish', and, as the episode involving the extraction of the tooth from the corpse of a highwayman suggests in Act One, the episodes involving her are often intended to be more comic than sinister.[19] Indeed, one of the most striking aspects of *The Knight from Olmedo* is the way in which the tragic tone of its final act are preceded in Acts One and Two by events which are markedly comic, and which largely derive from Fabia's scheming.

Tello, Alonso's servant, is, for the most part the traditional *gracioso*. Thus, in the incident involving the dead man's tooth he displays the cowardice associated with such a character and which is calculated to amuse the audience. He is also, in the same vein, materialistic. He is, however, like Mengo in *Fuente Ovejuna*, rather different from the traditional *gracioso*, for he is able to see things rather more clearly than his master and often advises him of the risks and hazards which accompany his affair with Inés—not so much from a moral point of view, but so that his master might negotiate those dangers in a more practical way. To this extent he can be seen as a foil to his less pragmatic master.

Rodrigo too is in some respects a stereotype: the traditional rejected lover cast into despair. But in this case his feelings go much deeper and are transformed in the course of the play's action into desperation, hatred of Alonso, and a growing resolve to murder him. This said, it can be argued that Rodrigo is not so much a cold-blooded villain as a man driven by his passions and overwhelmed by events over which he has no control. He can do nothing to oblige Inés to love him; he cannot prevent her from falling in love with Alonso; he finds himself in a situation in which he owes his life to his rival and in which, as a result of his heroism, Alonso also finds favour with the King. To this extent, Rodrigo is a victim of circumstance as well as a prisoner of his passions, and cannot but invite a

[19] Ibid. 53.

certain sympathy. The fact that he murders Alonso in the way he does—treacherously, with the assistance of accomplices—is in one sense a condemnation of his character, but it illustrates too the degree of desperation which has transformed a man of nobility into someone who is out of control. In a way, the tragedy which occurs is as much his as Alonso's.

The other characters have fairly standard roles, but the play as a whole points to the fact that, as in *Fuente Ovejuna*, Lope was fully capable of putting on stage characters who are not only lively and credible but who also, in many cases, have considerable depth.

Punishment Without Revenge

Punishment Without Revenge, as the autograph manuscript proves, was written in 1631 and is therefore one of Lope de Vega's late and truly mature plays. First published in Barcelona in 1634 in the form of a *suelta* (a single play), it appeared in 1635, the year of his death, in Volume 21 of his works. In a prologue to the 1634 edition Lope states that the play received only one performance. He does not specify the date nor give the reason for its withdrawal, but it is generally agreed that it was probably staged in the middle of May 1632, by the company of Manuel Vallejo, the latter also playing the part of the Duke. As for its withdrawal, several reasons have been suggested, in particular the possibility that in 1632 the subject matter proved offensive to a Spanish audience. It was an age, after all, in which standards of propriety were—at least officially—very vigorously enforced, and in which decorum on the stage was strictly observed. A play in which a newly married woman has a sexual relationship with her stepson must clearly have been somewhat sensational, though against this it has to be noted that in May 1632 a licence for the first performance had been granted by the censor Pedro Vargas de Machuca. Another possible reason for the play's suppression is that its subject matter was regarded as reflecting, albeit implicitly, on the actions of royal personages. In this respect the King himself, Philip IV, was not unlike Lope de Vega's Duke in seeking the company of women of ill-repute. Furthermore, the relationship in the play between Casandra, the Duke's wife, and his son Federico was not unlike that between Prince Carlos, son of Philip II, and Isabel, who became Philip's wife and Carlos's stepmother. Even though these events—the subject of Schiller's play, *Don Carlos* and Verdi's opera of the same name—belonged to the past, they were still sufficiently recent to have been a cause of possible embarrassment to the royal family. In this context it should also be borne in mind that, even if the action of the play is located in Italy, the actors would have worn contemporary Spanish costumes, which would have given the subject a decidedly Spanish flavour and resonance.[20]

The plot of *Punishment Without Revenge* derives, directly or indirectly, from a *novella* by the Italian writer Matteo Bandello (1485–1561) entitled *How Niccolò III, Marquis of Este, having found his son in an adulterous liaison with his stepmother, had them both beheaded on the same day in Ferrara*. A French version of Bandello's story had appeared in 1567 in *Histoires tragiques* by Bouistau and Belleforest, which in 1603 was published in a Spanish translation: *Historias trágicas exemplares de Pedro Bouistan y Francisco de Belleforest*, a book which Lope may well have read.[21] There may, of course, have been additional literary sources, and it is equally possible that Lope may have seen a dramatic performance of the story by one of the Italian theatre companies which during his lifetime often performed in Madrid.

Whatever Lope's source, he clearly followed the broad outline of the story but also introduced important changes. Apart from giving the characters names which are essentially Spanish—Bandello's Ugo became Federico, his stepmother Casandra (she is simply the Marchioness in the original story)—and elevating the Marquis to the status of Duke of Ferrara, Lope's innovations were intended to create more dramatic and theatrical situations. In Bandello, for example, Ugo and the Marchioness know each other before she resolves to seduce him in order to take revenge on her wayward husband. In Lope's Act One they meet suddenly, before the Duke's marriage, and also without knowing one another's identity—Federico rescues her when her carriage becomes stuck in a ford—and are immediately attracted to each other: a case of 'love at first sight'. There is thus an instinctive mutual attraction between the two young people

---

[20] On the single performance of the play and possible reasons for its suppression, see C. A. Jones (ed.), *Lope de Vega, El castigo sin venganza* (Oxford, 1966), 2–5.

[21] The version of the Bandello story in *Historias trágicas* is included in C. F. A. van Dam (ed.), *Lope de Vega, El castigo sin venganza* (Gronigen, 1928).

which is not present in the source, and which, when in Act Two Casandra has been abandoned by the Duke, makes her relationship with Federico much more than an act of revenge. Again, the Duke's absence from home at this vital juncture occurs in different circumstances, for here he is not called away for reasons of business but summoned by the Pope to assist him in the war against his enemies—a vital change which anticipates the Duke's return in Act Three as a reformed character, resolved to abandon his former way of life and to prove himself a good husband. Given his change of heart, the discovery of his wife's infidelity is the more ironic, and it is also brought about in the play in a more striking way—not through a servant but by the receipt of an anonymous note. And what happens subsequently is very different from the source material. There the Marquis has the young couple arrested, and they are executed after the Court has been made aware of their crime. In Lope's play the Duke secretly verifies their guilt and, having done so, incites Federico to murder an 'enemy' who is held prisoner in the next room and whose face is concealed. The enemy, unknown to Federico, is Casandra, and when the murder has been carried out the Duke summons his courtiers, accusing Federico of having killed Casandra because she is pregnant with the Duke's child and because he, being illegitimate, fears the loss of his inheritance. Federico is immediately seized and killed, therefore, without the incestuous relationship becoming public knowledge, and consequently without the Duke's honour and reputation being publicly damaged. To himself the Duke justifies the action not in terms of honour avenged but as a divine punishment which he, given his religious conversion, has been called upon to administer.

The punishment–revenge issue—its importance encapsulated in the play's title—is one which requires close consideration. Indeed, Lope himself seems to have hesitated over what to call his play, and to have made up his mind only when he had finished writing it. It has been suggested, for example, that the title is unsatisfactory because the punishment imposed on Casandra and Federico by the Duke is not without a strong element of personal revenge on his part.[22] On the other hand, it has been pointed out that Casandra and Federico deserve to be punished for the sin they have committed,

[22] See C. F. A. van Dam (ed.), *Lope de Vega, El castigo sin venganza* (Madrid, 1968), 20.

and to that extent the Duke's argument that he is acting as God's representative on earth is justified.[23] Accordingly, the title of the play points not to human revenge but to divine punishment, though it is perfectly true that the Duke's soliloquies are not devoid of 'thoughts of private vengeance and the laws of honour'.[24] The latter, demanding that an offence against one's honour and reputation be avenged, required too that, if the offence became public knowledge, the vengeance should be a public one, and that, if the offence remained secret, the vengeance should also be secret, thereby avoiding public disgrace. Indeed, no sooner has the Duke claimed that his actions will be a divine punishment than he refers specifically to the kind of revenge which honour demanded. In bringing about the deaths of Casandra and Federico in the way he does—a truly cunning and Machiavellian deception in both cases—the Duke effectively prevents their incestuous relationship and his own dishonour from becoming public knowledge, avenges the offence against himself, and at the same time leads the public at large to believe that the offence for which Federico dies is purely his murder of an innocent Casandra. In short, he is unable to separate punishment from revenge in spite of his attempts to do so. The argument has therefore been put forward that Lope's title was forced upon him by the contemporary Spanish concern with honour. Attracted by the Bandello story, Lope could not present the Duke's actions against the erring couple simply as a punishment—which is the case in the original—for their behaviour offends not merely against public morality but also against his personal honour. On the other hand, Lope did not wish the Duke's actions to be seen merely as a private revenge for lost honour when larger moral questions were involved. The title points to his concern with both issues.[25]

Another aspect of the play which requires comment is Lope's designation of it as a tragedy on the first page of the autograph manuscript. In the light of this, the question has often been asked:

[23] See E. M. Wilson 'Cuando Lope quiere, quiere', in *Cuadernos Hispanoamericanos*, 161–2 (1963), 265–98, repr. in *Spanish and English Literature of the 16th and 17th Centuries* (Cambridge, 1980), 155–83.

[24] Ibid. 180.

[25] See Jones, *El castigo sin venganza*, 12–13; T. E. May, 'Lope de Vega's *El castigo sin venganza*: The Idolatory of the Duke of Ferrara', *Bulletin of Hispanic Studies*, 37: 3 (1960), 154–82.

who is the tragic hero or heroine? One suggestion is that Casandra deserves to be regarded as such, for it is she who, slighted by the Duke, becomes entangled in a powerful but illicit relationship which brings upon her the most terrible consequences.[26] A different view is that the Duke should be regarded as the tragic protagonist, for all the events of the play stem from his actions and, although he does not die, he is left at the end with his life in ruins.[27] Against this, it can be argued that Lope's conception of tragedy did not, perhaps, demand a single tragic hero or heroine, and that the tragedy of the play consists of the situation itself, 'in which all the main characters are implicated, and in which all share in both guilt and loss, whether the loss be of life or of what makes life worth while'.[28]

This view of the play, with its emphasis on guilt, suggests, of course, that the play's tragic outcome stems purely from the moral defects and wrongdoing of its principal characters. Thus, the Duke is a libertine who, unwilling to put up with an arranged marriage to Casandra, shamelessly neglects her and quickly returns to his former way of life. She, upset by his callous treatment of her, seeks revenge on him and compensation for herself in an affair with her stepson Federico, while he, the illegitimate child of one of his father's innumerable escapades, and cast into deep depression by the thought that the marriage will deprive him of his inheritance, is not sufficiently strong-willed to reject his stepmother's advances. When the Duke learns of the incestuous affair he devises the cunning plan to punish the guilty couple for their crime and simultaneously avenge his honour, and in so doing is motivated in no small measure by an awareness of his own contribution to all that has happened. Thus, all the events of the play, each dependent on the other, are seen to involve selfish and imprudent motives. This is not, though, the only way of considering Lope's tragedy, for a closer examination will reveal that various factors outside the control of the characters— other people, social pressures, chance events —also play an important and even crucial part in the shaping of events.

[26] See C. F. A. van Dam, *Lope de Vega, El castigo sin venganza*, both editions.
[27] See A. A. Parker, *The Approach to the Spanish Drama of the Golden Age* (London, 1957), 15–16. A revised version, 'The Spanish Drama of the Golden Age: A Method of Analysis and Interpretation', appeared in Eric Bentley (ed.), *The Great Playwrights: Twenty-five Plays with Commentaries by Critics and Scholars* (New York, 1970), 697–707.
[28] Jones, *El castigo sin venganza*, 16–17.

It cannot be denied that to a considerable degree each of the major characters' lives is influenced by other people to the point where their own choices count for little. The Duke, having sought to avoid marriage, is forced into it by his subjects, who will not accept the illegitimate Federico as his heir. Entrapment in a marriage he does not want intensifies his resolve to return to his old ways and, in turn, creates a set of circumstances whose repercussions cannot be avoided. Again, on a social level the Duke cannot escape the demands of the honour code once his honour has been offended. As for Federico, he is from the outset unable to escape the consequences of his illegitimate status, for he is rejected by the Duke's subjects as heir to his possessions, and feels intensely the bitterness attendant on his possible disinheritance. Later he seems powerless to escape Casandra's hold upon him, and when their affair becomes known to the Duke, he is trapped by the implacable demands of honour and vengeance. Casandra is the pawn both of her father and her husband, pressurized by the former into a marriage she does not want and, as a wife, cast aside by a man who prefers women of the streets. In the affair with Federico she then becomes the prisoner of her own powerful emotions, and finally, like Federico, the victim of honour's tyranny. By the end of the play the three principal characters are manipulated by forces and pressures stronger than themselves.

Circumstance is another important shaping factor in their lives. When Casandra and Federico first meet —when her carriage becomes stuck in the ford—they do so in total ignorance of each other's identity, which means that their attraction to each other is spontaneous and uninhibited by those constraints which a knowledge of their true relationship would impose upon them. First impressions are indeed powerful. Again, the Duke's unexpected departure from home comes at the crucial moment when Casandra, though offended by the Duke's neglect of her, has so far succeeded in containing her feelings for her stepson. The Duke's sudden absence literally throws the young couple into each other's arms and pushes them further along the path which leads to their tragic destiny.

In short, the argument which suggests that the outcome of Lope's tragedy is determined by the moral defects and wrongdoing of the principal characters is a very narrow one, and can be countered, or at least modified, by an approach to the play which emphasizes other factors outside the control of those characters. They may indeed have to make moral choices, but to make the right choice in the circumstances in which they find themselves would be a course of action better suited to saints than ordinary human beings. It is the interplay of individual motives and external events which therefore makes *Punishment Without Revenge* the great and complex play that it is, for the tragic pattern which it reveals is in many ways that of Greek and Shakespearean tragedy.[29]

It is clear from what has been said already that in this play Lope created his most rounded and fascinating characters. The Duke, Casandra, and Federico develop and change in the light of the circumstances in which they find themselves. Their complexity is self-evident, and it is no accident that there should be so many soliloquies, for at such moments characters reveal their most private thoughts. By the time Lope wrote this play—he was 69—his experience of life and of love was considerable, and it shows.

[29] For a more detailed analysis of the play from this point of view, see Gwynne Edwards, 'Lope and Calderón: The Tragic Pattern of *El castigo sin venganza*', *Bulletin of the Comediantes*, 33: 2 (1981), 107–20.

THE STAGING OF
GOLDEN AGE PLAYS

All three plays presented in this volume were written for and performed in the public theatres or *corrales* which developed in Spain,
particularly in Madrid, in the last quarter of the sixteenth century.[1]
These were, as the word suggests, large rectangular courtyards in
which the stage, with its projecting apron, was placed at one end.
For economic reasons the staging of plays was relatively simple, and
such great emphasis was placed on quick-moving action that complex scene-changes would have been impossible. Much was left,
therefore, to the imagination of the audience.

These factors result, in *Fuente Ovejuna*, for example, in a seam-
less, almost cinematic flow of action, a new scene beginning where
the previous one ends without any interruption; the fact that the
location has moved from, say, the village to the house of Fernán
Gómez, or to the Court of the Catholic Kings, is indicated only by
the appearance on stage of the relevant characters. Sometimes the
location of a scene is pinpointed as well in the dialogue, as in Act
One of *The Knight from Olmedo* when Rodrigo and Fernando keep
watch on Inés's house: 'Why come here merely to see the house?'
(1.514). Again, the fact that in Act Three Alonso travels to Olmedo
not long before dawn is suggested by the text: 'How dark it is! So
full|Of fearful shadows till the dawn|Begins to place its golden
feet|On bright and flowered carpets' (3.461–4). In this context it is,
of course, important to remember that, in the absence of stage-
lighting, the performances of plays in the *corrales* took place during
daytime. Audiences were therefore required to imagine that the
stage-action in a particular scene was set at night, and were clearly
attuned to doing so.

Although use could be made of the balconies and windows of the
buildings immediately behind the stage of the *corrales*, the three

---

[1] The most detailed studies of the physical characteristics of the Spanish stage, as
well as of its development during the Golden Age, are those by H. A. Rennert, *The
Spanish Stage in the Time of Lope de Vega* (New York, 1909; 2nd edn. 1963), and N. D.
Shergold, *A History of the Spanish Stage from Medieval Times until the End of the
Seventeenth Century* (Oxford, 1967).

plays translated here suggest that only the main stage was used for their performance. This said, there are several occasions when the curtained 'discovery space' at the back of the stage might have been used. At the end of Act One of *Fuente Ovejuna*, for example, Frondoso could have hidden there from the Commander, as could Frondoso and Laurencia in Act Two when her father and uncle approach. In the final act of *Punishment Without Revenge*, the Duke may have hidden there to listen to the conversation of Federico and Casandra, and later in the act it was probably the place where '*The bodies are revealed*' (3.978), the curtains being dramatically pulled back to reveal the bloodstained corpses.

Stage furniture, like scenery, was reduced to a minimum. In *Fuente Ovejuna* it seems likely that the only furniture required would have been benches on which the villagers would sit at the beginning of Act Two and for the council meeting in Act Three, and more impressive chairs for the Catholic Kings in the scenes at Court. Much more importance, however, would have been given to the visual and symbolic impact of costumes. The Commander's red cross, embroidered on his doublet, would have been a vivid visual reminder of the Order to which he belongs and of the ideals he fails to put into practice. The Master would also have been richly dressed, and the Catholic Kings, of course, would have worn costumes appropriate to their station and intended to impress a contemporary audience. The peasants, by contrast, would have worn simple costumes, reflecting their way of life, except for the wedding at the end of Act Two. At the beginning of *Punishment Without Revenge* the Duke appears 'disguised' (1.89), undoubtedly dressed in dark clothes which are not merely suited to the late hour at which he is consorting with prostitutes, but are also a symbolic pointer to the darker side of his nature. In Act Three, by contrast, he is '*handsomely dressed as a soldier*' (3.255), his military uniform a visual image of his role on the battlefield as the 'mighty lion of the Church' and also of the victory which he claims to have won over his baser instincts. In *The Knight from Olmedo* the dark clothing worn by Alonso when he visits Inés at night in Act One, and by Rodrigo when he watches her house, are traditional enough, but also point, in Alonso's case, to the less-than-innocent nature of his behaviour, and in Rodrigo's, to the dangerous character of his jealousy. And in Act Two, when Fabia enters '*with a rosary and walking-stick and wearing spectacles*' (2.451) and Tello '*wearing a scholar's cap*' (2.491), the effect may be comic, but their costumes also suggest the disparity between what the two individuals are and what they are pretending to be.

In Golden Age theatre music also played a significant part. During the interval between the acts of plays musical interludes were often introduced, but the plays themselves also contained music of different kinds. In Act One of *Fuente Ovejuna* the peasants sing a song of welcome to the Commander (1.405–19); in Act Two they have two songs in celebration of the wedding of Laurencia and Frondoso (2.509–16, 546–69); and in Act Three, after the Commander's death, their song expresses their loyalty to the Catholic Kings and wishes them a long life. In each case, music is used in order to celebrate love and harmony and, to that extent, is an earthly image of that perfect harmony which characterizes a divinely inspired universe.[2] *The Knight from Olmedo* has fewer songs, but all are important, in particular the doom-laden song sung by the peasant in Act Three (3.473–6, 484–9). In *Punishment Without Revenge* the Duke alludes in Act One to music as a remedy for melancholy (1.184). Towards the end of the act music would undoubtedly have accompanied the arrival of Casandra at the Duke's estate when the party enters '*with pomp and splendour*' (1.809). Its suggestion of the harmony which ought to accompany their marriage is, of course, ironically at odds with the private feelings of the individuals concerned.

[2] See Victor Dixon, *Lope de Vega, Fuente Ovejuna* (Warminster, 1989), 29–30.

TRANSLATOR'S NOTE

Spanish Golden Age drama is written almost entirely in verse. Unlike their Elizabethan counterparts, Lope de Vega and his contemporaries favoured an octosyllabic line, in part because it allowed for lightness and speed and enabled the play to unfold with the pace which restless and easily bored Spanish audiences demanded. In addition, all the Spanish playwrights, following Lope's example, employed a variety of stanza forms, which ranged from three to ten lines and which were characterized by complex rhyme schemes, or else by a pattern of assonance in the last word of alternate lines which was easily achieved in Spanish and which also had a rhyming effect. English translators of Spanish plays have frequently abandoned both the octosyllabic line and rhyme in the belief that unrhymed iambic pentameter is more suited to English or British actors, but this only creates further problems. In general, Spanish words are longer than their English equivalents, which means that in translation there would be more English than Spanish words in a line of eight syllables, and more again in a line of ten syllables. To opt for the latter invariably means that the translator has to introduce unecessary extra words.

In the plays printed here I have of course attempted to convey the meaning of the original Spanish, but they are not 'literal' translations and there will, inevitably, be some small differences. As far as line-length is concerned, I have opted in the main for an octosyllabic line in an attempt to preserve the quick pace of Lope's original, though there are too a number of lines of ten syllables. In general, absolute consistency in the number of syllables seems less important than a sense of flow and rhythm. Furthermore, I have avoided any attempt to reproduce the rhyming patterns of the original, since to try to do that would lead in English to distortion of the syntax and a clumsiness which is at odds with the musicality of the Spanish. My policy has been to use occasional rhyme both at the end of lines and within lines, but in a way which allows the verse to flow naturally. Above all, because the plays of the Golden Age were written in verse and employed rhyme, they have a sense of discipline and style. It is important in translation that that sense of style—of verse which is musical and pleasing on the lips of an actor and the ears of an audience—be preserved. This, in the end, has been my main concern.

In the case of *Fuente Ovejuna*, my translation is based on the Spanish text published in Madrid in 1619 in the *Dozena Parte de las Comedias de Lope de Vega Carpio*, of which there is a copy in the British Library (1072.i.12). A modern edition is *Lope de Vega: Fuente Ovejuna*, ed. and trans. Victor Dixon (Warminster, 1989). For the translation of *The Knight from Olmedo*, I have followed the Spanish text published in 1641 in Zaragoza in the *Veintiquatro Parte Perfecta de las Comedias del Fénix de España, Frey Lope Félix de Vega Carpio*, of which there is a copy in the Biblioteca Nacional, Madrid (R. 13875). A good modern edition is *El caballero de Olmedo*, ed. Francisco Rico (Madrid, 1981). *Punishment Without Revenge* is based on the autograph manuscript of the play dated 1 August 1631 and now in the Ticknor Library in Boston. A modern edition is *El castigo sin venganza*, ed. C. A. Jones (Oxford, 1966).

SELECT BIBLIOGRAPHY

General Studies on Lope de Vega

Castro, A. and Rennert, H. A., *Vida de Lope de Vega (1562–1635)* (Salamanca, 1969).

McKendrick, Melveena, *Theatre in Spain 1490–1700* (Cambridge, 1989). See chapter 4.

Rennert, H. A., *The Life of Lope de Vega (1562–1635)* (Glasgow, 1904).
—— *The Spanish Stage in the Time of Lope de Vega* (New York, 1909).

Shergold, N. D., *A History of the Spanish Stage from Medieval Times until the End of the Seventeenth Century* (Oxford, 1967). See chapters 7 and 8.

Vossler, K., *Lope de Vega y su tiempo* (Madrid, 1940).

Wilson, E. M. and Moir, D., *A Literary History of Spain, the Golden Age: Drama 1492–1700* (London, 1971). See chapter 3.

Wilson, Margaret, *Spanish Drama of the Golden Age* (Oxford and London, 1969). See chapters 4 and 5.

Studies of Fuente Ovejuna

Anibal, C. E., 'The Historical Elements of Lope de Vega's *Fuente Ovejuna*', *Publications of the Modern Language Association of America*, 49 (1934), 657–718.

Carter, Robin, '*Fuente Ovejuna* and Tyranny: Some Problems of Linking Drama with Political Theory', *Forum for Modern Language Studies*, 13 (1977), 313–35.

Darst, David H., 'The Awareness of Higher Authority in *Fuente Ovejuna*', *Oelschläger Festschrift*, Estudios de Hispanófila, 36 (Chapel Hill, NC, 1976), 143–9.

Dixon, Victor, *Lope de Vega, Fuente Ovejuna* (Warminster, 1989).

Gerli, E. Michael, 'The Hunt of Love: The Literalization of a Metaphor in *Fuente Ovejuna*', *Neophilologus*, 63 (1979), 54–8.

Hall, J. B., *Lope de Vega, Fuente Ovejuna, Critical Guides to Spanish Texts* (London, 1985).
—— 'Theme and Structure in Lope's *Fuente Ovejuna*', *Forum for Modern Language Studies*, 10 (1974), 57–66.

Herrero, Javier, 'The New Monarchy: A Structural Reinterpretation of *Fuente Ovejuna*', *Revista Hispánica Moderna*, 36 (1970–1), 173–85.

Larson, Donald R., *The Honor Plays of Lope de Vega* (Cambridge, Mass., 1977).

McCrary, William C., '*Fuente Ovejuna*: Its Platonic Vision and Execution', *Studies in Philology*, 58 (1961), 179–92.

Moir, Duncan W., 'Lope de Vega's *Fuente Ovejuna* and the *Emblemas morales* of Sebastián de Covarrubias Horozco . . .', in *Homenaje a William L. Fichter*, ed. A. David Kossof and José Amor y Vázquez (Madrid, 1971), 537–46.

Pring-Mill, R. D. F., 'Sententiousness in *Fuente Ovejuna*', *Tulane Drama Review*, 7 (1962), 5–37.

Ribbans, G. W., 'The Meaning and Structure of Lope's *Fuente Ovejuna*', *Bulletin of Hispanic Studies*, 30 (1953), 150–70.

Studies of The Knight from Olmedo

Brownstein, Leonard A., 'Comedy in *El Caballero de Olmedo*', in *Perspectivas de la comedia*, 2 (Valencia–Chapel Hill, 1979), 27–37.

Casa, Frank P., 'The Dramatic Unity of *El caballero de Olmedo*', *Neophilologus*, 50 (1966), 234–43.

Gerard, A. S., 'Baroque Unity and the Dualities of *El caballero de Olmedo*', *The Romanic Review*, 56 (1965), 92–106.

Hesse, Everet W., 'The Role of the Mind in Lope's *El caballero de Olmedo*', *Symposium*, 19 (1965), 58–66.

Jones, Sonia, 'The Tragedy of Passion: Lope's *El caballero de Olmedo*', *Reflexion*, 3–4 (1974–5), 138–45.

King, Lloyd, 'The Darkest Justice of Death in Lope's *El caballero de Olmedo*', *Forum for Modern Language Studies*, 5 (1969), 388–94.

King, Villard F., '*El caballero de Olmedo: Poetic Justice or Destiny*', in *Homenaje a William L. Fichter*, ed. A. David Kossoff and José Amor y Vázquez (Madrid, 1971), 367–79.

McCrary, C., *The Goldfinch and the Hawk: A Study of Lope de Vega's Tragedy, El caballero de Olmedo* (Chapel Hill, 1966).

McGaha, Michael, 'The Structure of *El caballero de Olmedo*', *Hispania*, 61 (1978), 451–8.

Powers, Harriet B., 'Unity in *El caballero de Olmedo*', *Bulletin of the Comediantes*, 27 (1974), 52–9.

Schafer, Alice E., 'Fate versus Responsibility in Lope's *El caballero de Olmedo*', *Revista canadiense de estudios hispánicos*, 3 (1972), 26–39.

Soons, Alan, 'Towards an Interpretation of *El caballero de Olmedo*', *Romanische Forschungen*, 73 (1961), 160–8.

Turner, Alison, 'The Dramatic Function of Imagery and Symbolism in *Peribáñez* and *El caballero de Olmedo*', *Symposium*, 20 (1966), 174–85.

Wardropper, Bruce W., 'The Criticism of the Spanish Comedia: *El caballero de Olmedo* as Object Lesson', *Philological Quarterly*, 51 (1972), 177–96.

Wilson, Edward M., 'The Exemplary Nature of *El caballero de Olmedo*', in *Spanish and English Literature of the 16th and 17th Centuries* (Cambridge, 1980), 184–200.

Yates, Donald A., 'The Poetry of the Fantastic in *El caballero de Olmedo*', *Hispania*, 43 (1960), 503–7.

Studies of Punishment Without Revenge

Bianco, F. J., 'Lope de Vega's *El castigo sin venganza* and Free Will', *Kentucky Romance Quarterly*, 26 (1979), 461–8.

Dixon, Victor, '*El castigo sin venganza*: The Artistry of Lope de Vega', in *Studies in Spanish Literature of the Golden Age Presented to Edward M. Wilson*, ed. R. O. Jones (London, 1973), 63–81.

—— and Parker, A. A., 'Two Lines, Two Interpretations', *Modern Language Notes*, 85 (1970), 157–66.

Edwards, Gwynne, 'Lope and Calderón: The Tragic Pattern of *El castigo sin venganza*', *Bulletin of the Comediantes*, 33: 2 (1981), 107–20.

Evans, W. P., 'Character and Context in *El castigo sin venganza*', *Modern Language Review*, 74 (1979), 321–34.

May, T. E., 'Lope de Vega's *El castigo sin venganza: The Idolatry of the Duke of Ferrara*', *Bulletin of Hispanic Studies*, 37 (1960), 154–82.

Morris, C. B., 'Lope de Vega's *El castigo sin venganza* and Poetic Tradition', *Bulletin of Hispanic Studies*, 40 (1963), 69–78.

Pring-Mill, D. F., Introduction to *Lope de Vega: Five Plays*, trans. Jill Booty (New York, 1961).

Wade, Gerald E., 'Lope de Vega's *El castigo sin venganza*: Its Composition and Presentation', *Kentucky Romance Quarterly*, 23 (1976), 357–64.

Wilson, E. M., 'Cuando Lope quiere, quiere', in *Spanish and English Literature of the 16th and 17th Centuries* (Cambridge, 1980), 155–83.

Further Reading in Oxford World's Classics

Luís Vaz de Camões, *The Lusiads*, trans. and ed. Landeg White.

Miguel de Cervantes, *Don Quixote de la Mancha*, trans. Charles Jarvis, ed. E. C. Riley.

—— *Exemplary Stories*, trans. and ed. Lesley Lipson.

CHRONOLOGY OF
LOPE DE VEGA'S LIFE

1562   Lope Félix de Vega Carpio born 25 November in Madrid.

1577   A student at the University of Alcalá de Henares.

1581? Birth of Tirso de Molina, another major Golden Age dramatist.

1582   Leaves Alcalá de Henares.

1583   Begins a five-year affair with Elena Osorio, daughter of an actor-manager.

1588   Banished from Madrid for eight years and from Castile for two years as a result of libellous attacks on Elena Osorio and her family. Marries Isabel de Urbina by proxy. Sails with the Armada in the attack on England and is one of the few survivors.

1595   Death of Isabel de Urbina.

1596   Relationship with Antonia Trillo de Armento leads to prosecution.

1598   Lope marries Juana de Guarda, daughter of a Madrid butcher. Extra-marital affair with Micaela de Luján, wife of an actor. Death of Philip II, succeeded by his son, Philip III.

1600   Birth in Madrid of Calderón de la Barca, one of the great Golden Age dramatists.

1605   Lope's *Peribáñez* possibly written in this year. Part I of Cervantes's *Don Quijote*.

1609   Publication in Madrid of Lope's poetic essay, *The New Art of Writing Plays*.

1612? Lope's *Fuente Ovejuna*.

1613   Death of Juana de Guarda. Lope becomes a priest. Writes *The Dog in the Manger*. Cervantes's *Exemplary Novels* published.

1615   Extra-marital affair with Marta de Nevares Santoyo. Publication of Part II of Cervantes's *Don Quijote*.

1616   Death of Cervantes.

1620   Possible date for Lope's *The King is the Best Judge* and *The Knight from Olmedo*.

1621   Death of Philip III, succeeded by Philip IV.

1630   Publication of Tirso de Molina's Don Juan play, *The Trickster of Seville*.

1631   Writes *Punishment Without Revenge*.

1632   Death of Marta de Nevares Santoyo.

1634   Lope's daughter, Antonia, elopes with a courtier, and his son, Lope, is drowned in the Caribbean.

1635   Lope dies in Madrid on 27 August, aged 72.

FUENTE OVEJUNA

THE CHARACTERS OF THE PLAY

Fernán Gómez, the Grand Commander of Calatrava
{ Ortuño
{ Flores, his servants
The Master of Calatrava, Rodrigo Téllez Girón
{ Pascuala
{ Laurencia, peasant-women
{ Mengo
{ Barrildo
{ Frondoso, peasants
Juan Rojo, alderman, Laurencia's uncle
Esteban, magistrate, Laurencia's father
Alonso, magistrate
King Fernando of Aragón
Queen Isabel of Castile
Manrique, Master of Santiago
An Alderman*
Cimbranos, a soldier
Jacinta, a peasant-woman
Boy
Peasants
A Judge
Musicians

ACT ONE*

Enter the COMMANDER, *with his servants* FLORES *and* ORTUÑO.

COMMANDER. Doesn't the Master* know I'm here?

FLORES. He does.

ORTUÑO.   Now that he's older, he's much
More high and mighty.

COMMANDER.   But he surely knows
That I am Fernán Gómez de Guzmán?

FLORES. He's still a boy. It's not surprising.   5

COMMANDER. But if not my name, my rank of Grand
Commander.*

ORTUÑO.   There are those who advise
Him not to show respect.

COMMANDER.   Then he'll not
Win much affection. Respect's the key
To men's good will; discourtesy merely   10
Makes enemies.

ORTUÑO.   If such men knew
How everyone detests them and longs
To see them grovel, they'd sooner die.

FLORES. Such people are so hard to take!
Such surliness and lack of manners.   15
Amongst equals it's pure folly;
Towards inferiors sheer tyranny.
But you shouldn't take it to heart, sir.
He's still too young to know what it means
To be loved by others.

COMMANDER.   The day   20
The sword was placed around his waist,

The cross of Calatrava* on
His breast, it should have been enough
To teach him due respect.

FLORES.   You'll soon know
If they've turned him against you.

ORTUÑO.   Look   25
This way. Find out for yourself.

COMMANDER.   Let's hear
What he has to say.

The MASTER *enters with his attendants.*

MASTER. Forgive me, Fernán Gómez de Guzmán!
I've only just been told
Of your arrival.

COMMANDER.   I have good reason to   30
Complain. My love and background led
Me to expect much more respect
From you, Master of Calatrava,
Towards your most obedient servant and
Commander.

MASTER.   I was expecting the warmest   35
Of welcomes, Fernando.* Let me
Embrace you.

COMMANDER.   You are right to honour me.
How often have I risked my life
On your account, before the Pope
Acknowledged you had come of age!   40

MASTER. Of course! And I swear by the cross
Displayed on your breast and mine
That I am grateful, and honour you
As much as my own father.

COMMANDER.   Then I
Am happy.

MASTER.   What news of the war?   45

COMMANDER. Hear my account and you shall learn
    Where your duty lies.

MASTER.   Proceed, then. I
    Am listening.

COMMANDER.   Rodrigo Téllez
    Girón, Master of Calatrava,
    You owe your high position to   50
    Your brave and famous father.* When you
    Were only eight, he stepped
    Aside, granting you his great authority,
    Which was then ratified by kings
    And great commanders too, as well   55
    As papal bulls, first from Pius,* then
    From Paul,* but on condition that Juan
    Pacheco, Master of Santiago, shared
    Your rule. Now that he's dead and you,
    Though still so young, govern alone,   60
    Do not forget that you are duty bound
    To carry out the wishes of
    Your family. They insist that, after
    The death of King Henry the Fourth,*
    His subjects swear allegiance to   65
    Alonso King of Portugal,
    Who, through his wife and consort, Juana,*
    The child of Henry, rightly claims
    Castile. And though Fernando,* Prince
    Of Aragon, contests that claim,   70
    And seeks the kingdom for his wife,
    And Henry's sister, Isabel,*
    Your family favours Juana, at present in
    Your cousin's power, denying that
    Her claims are false. So I am here   75
    To urge you call upon the Knights
    Of Calatrava, assemble them in
    Almagro, and take Ciudad Real,*
    A town that, placed between Castile
    And Andalusia, faces both.   80
    We'll not need many men. The soldiers who

Protect it are its own inhabitants,
Together with some minor nobles,
Who both defend the name of Isabel
And call Fernando their king. 85
You would do well, Rodrigo, to astonish those
Who think you are too young and that
Great Cross too much for you to bear.
Remember your ancestors,
The Counts of Urueña,* and take 90
As your example their great deeds.
Villena's Marquesses* as well,
And other captains too whose feats
The wings of Fame can scarcely bear.
Take your sword, so far unstained 95
By blood, and turn it red as the Cross
Upon your breast. How else can I
Address you as Master of the Cross
If the one is red and not the other?
Let both of them be crimson, and you, 100
Worthy Girón, crown the immortal temple of
Your famous ancestors.

MASTER.   Fernán Gómez,
You may be sure that in this conflict I
Support my family, for their cause
Is just. If you want proof, you'll see 105
Me march upon Ciudad Real,
And like a bolt from heaven, destroy
Its walls. My uncle may be dead,
But no one should assume, because
I'm still so young, that with his death 110
My courage vanished too. I'll take
My sword and make the brightness of
Its blade the colour of this Cross,
Bathed in blood. From where you govern, can
You provide some soldiers?

COMMANDER.   Not many; 115
In fact my vassals. But if they are obliged,
They'll fight as fiercely as lions.

In Fuente Ovejuna* they
Are humble people, more used to fields
And ploughshares than battles.

MASTER.   Is that   120
Where you live?

COMMANDER.   In times as dangerous
As these, it's where I chose to live. Summon
Your men. No one shall remain behind.

MASTER. You shall see me ride out, my lance
At the ready.   125

They exit* and PASCUALA *and* LAURENCIA *enter.*

LAURENCIA. Let's hope he never comes back!

PASCUALA.   Well, I'm damned!
I thought you'd be broken-hearted at
The news.

LAURENCIA. Heaven forbid! I'd rather not
See him again in Fuente Ovejuna!

PASCUALA. Believe me, Laurencia, I've seen others   130
As fierce as you, some fiercer still,
And underneath a heart as soft
As butter.

LAURENCIA. Have you seen an oak
As dry and hard as myself?

PASCUALA.   Oh, get
Away with you! No one should say   135
'I'll never drink that water!'

LAURENCIA.   Well I
Shan't, though others may say differently.
What good would it do me to fall
For Fernando? Do you think he'd marry me?

PASCUALA. No.

LAURENCIA.   Then I'll have nothing to do   140

With him. How many girls in our village
Have put their trust in the Commander,
And seen their reputation shot
To pieces?

PASCUALA. I'll be amazed if you
Escape his clutches.

LAURENCIA.   You shouldn't believe   145
Everything you see. He's chased me for
A month, Pascuala, and still got nowhere.
Flores, his pimp, and that scoundrel, Ortuño,
They showed me a bodice, a necklace, and
A bonnet, and said so many things   150
About their master, Fernando,
They frightened me really, but they won't
Persuade me.

PASCUALA.   So where did this take place?

LAURENCIA. There by the stream.* Six days ago.

PASCUALA. Well, I fancy they'll change your mind,   155
Laurencia.

LAURENCIA. What, me?

PASCUALA.   I don't mean the priest,
Now do I?

LAURENCIA. I'm a young bird, true, but far
Too tough for his holiness. Believe me,
Pascuala, for breakfast I'd much
Rather have a nice slice of bacon,   160
With a piece of bread from a loaf
I've baked myself, and pinch a glass
Of wine from my mother's jar. At noon
I'd rather see beef and cabbage
Dancing to a merry, bubbling tune,*   165
And when I'm tired from travelling,
A slice of bacon wedded to
An aubergine. Then later on,
While supper's cooking, a bunch of grapes

(God protect the vines from hailstones!),   170
And, when it's ready, a tasty fry
Of chopped-up meat with oil and peppers.
And so at last happily to bed,
To say my prayers, including 'lead
Me not into temptation!' I much   175
Prefer all this to the tricks and lies
Of rogues with all their talk and promises
Of love. Their only aim's to leave
Us in the lurch. They take us to bed
For their pleasure; when morning comes,   180
It's 'Goodbye, treasure!'

PASQUALA.   Quite right, Laurencia.
When they stop loving, men are more
Ungrateful than the sparrows. In winter,
When the fields are frozen, they come down
From the rooftops—'chirp, chirp'—and eat   185
The crumbs from your kitchen table.
But once the cold of winter's passed,
And they see the fields grow green at last,
It's not 'chirp, chirp' any longer; more
'Twerp, twerp',* from the safety of the rooftops,   190
All the farmer's kindness quite forgotten.
Such are men! Whenever they need us, we
Are their lives, their entire being;
Because of us their life has meaning.
But once their fire starts to cool,   195
They act just like those sparrows.* Never again
Will you hear 'sweetheart'! Suddenly,
You become just a tart!

LAURENCIA.   Never trust
A man!

PASQUALA. Oh, I agree, Laurencia!

Enter MENGO, BARRILDO, *and* FRONDOSO.

FRONDOSO. Your argument's ridiculous,   200
Barrildo.

BARRILDO. At least there's someone here
  Who'll settle it.

MENGO.   Before you ask,
  Let's come to an agreement. If they
  Decide I'm right you both pay up
  The prize for winning.

BARRILDO.   Fair enough.   205
  But if you lose, you'll give us something.

MENGO. You can have this fiddle.* It's worth
  A granary, and to me much more
  Than that.

BARRILDO.   Agreed then.

FRONDOSO.   Let's do it!
  God be with you, lovely ladies!   210

LAURENCIA. Since when, Frondoso, do you call us ladies?

FRONDOSO. We are followers of fashion.
  Nowadays your schoolboy's called a graduate,
  Your blind as a bat, myopic;
  Your cross-eyed man has just a squint,   215
  And your totally lame's arthritic.
  The couldn't-care-less are upright chaps,
  The stupid are called clever;
  A pig of a man's described as bold,
  And a big mouth an entertainer.   220
  A beady eye is said to be sharp,
  Argumentative people try hard;
  A silly ass is amusing,
  And a chatterbox is a card.
  A common upstart, oh, he's brave,   225
  A coward lacks initiative;
  Your hothead, well, he's really dashing,
  And your dolt is someone well worth knowing.
  If you're off your head, you're free as air,
  If down in the dumps, just full of care;   230
  If you're bald, you have authority,

If you're stupid, oh, so very witty.
Big feet are the sign of a solid man,
The pox is only a runny nose,
Arrogance is but reserve,   235
And a hunchback wears bad-fitting clothes.
This is why, you see, I call you ladies.
I shan't say more or I might go on
Forever.

LAURENCIA. That's city talk* when they want
To be polite. But take my word   240
For it, they use a different style
When they insult you.

FRONDOSO.   How exactly?

LAURENCIA. Everything's just the opposite.
They call a serious man a bore,
You speak your mind and you are rash;   245
A thoughtful person's melancholic,
You criticize, and you are brash.
You give advice, it's pure cheek,
Be generous, you stick your nose in;
If you are just, you're seen as cruel,   250
Show mercy and you're just a weakling.
Be constant and they call you boring,
Polite and you're a flatterer;
Be kind and you're a hypocrite,
A Christian's someone seeking favour.   255
If you've got talent, that's just lucky,
You tell the truth, that's impudence;
Put up with things and you're a coward,
When things go wrong, it's your come-uppance.
A modest woman is a fool,   260
Pretty but chaste, she's into seduction;
If she's virtuous, she's . . . no, no,
That's it, end of demonstration!

MENGO. I swear you are a little devil.

BARRILDO. In the name of God, that wasn't bad!   265

MENGO. You must have been christened with something
   Much saltier than water.*

LAURENCIA.   Anyway,
   What were you arguing about?

FRONDOSO. I'll tell you.

LAURENCIA.   Right.

FRONDOSO.   Pay attention.

LAURENCIA. You have it, for nothing. I'm all ears.   270

FRONDOSO. I put my faith in your judgement.

LAURENCIA. So what's the argument?

FRONDOSO.   It's me
   And Barrildo against Mengo.

LAURENCIA.   About what?

BARRILDO. Something that, though obviously true, he
   Denies.

MENGO. Only because I know I'm right.   275

LAURENCIA. So what's he say?

BARRILDO.   That love does not
   Exist.

LAURENCIA. That's very sweeping.

BARRILDO.   As well
   As stupid. If love did not exist,
   Neither would this world of ours.

MENGO. I'm no philosopher and, more's   280
   The pity, I can't read. But if
   The elements are always in
   A state of war, and our bodies—blood,
   Phlegm, melancholy, choler*—draw
   Their sustenance from them—where   285
   Is love?

BARRILDO. In this world and the next,
My friend, there's perfect harmony.*
And harmony is love, since love's
Harmonious.

MENGO.   Oh, I don't deny
That love is natural and has   290
Great power. It governs everything,
And everything we see it keeps
In balance. Nor have I ever said
That love does not exist in every man,
According to his humour, and that's   295
What helps him to survive. If someone aims
A punch at me, my hand protects
My face. If danger comes, my feet
Will help me to escape it; if something
Approaches my eyes, my lids close sharpish.   300
That's natural love.

PASCUALA.   So what's the point
You want to make?

MENGO.   That we love ourselves
And no one else.

PASCUALA.   Excuse me, Mengo,
But that's plain daft. The proof lies in
The fact that men and women love   305
Each other passionately, as does
An animal its mate.

MENGO.   That's still
Self-love, not love. Tell me what love is.

LAURENCIA. A desire for beauty.

MENGO.   And why
Does love desire it?

LAURENCIA.   To enjoy it.   310

MENGO. Right. And doesn't it want that pleasure for
Itself?

LAURENCIA. Well, yes.

MENGO.   In other words, because
It loves itself, it seeks enjoyment for
Itself?

LAURENCIA. I suppose so.

MENGO.   Well, there you have it.
Self-love's the only kind of love.   315
I seek it just for my own pleasure.
I'm the object of the whole endeavour.

BARRILDO. But I remember the village priest
Once talked in his sermon about
A certain Plato* and what he said   320
On love, which was that we should love
Only the soul and virtue of
The one we love.

PASCUALA.   Such topics frazzle
The brains of wise professors in
Our colleges and great academies.   325

LAURENCIA. She's right. So don't get tangled up
Yourself, supporting their idiocies.
Be thankful, Mengo, you weren't made
To love.

MENGO.   So who do you love?

LAURENCIA.   Only
My honour.

FRONDOSO.   Then may God punish you   330
And make you jealous!

BARRILDO.   So who's the winner?

PASCUALA. You'd best go to the sacristan.
He or the priest are bound to have
An answer. As for the two of us,
Laurencia's not in love and I've   335
Got no experience. We can't judge.

FRONDOSO. Her coldness is my answer!

Enter FLORES.

FLORES. May God be with you, good people!

PASCUALA. It's the Commander's lackey.

LAURENCIA. Such a fine falcon!* So where have you come   340
    From, friend?

FLORES.   Can't you tell by my uniform?

LAURENCIA. Is Don Fernando here as well?

FLORES. The battle's finished. It's cost us friends
    And no little blood.

FRONDOSO.   So give us an account
    Of it.

FLORES. Who better if my eyes   345
    Were witness to it all? In order to
    Prepare for that campaign against the town,
    Ciudad Real, the gallant Master chose
    From all his valiant followers
    Two thousand infantry, supported by   350
    Three hundred men on horseback, secular
    And clerical—for if they wear
    The Cross upon their breast, they are
    Obliged, though they be friars,* to take
    Up arms against the Moorish infidel.   355
    The young man was a splendid sight,
    His doublet green with gold embroidery,
    Revealing at the sleeves armlets held
    In place by six bright fastenings.
    He sat astride a mighty stallion,   360
    In colour dapple-grey, which drank
    From the Guadalquivir* and grazed
    Upon the fertile pasture of its banks.
    Its tail was bound by strips of leather,
    Its mane adorned by bows that in   365
    Their whiteness matched the dappled pattern of

Its skin. And at the Master's side
Fernán Gómez, your overlord, upon
A strong and honey-coloured steed,
Its hooves black, its mouth white. Over   370
A coat of mail in Turkish style,
Brightest armour front and back,
And an orange doublet, and set atop
All this a helmet whose white plumes
Seemed, against that orange, more   375
Like blossoms. About his arm a band
Of red and white, couching a lance
Which seemed a mighty oak before
Which all Granada* trembles. Ciudad Real
Then took to arms, its people claiming they   380
Were loyal to the Crown and would
Defend their rights to so remain.
Despite all this, the Master seized
The town, and those who had offended his
Good name soon had their heads cut off,   385
While those of lesser worth were gagged
And flogged in public view. He is
So feared there and yet so loved,
They all believe that one who, though
So young, can fight and overwhelm   390
His enemies, will one day be
The scourge of Moorish Africa, forcing
Those blue and crescent moons to yield
To his red Cross. He has displayed
Such generosity to all—   395
To our Commander too—the sacking of
The town seems more the plunder of
His own estate. But now the music sounds.
Receive him joyfully! Goodwill
Is easily the best reward   400
For such a triumph.

Enter the COMMANDER *and* ORTUÑO; MUSICIANS;
JUAN ROJO; *and* ESTEBAN *and* ALONSO,
magistrates.

MUSICIANS [*sing*]. *All hail our great Commander,*
   We welcome him most warmly;
   He conquers foreign lands for us,
   And overcomes our enemy.   405
   Long live all the Guzmanes!
   Long live all the Girones!
   In peace he is so gentle,
   He speaks his words so sweetly;
   But when it comes to killing Moors,   410
   As strong as any oak-tree!
   He comes now from Ciudad Real,
   The great and glorious victor;
   He brings his banners with him
   To Fuente Ovejuna!   415
   May he enjoy long life!
   All hail Fernán Gómez!

COMMANDER. People of this town, I duly thank
   You for this demonstration of
   Your love.

ALONSO.   It is but part of what   420
   We feel. But since you are deserving of
   Our love, why be surprised by it?

ESTEBAN. Fuente Ovejuna and its councillors,
   Whom you so honour, now request
   That you receive the humble offerings   425
   Brought by these carts* in all due modesty,
   For they, adorned by leafy boughs,
   Contain not costly gifts but much
   Goodwill. First, two baskets filled
   With polished pots of clay. And then   430
   An entire flock of geese who stretch
   Their necks through nets, eager to sing
   Of your warlike deeds. Ten salted hogs,
   Choice animals, as well as other kinds
   Of cured meats whose skins are sweet   435
   As amber-scented gloves. A hundred pairs
   Of hens and capons, whose widowed spouses can

Be found in all our neighbouring villages.
They cannot offer arms or horses,
Or bridles edged with pure gold,   440
And yet your vassals' love is in
Itself the purest gold. And since
I mention 'pure', I promise you that these
Twelve wineskins would, if your troops
But drank from them, give them such strength   445
That they, though naked in the midst
Of winter, could defend a battlement
Much better than the hardest steel.
For wine can truly give a man
The extra steel he needs. As for   450
The cheeses and the other smaller gifts,
I'll not describe them; merely say
They are the offerings of all
The love that you deserve. And so,
May they provide good cheer for   455
Your household and yourself!

COMMANDER. My heartfelt thanks! Good councillors,
You may depart!

ALONSO.　　　　　And you, my lord,
May take your ease. You are most welcome.
If it were possible, we'd turn   460
The reeds and rushes at your door
To purest pearl, though you deserve
Much better still.

COMMANDER.　　　　I really do
Believe you, gentlemen. God be with you.

ESTEBAN. Singers, come! The song again!   465

MUSICIANS [sing]. *All hail our great Commander,*
We welcome him most warmly;
He conquers foreign lands for us,
And overcomes our enemies . . .

[*They leave*

COMMANDER. You two, stay!

LAURENCIA.   What's your lordship want   470
  Of us?

COMMANDER. You were quite cool the other day,
  And towards me!

LAURENCIA.   Does he mean you,
  Pascuala?

PASCUALA. Me? Oh, don't be silly!

COMMANDER. I'm talking to you, my pretty creature,
  And to your friend. You belong to me,   475
  Do you not?

PASCUALA.   We do, my lord, but not
  In the way you mean.

COMMANDER.   Step inside.
  My men are there. Don't be afraid.

LAURENCIA. I shall if the magistrates come too.
  One of them's my father, but otherwise . . .   480

COMMANDER. Flores!

FLORES.   Yes, sir?

COMMANDER.   Why aren't they doing what
  I say?

FLORES. Get in there!

LAURENCIA.   Get your hands
  Off us!

FLORES. Come on, you stupid girls!

PASCUALA. Whoa now!* For you to lock the stable-door?

FLORES. Inside! He wants to show you all   485
  The spoils of war.

COMMANDER [*aside, as he exits*]. Ortuño, once
  Inside, you'll lock them in.

LAURENCIA.   Flores,
Get out of our way!

ORTUÑO.   But you are part
Of all his presents.

PASCUALA.   I don't believe it!
Move yourself, or you'll get it!

FLORES.   Alright,   490
They are too excitable.

LAURENCIA.   Your master's had
Enough flesh for today!

ORTUÑO.   It's yours
He fancies most!

LAURENCIA.   Let's hope he chokes!

                                          [*They leave*

FLORES. Wait till we give him this good news!
Imagine what he'll say when we   495
Turn up without them!

ORTUÑO.   That's the way
Things are for those who serve. If you want
To get on, put up with it; otherwise,
Best out of it, and quick!

                                          [*They leave*

Enter KING FERNANDO, QUEEN ISABEL, MANRIQUE, *and*
                    ATTENDANTS.

ISABEL. My lord, there must be no delay   500
In this. Alfonso is well placed
And even now prepares his troops.
Before he strikes at us, it's best
We strike at him. If we do not,
The risk is clear.

KING.   We can rely   505
On both Navarre and Aragon for our

Support. When I have managed to control
Castile, our victory will be
Assured.

ISABEL.   I know, my lord, all this
Will guarantee our triumph.

MANRIQUE.   Your Majesty,   510
Two aldermen who represent
Ciudad Real. Will you see them?

KING. Of course. You'll show them in.

Enter two ALDERMEN *from Ciudad Real.*

FIRST ALDERMAN. Most Catholic King Fernando,
Whom Heaven has sent from Aragon   515
To be our help and saviour in
Castile, we come as spokesmen from
Ciudad Real to seek in all
Humility your royal favour.
To be your subjects was for us   520
The greatest happiness, but now
We are deprived of that by cruel fate.
Rodrigo Téllez Girón, renowned,
Though still so young, for such great bravery,
And seeking to enhance his name   525
As Master of Calatrava, attacked
Our city. We fought as best we could;
Resisted him till all our streams
Ran red with our blood. At last
He seized the town, but would have failed   530
Without the help and good advice
Of Fernán Gómez. And so he has
Possession of the town and we
Will be his vassals soon unless
Your majesty decides to help us.   535

KING. Where is Fernán Gómez?

FIRST ALDERMAN.   I think
In Fuente Ovejuna. He is

Its overlord and has his house
And seat of power there. He rules
The place just as he wishes, denying   540
His subjects any kind of happiness.

KING. Do you have a leader?

SECOND ALDERMAN.   We do not,
Your Majesty. Every nobleman
Was captured, hurt, or killed.

ISABEL.   Then we
Should not delay. To do so is   545
To give the enemy encouragement
And greater heart. Extremadura* is
The door whereby the King of Portugal
Can now advance and damage us.

KING. Don Manrique, prepare to leave.   550
You'll take two companies and curb
The enemy's excesses. Not
A moment's respite, understand?
The Count of Cabra goes with you.
A man of valour, Córdoba.*   555
The whole world knows how brave he is.
In the circumstances, this is the best
Way forward.

MANRIQUE.   A bold decision, my lord.
I'll put an end to their arrogance,
As long as I have breath in me.   560

ISABEL. Your presence there will guarantee
Our triumph.

          Exit all. Enter LAURENCIA *and* FRONDOSO.

LAURENCIA.   I had to leave the stream,
My clothes half done, because of you!
You are too bold, Frondoso, yet well
You know how people love to talk.*   565
'She fancies him', 'He fancies her',
All over town, their eyes on stalks

To see if it is true or not.
And since you are . . . well . . . better looking than
The rest, and dress more smartly, there's not   570
A single person in the place*
Who doesn't think we're as good as spliced
Already, and waiting for the day
When Juan Chamorro, our sacristan,
Stops playing his bassoon to announce   575
Instead our marriage-bans. But they,
As far as I'm concerned, would be
Much better occupied in stocking up
Their barns with golden grain, their vats
With wine, than harbouring such wild   580
Imaginings. To tell the truth,
I never gave this marriage thing
A second thought.

FRONDOSO.   This coldness* does
   Me such an injury, Laurencia,
   I risk my life each time I look   585
   At you. If you already know
   I want to marry you, does my
   Good faith deserve such scant reward?

LAURENCIA. There is no other I can give.

FRONDOSO. Does not the state I'm in succeed   590
   In moving you at all? Or knowing that,
   Because of you, I cannot eat
   Or drink or sleep? How can an angel's face*
   Contain such coldness? By God, I shall
   Go mad!

LAURENCIA. Then see a doctor.

FRONDOSO.   But you,   595
   Laurencia, are my cure. When we
   Get married, we'll be like turtle-doves,*
   Our little beaks together, making sweet
   And soothing music.

LAURENCIA.   Go tell it to

My uncle John! You know full well   600
I'm not in love with you, but maybe there's . . .
Well . . . just a little spark . . .

FRONDOSO.   Look there!
The Commander!

LAURENCIA.   He must be hunting deer.
Hide in the trees!

FRONDOSO.   I shall, and burn
With jealousy!

The COMMANDER *enters.*

COMMANDER.   Well who'd have thought   605
That, in pursuit of frightened deer,*
I'd come across much prettier game?

LAURENCIA. I'm having a break from washing clothes.
I'll get back to the stream if you
Don't mind, sir.

COMMANDER.   Such coldness, my sweet   610
Laurencia, offends the beauty God
Has given you. It makes of you
A real monster. But if at other times
You've managed to escape my amorous
Requests, this place shall now become   615
Their silent witness. I cannot think
That, since we are alone, you are
So proud as to reject your lord
And master, turning away from me!
Sebastiana, Pedro Redondo's wife,   620
Surrendered willingly, as did
Martin del Pozo's after just
Two days of marriage.

LAURENCIA.   Both of them
Had been along that road before,
My lord. They knew exactly how   625
To please you. So God go with you
In the hunt, sir . . . I mean for deer.

If it weren't for that cross upon
Your chest, I'd take you for the devil, such
Is your pursuit of me!

COMMANDER.   Such language is   630
Offensive! I'll put my bow* aside
And let my hands overcome those airs
And graces!

LAURENCIA.   What are you doing? Have you
Gone mad?

Enter FRONDOSO, *picking up the crossbow.*

COMMANDER. Stop struggling!

FRONDOSO.   The bow!
Please God I shan't be forced to use it!   635

COMMANDER. Come on! No point resisting!

LAURENCIA.   Oh, God,
Please help me!

COMMANDER.   We're all alone. No need
To be afraid!

FRONDOSO.   Noble Commander, leave her!
Despite my reverence for the Cross,
My anger will not hesitate   640
To make your breast the arrow's target.

COMMANDER. You peasant dog!

FRONDOSO.   I don't see any dog, sir.
Laurencia, run!

LAURENCIA.   Frondoso, be careful!

FRONDOSO.   Go!

[*She leaves*

COMMANDER. The man's a fool who leaves his sword
Behind. I left it, thinking it   645
Would scare my quarry.

FRONDOSO.   I only need
  To press the trigger and it's your feet
  They'll be tying together.*

COMMANDER.   She's gone,
  You fool! Give me the bow! Release it!

FRONDOSO.   Why?
  So you can kill me? Have you forgotten love   650
  Is deaf? Where it rules it doesn't listen.

COMMANDER. Am I, a man of worth, to turn
  My back upon a peasant? I shall not break
  The rules of chivalry!*

FRONDOSO.   I don't
  Intend to kill you. I know my place.   655
  But since I need to stay alive,
  I'll keep the crossbow.

                                          [*Exit* FRONDOSO

COMMANDER.   That was, indeed,
  A close-run thing! But I shall take
  Revenge on him for this, both for
  The insult and the interruption.   660
  I should have tackled him! That I
  Did not adds further to my sense of shame!

                                    [*Exit the* COMMANDER

ACT TWO

Enter ESTEBAN *and* FIRST ALDERMAN.*

ESTEBAN. I think it wiser if we do
  Not draw upon our stocks of grain.
  The year bodes ill, the weather worsens.
  Although the others don't agree,
  We need to keep the grain we have.   5

FIRST ALDERMAN. That's always been my policy
  In seeking to govern properly.

ESTEBAN. Then let's approach Fernán Gómez.
  I cannot stand these forecasters*
  Who, knowing nothing, claim that they   10
  Can tell the future, making us
  Believe that they alone have access to
  God's secrets. They carry on like theologians,
  Debating what has and will occur,
  But, as for the present, which is   15
  What matters most to us, the one who seems
  The wisest is the greatest fool.
  You'd think the clouds and all the movements of
  The stars are their property!
  How can they know what's happening   20
  Above to worry us to death
  With their prophecies? They tell
  Us what and when we ought to sow:
  Your wheat here, your barley there; your veg,
  Your mustard, cucumbers, pumpkins.   25
  Ask me, it's them that are pumpkins!
  They forecast the death of some great leader;
  It happens, yes, but in Transylvania.*
  As for wine, they tell us there won't be any,
  But the beer's alright—in Germany!   30
  In Gascony all the cherries will freeze,

In Hircania* tigers will grow on trees!
But sow or not, does it really matter
If we know every year ends in December?

Enter LEONELO, *a graduate, and* BARRILDO.

LEONELO. No way you'll be teacher's pet today.   35
The others have got there before us.

BARRILDO. How was it in Salamanca?*

LEONELO.   So, so.

BARRILDO. You'll know as much as Bartolo,* then.

LEONELO. But not as much as your local barber.
Everything I told you's known   40
To everyone.

BARRILDO.   But even so,
You've come back educated.

LEONELO.   I've tried
To learn the things that matter.

BARRILDO.   There's such
A lot of books these days, everyone thinks
He's an expert.

LEONELO.   Which is why I think   45
They know far less. It's not condensed
Enough, you see. Instead of summaries,
It's all long-winded stuff, all froth
That only leads to more confusion.
The experienced reader sees so many books,   50
He ends up driven to distraction.
I don't deny, of course, that printing has
Allowed true genius to emerge,
And furthermore protects great works
Against the ruthless march of time,   55
Making them known throughout the world.
It was invented by a German,
A certain Gutenberg from Mainz,*
Whose place in history is thus

Assured. But many men, who were   60
Regarded as important, lost
Their reputation when their works
Appeared in print. As well as this,
There are those so-called experts who
Have published pure rubbish in   65
The guise of wisdom, and those who,
Driven by envy, publish in the name*
Of someone else they hate, merely to harm
His reputation.

BARRILDO.   I disagree
With you.

LEONELO.   You think it right that fools   70
Should take revenge on men of talent?

BARRILDO. But Leonelo, printing is progress.

LEONELO. For centuries we've done without it.
What's more, this century of ours,
It hasn't given us another Saint Jerome   75
Or an Augustine!

BARRILDO.   Let's leave it! Take
A seat! No point in arguing.

Enter JUAN ROJO *and another* PEASANT.

JUAN ROJO. Believe me, nowadays you'd need
To sell four farms to give a girl
A proper dowry. The people here   80
Can criticize, but really they
Have no idea.

PEASANT.   Any news
Of the Commander? Did I say something
I shouldn't?

JUAN ROJO.   You heard how he treated
Laurencia!

PEASANT.   The man's a beast!   85
I'd have him swing from that olive-tree!

Enter the COMMANDER, ORTUÑO, *and* FLORES.

COMMANDER. God be with you all!

ALDERMAN.   My good lord!

COMMANDER. I beg you, do not rise!*

ALDERMAN.   But let
  Your lordship sit as usual.
  The rest of us are better standing.   90

COMMANDER. I insist, you must be seated.

ESTEBAN.   It falls
  To noblemen to grant true honour. Those
  Who have no honour cannot grant it.

COMMANDER. Come now, sit! There are matters to discuss.

ESTEBAN. Did your lordship see the greyhound?*   95

COMMANDER. My men were quite amazed to see
  How fleet of foot it was.

ESTEBAN.   In truth,
  An amazing creature. As fast
  As any runaway thief or coward's tongue.

COMMANDER. I'd like to have you set it on   100
  A hare* that keeps escaping me.

ESTEBAN. It shall be done. Where is it?

COMMANDER.   There!
  Your daughter!

ESTEBAN.   My daughter? You think
  She merits being chased by you?

COMMANDER. She needs a talking to!

ESTEBAN.   But why?   105

COMMANDER. She persists in annoying me.
  One of the other women here,
  The wife of someone in this square,

And quite important, saw how taken I was
With her and let herself be taken. 110

ESTEBAN. Then she did wrong. And you, my lord,
Do wrong in speaking quite so freely.

COMMANDER. Oh, what an eloquent peasant you are!
Flores! Arrange for him to have
A copy of Aristotle's *Politics*.* 115
He has to read it.

ESTEBAN. This town, my lord,
Is happy to be governed by you.
But there are people of great worth
In Fuente Ovejuna.

LEONELO. Was there ever
Such scant respect?

COMMANDER. Alderman, have I 120
Said something to upset you?

ALDERMAN. You speak
Unjustly. To speak of us like that
Is to deny us honour.

COMMANDER. You believe
You have honour?* You'll be claiming next
You are knights of Calatrava! 125

ALDERMAN. There are doubtless some who wear the Cross
You place upon their breast whose blood
Is far less pure* than ours.

COMMANDER. You think
My blood makes yours more impure?

ALDERMAN. Bad deeds have never cleansed, my lord. 130
They merely stain.

COMMANDER. At all events,
I honour your women.

MAGISTRATE. Your words
Dishonour them, your actions even more.

COMMANDER. Such tedious peasant values! Thank God
   For cities! There at least a man   135
   Of quality enjoys himself
   Without hindrance. Why, married men
   Are glad to see their wives favoured.

ESTEBAN. I'm sure they aren't. You are saying this
   To put us off our guard. God lives   140
   In cities too, and punishment
   Can come with even greater speed.

COMMANDER. Away with you!

MAGISTRATE.   How dare he speak to us
   Like this!

COMMANDER. Get out of the square! All of you!

ESTEBAN. We are going.

COMMANDER.   And show more respect!   145

FLORES. Please, sir, calm down!

COMMANDER.   They intend to hatch
   Some plot behind my back!

ORTUÑO.   Patience, sir!

COMMANDER. I can't believe I *am* so patient!
   Go back to your houses . . . separately!

LEONELO. Heavens, can you endure this?   150

ESTEBAN. I'm going this way.

                    [*Exit* PEASANTS

COMMANDER.   What can one say
   Of such people?

ORTUÑO.   You never hide
   The fact you can't be bothered listening
   When they complain.

COMMANDER.   Are they my equals?

FLORES. It's not a question of being equal, sir.   155

COMMANDER. And the peasant who stole my bow!
    Is he to go unpunished?

FLORES.   I think
    I saw him at Laurencia's door
    Last night, or at the very least
    Someone whose cloak looked just like his.   160
    I gave him a present—from ear
    To ear—to mark the occasion.

COMMANDER. Where is the fellow now?

FLORES.   I'm told
    He's around, sir.

COMMANDER.   He has a nerve!
    Still here after trying to kill me!   165

FLORES. We'll get him soon, like a bird in a snare
    Or a fish on a hook.

COMMANDER.   Before my sword
    Granada and Córdoba* both tremble,
    Yet this boy, this peasant, dares point
    An arrow at my breast! The world   170
    Has gone mad, Flores.

FLORES.   The power of love,
    My lord. But since he let you live,
    You're in his debt.

COMMANDER.   I've controlled myself,
    Ortuño. If I had not, this town
    In two short hours would have been   175
    Reduced to ashes. Until the time
    Is ripe, I shall rein in my longing for
    Revenge. What did Pascuala* have
    To say?

FLORES. She says she's soon to be married.

COMMANDER. And does she plan to settle her account?   180

FLORES. She says you can have it in cash, sir.

COMMANDER. And Olalla?

ORTUÑO.   An amusing answer.

COMMANDER. She's a spirited creature.

ORTUÑO.   She says
   Her fiancé's on his guard, because
   You send her messages and visit her   185
   So often with your servants. But when
   He's looking the other way, she'll let
   You enter.

COMMANDER. Excellent! But the yokel's careful?

ORTUÑO. He is, but his head's in the clouds.

COMMANDER. And what about Inés?

FLORES.   Which one?   190

COMMANDER. Antón's wife.

FLORES.   You can have her any time.
   I spoke to her in the stable-yard.
   It's the back way in with her!

COMMANDER.   I love
   These easy women well and pay them ill.
   Ah, Flores, if they only knew   195
   Their true worth!

FLORES.   A woman's coolness makes
   For better satisfaction. She yields
   Too soon, it spoils anticipation.
   There are some, as Aristotle* says,
   Who long for men as matter longs   200
   For form. But where's the surprise
   In that?

COMMANDER. A man who's driven mad
   By passion cannot complain if she
   Yields quickly, even though he then

Has little time for her. The things   205
We long for, easily obtained,
Are easily forgotten.

Enter CIMBRANOS, *a soldier.*

CIMBRANOS.   Is
The Commander here?

ORTUÑO.   He stands before you.

CIMBRANOS. Fernán Gómez, bravest of men.
Remove at once this cap of green,   210
This cloak, and in their place put on
Your shining helmet, your suit of armour.
The Master of Santiago,* aided by
The Count of Cabra, both of them
Supporting Isabella's cause,   215
Surround Ciudad Real and thus
Girón. We run the risk of losing what
For Calatrava has cost us so
Much blood. From high upon the battlements
Torchlights illuminate the lions   220
And castles of Castile, the bars
Of Aragon.* And though the King
Of Portugal supports Girón,
He will do well if he survives
To see Almagro. Ride out, my Lord.   225
The very sight of you will make
Them turn and seek the safety of Castile.

COMMANDER. We'll hear no more. Ortuño, let
The trumpet sound in the square at once.
What soldiers do we have?

ORTUÑO.   Some fifty, sir.   230

COMMANDER. Let all of them be mounted.

CIMBRANOS.   Unless
You hurry, Castile will take Ciudad Real.

COMMANDER. I promise you, it will not fall!

Exit all. Enter MENGO, *and* LAURENCIA *and* PASCUALA *running.*

PASCUALA. Mengo, stay with us!

MENGO.   But why so frightened here?

LAURENCIA. It's safest if we go to town   235
　　Together, when there aren't any men,
　　In case we meet him.

MENGO.   The devil's* ruining
　　Our lives!

LAURENCIA. He gives us no peace by night
　　Or day.

MENGO.   If only a bolt from Heaven
　　Would strike this madman!

LAURENCIA.   More beast   240
　　Than madman! Foul pestilence poisoning
　　Our village.

MENGO.   I'm told Frondoso, in this
　　Meadow, to save you from him, aimed
　　An arrow at his black heart.

LAURENCIA.   I hated men,
　　As you well know, but since that day   245
　　I see them differently. Frondoso was
　　So brave. And yet he could pay dearly
　　For that.

MENGO.   It's best he gets away
　　From here.

LAURENCIA.   I've told him so, as fond
　　Of him as I've become. But when   250
　　I try to speak to him, it puts
　　Him in a furious temper, even though
　　The Commander's sworn to hang him upside down.

PASCUALA. Let's hope that someone strangles him!

MENGO. I'd rather see him stoned to death.   255

I swear to God, if I let loose
The stone I carry in my sling,*
You'd hear the crack as it split his skull
In two. That Roman Sabalus
Wasn't half as vicious.

LAURENCIA.   I think you must   260
  Mean Heliogabalus.* He was a real beast.

MENGO. Sabalus, Gabalus, whatever!
  I'm no historian. But he was nothing
  Compared with this one. Nothing in
  The whole of Nature can compare   265
  With Fernán Gómez.

PASCUALA.   True enough.
  He has the nature of a tigress.

Enter JACINTA.

JACINTA. My friends, you have to help me, please!

LAURENCIA. Jacinta, what's the matter?

PASCUALA.   You know
  We are your friends.

JACINTA.   The Commander's servants . . .   270
  They're on their way to Ciudad Real.
  Armed less with noble steel than with
  Their vile and sordid wickedness,
  They plan to take me to him!

LAURENCIA.   In that
  Case, God be with you! If he's going   275
  To take advantage of you, I dread
  To think what he'd do to me!

                                            [*She leaves*

PASCUALA.   And since
  I'm not a man, Jacinta, I
  Can't help you, either.

                                            [*She leaves*

MENGO. But I am,
And I will. Come here, stand close to me! 280

JACINTA. Do you have any weapons to defend us?

MENGO. The first God made.

JACINTA. You mean you don't?

MENGO. These stones, Jacinta. Lots of them!

Enter FLORES *and* ORTUÑO.

FLORES. Did you think you could run away
From us?

JACINTA. Mengo, I'm done for!

MENGO. Gentlemen, 285
We are poor peasants!

ORTUÑO. Are you
Intending to defend the girl?

MENGO. I'm asking you to leave her be.
She's a relative. It's my duty to
Protect her.

FLORES. Kill him!

MENGO. I swear to God, 290
Provoke me and I'll use my sling!
It's your life that will be lost!

Enter the COMMANDER *and* CIMBRANOS.

COMMANDER. What's going on? You get me to dismount
For this?

FLORES. These village scum defy us!
You'd do well to raze their village to 295
The ground. They are nothing but trouble.

MENGO. My lord, I beg you. Punish these men
For what they try to do to us.
In your name they would take this girl
Away with them, despite the fact 300

She's married and has honourable parents.
I ask for leave to take her home.

COMMANDER. I give them leave to take revenge
On you. Hand over the sling at once!

MENGO. My lord!

COMMANDER.   Flores, Ortuño, Cimbranos,   305
Use it to tie his hands.

MENGO.   Is this
How you defend her honour?

COMMANDER.   Who
Does Fuente Ovejuna and its rabble think
I am?

MENGO. But how have I or any of
The villagers offended you?   310

FLORES. Is he to die?

COMMANDER.   Don't tarnish your swords
On him! They'll find more honourable tasks
Ahead.

ORTUÑO. What, then?

COMMANDER.   He shall be flogged!
That oak tree there! Tie him fast, remove
His clothes, and use these reins!

MENGO.   My lord,   315
Have pity! You are a noble man.

COMMANDER. Beat him, until the studs fly free
From their stitching!

MENGO.   Oh, Heavens, will you
Allow such cruel deeds to go
Unpunished?

                              [*Exit* MENGO *and the* SERVANTS

COMMANDER. Well now, my pretty peasant,   320

Why run away? Would you prefer
A yokel to a man of my
Great rank?

JACINTA.   They offended my honour.
To take me for yourself is not
The way to give it back to me.   325

COMMANDER. To take you for myself?

JACINTA.   My father is
An honourable man. Not of
Such noble birth as you, my lord,
But nobler in his deeds and actions.

COMMANDER. You think these peasant insults will   330
Dispel my anger? Come!

JACINTA.   Come where?

COMMANDER. With me!

JACINTA.   Consider this well, my lord.

COMMANDER. I consider it ill for you, my dear.
You shan't be mine. You shall become
My soldiers' baggage.*

JACINTA.   As long as I   335
Have life, there's no one in the world
Can do me wrong.

COMMANDER.   Get moving!

JACINTA.   Have pity!

COMMANDER. You'll find none here!

JACINTA.   I call on Heaven
To punish your cruelty!

*[They carry her off. All exit**

Enter LAURENCIA *and* FRONDOSO.

LAURENCIA. You know how dangerous it is,   340
And yet you dare to come here.

FRONDOSO.   Which goes
  To show how fond of you I am.
  I was up there on the hill. I saw
  The Commander leave. My faith in you
  Got rid of all my fear. Let's hope   345
  He never comes back and rots in Hell!

LAURENCIA. No point in cursing him. They say
  The one you want to die lives longest.

FRONDOSO. Then let him live a thousand years
  And die the quickest! Laurencia, I want   350
  To know if you care for me at all;
  If the loyalty I've shown has made
  Me in the least deserving. The town
  Already sees the two of us as one
  And cannot understand why we   355
  Are not. Why not forget all past
  Disdain? I'm asking you to marry me?

LAURENCIA. Then you and all the village too
  Had better know . . . that I agree.

FRONDOSO. I kiss your feet* for such a favour.   360
  I promise you it gives my life
  New meaning.

LAURENCIA.   All right, enough of that.
  The thing you have to do is ask
  My father. Oh, look! He's coming with
  My uncle. Don't worry, Frondoso!   365
  I'll be your wife, no problem.

FRONDOSO. I place my trust in God.

                She hides. Enter ESTEBAN *the magistrate
                    and the* ALDERMAN.*

ESTEBAN. The way that he behaved upset
  The entire crowd. His actions were
  Outrageous. No one is surprised   370
  By his excesses. And now Jacinta's made
  To suffer for it.

ALDERMAN.   The Catholic Kings*—
The people call them that already—
Will soon have Spain obedient to their laws.
Santiago, their Captain-General,   375
Already rides against Girón,
Who holds Ciudad Real. But yes,
Jacinta is a decent girl.
I do feel sorry for her.

ESTEBAN.   And Mengo too
Was flogged?

ALDERMAN.   His body the colour of   380
The blackest cloth or ink.

ESTEBAN.   I'll hear
No more. It makes me boil to see
Such wickedness. Everyone speaks ill
Of him. As for myself, what use
Is this rod of office?*

ALDERMAN.   But if   385
His servants were to blame, why be
Upset?

ESTEBAN. You'd like to hear more? I'm told
The other day they came across
Pedro Redondo's wife, down in
The valley, and when he'd had his way   390
With her, he gave her to his servants.

ALDERMAN. There's someone there! Who is it?

FRONDOSO.   It's me,
Frondoso. I'd like permission to speak
With you.

ESTEBAN.   Since when do family
Require permission? Your father gave   395
You life and I much love. I've seen
You grow. To me you are a son.

FRONDOSO. Then, trusting in your love, I'd ask

Of you the greatest favour. You know
My father . . .

ESTEBAN. Has this Fernán Gómez wronged you? 400

FRONDOSO. He has.

ESTEBAN. I thought as much.

FRONDOSO. The fact is, sir,
That knowledge of your love for me
Makes me so bold as to declare
I love Laurencia and wish
To marry her. Forgive me if, 405
In asking for her hand, my tongue
Has run away with me or my
Request seems over-bold.

ESTEBAN. No, not
At all, Frondoso. You give me another lease
Of life, allaying my greatest fear. 410
I thank the heavens that you do me
This honour; am grateful to your love
That you have shown such honesty.
But now it's only right, of course,
Your father is informed. If he 415
Does not object, I am agreed.
That being so, you have my blessing.

ALDERMAN. Should not the girl be asked, before
You agree to anything?

ESTEBAN. Oh, don't
You worry, they'll have seen to that, 420
Agreed between themselves before
It's gone this far. We could discuss
The dowry if you want. I'd like
To give you money.

FRONDOSO. But I don't need
A dowry, sir. It's not important. 425

ALDERMAN. Be thankful, Esteban, he'll take

Her as God made her.

ESTEBAN.   I think it best
I ask her what she thinks.

FRONDOSO.   Of course.
No point in going against a person's wishes.

ESTEBAN. Daughter! Laurencia!

LAURENCIA.   Yes, father?   430

ESTEBAN. You see how she always obeys me?*
Laurencia, my dear, there's something I'd like
To ask you ... (come over here a moment) ...
How do you feel about your friend, Gila,
Taking Frondoso as a husband?   435
He's an honourable boy, as good
As any in Fuente Ovejuna.

LAURENCIA. Gila ... ?

ESTEBAN.   A deserving girl, a match
For him in every respect.

LAURENCIA.   Well, yes, father,
I have to agree.

ESTEBAN.   But even so,   440
As ugly as sin! Frondoso's far
Better off with you.

LAURENCIA.   Father, that's such
A rotten trick, and at your age!*

ESTEBAN. You love him?

LAURENCIA.   I'm very fond of him
And have grown fonder still. But as   445
You know ...

ESTEBAN.   You want me to say 'yes'?

LAURENCIA. On my behalf.

ESTEBAN.   It's in my hands?

All right, that's settled. Come on, we'll find
My old friend in the square.

ALDERMAN.   Let's go.

ESTEBAN. My boy, the question of the dowry.   450
   What shall we say to him? I'm quite prepared
   To give you four thousand maravedis.*

FRONDOSO. But, sir, to accept it would offend me.

ESTEBAN. Oh, come along. Such things are soon
   Forgotten. If there's no dowry, I tell   455
   You you'll regret it afterwards.

> [*Exit* ESTEBAN *and the* ALDERMAN. FRONDOSO
> *and* LAURENCIA *remain*

LAURENCIA. Are you happy, Frondoso?

FRONDOSO.   Why would
   I not be? I'm head over heels with joy!
   My eyes reveal the feelings of
   My heart when they see you are mine,   460
   My sweet Laurencia!

> *They leave. Enter the* MASTER,* *the* COMMANDER,
> FLORES, *and* ORTUÑO.

COMMANDER. You must escape. There's nothing else
   To do.

MASTER. The wall was weak, the enemy
   Immensely powerful.

COMMANDER.   Even so,
   They paid for it in blood and lives.   465

MASTER. Nor can they boast that their spoils
   Include the flag of Calatrava.*
   That would have crowned their enterprise
   And been their greatest victory.

COMMANDER. But still, Girón, your hopes now lie   470
   In ruins.

MASTER.   What can I do if Fortune is
So blind that he who tastes success
Today, must see it snatched away
Tomorrow?

VOICES [*off*].   All hail Castile's great victory!

MASTER. Their torches crown the battlements.   475
The flags of victory adorn
The windows of the highest towers.*

COMMANDER. They could as easily adorn
Them with their blood. This is more tragedy
Than celebration.

MASTER.   I shall return   480
To Calatrava.

COMMANDER.   And I to Fuente Ovejuna.
You must decide if you'll pursue
Your kinsman's cause or now accept
The Catholic Kings.

MASTER.   I'll write and let
You know.

COMMANDER. Time will help you make the right   485
Decision.

MASTER.   Unless, as often happens in
Our youth, it proves the agent of deception.

> *They leave. Enter the wedding party:* MUSICIANS,
> MENGO, FRONDOSO, LAURENCIA, PASCUALA,
> BARRILDO, ESTEBAN, MAGISTRATE, *and* JUAN ROJO.*

MUSICIANS. *Long life to them,*
The newly-weds!
Long life!   490

MENGO. Come on, you lot! It's the song that needs
More life.

BARRILDO. No doubt you think you could write
A better one!

FRONDOSO.   Mengo knows more
  Of whipping than composing.

MENGO.   That's true,
  But there down in the valley there's   495
  A chap the Commander . . .

BARRILDO.   No! Say
  No more! The man's an animal,
  Dishonours all of us!

MENGO.   He had
  A hundred soldiers beat me! I had
  A sling, that's all. It was terrible!   500
  But not as bad as this other fellow, who shall
  Be nameless. They pumped* black ink
  And stones right up his backside. Can you
  Imagine?

BARRILDO. It must have been a joke!

MENGO. Since when are enemas a joke!   505
  They may be good for you, but I think
  It would kill me.

FRONDOSO.   Anyway, let's hear
  The song now, let's see how good it is.

BARRILDO [sings]. *I pray to God that their life
  Be long and always happy;*   510
  That they will never come to blows
  On account of jealousy.
  Oh, let them go to their graves,
  Worn out by being carefree.
  I pray to God that their life   515
  Be long and always happy.

MENGO. And the devil take the author of
  Such dreadful poetry!*

BARRILDO.   I had to get
  It written quickly!

MENGO.   I'll tell you what

I think of such poets. You must   520
Have seen a fellow making fritters.
He throws great lumps of dough into
A pan of boiling oil until its full.
Some come out swollen, some deformed,
Some totally misshapen, some   525
Are fine, others not, some burnt to death,
Some soggy. And that's your poetry too.
The subject matter is the poet's dough.
He throws it in the pan, which is
His paper, and after it spoonfuls   530
Of honey to cover up the taste
And make it sweeter. Trouble is,
There's no one wants to try it when
It's done. So he's the one who's left
With indigestion.

BARRILDO.   Stop fooling about.   535
Let the young lovers speak.

LAURENCIA.   Let me kiss
Your hand.

JUAN ROJO.   My hand? But why, Laurencia?
You should kiss your father's hand,
In gratitude for what he's done
For you and for Frondoso.

ESTEBAN.   My friend,   540
I pray that Heaven will offer them
Its hand and constant blessing.

FRONDOSO.   Why don't
The two of you bless both of us?

JUAN ROJO.   Come on! Let's have some music. Sing!
They are as one!*   545

MUSICIANS [*sing*]. *The village-girl* came down the path*
From Fuente Ovejuna.
She was soon followed by the knight
Who came from Calatrava.

She hid amongst the branches there,   550
She felt such shame and fear;
Pretending she had not seen him,
She drew the leaves around her.
'Why try to hide yourself away?
You really are quite pretty.   555
My eyes can see through walls of stone
When someone takes my fancy'.
And so the knight went up to her,
And she grew still more terrified;
She used the trees to form a screen,   560
Behind which she could safely hide.
But, as you know, a man in love
Can conquer any mountain;
There's nothing can keep him at bay,
And so he spoke to her again: 565
'Why try to hide yourself away?
You really are quite pretty;
My eyes can see through walls of stone
When someone takes my fancy'.

Enter the COMMANDER*, FLORES, ORTUÑO, *and* CIMBRANOS.

COMMANDER. Stop these celebrations now!   570
Let no one cause any trouble here.

JUAN ROJO. This is a serious business, sir,
But if that's what you want. Perhaps
You'd like to join us? But why this show
Of arms? I take it you have been   575
Victorious.

FRONDOSO.   Heaven help me! I'm as good
As dead!

LAURENCIA. That way, Frondoso! Run!

COMMANDER. Get hold of him and tie him up!

JUAN ROJO. Best give yourself up, lad!

FRONDOSO.   You mean
You'll let them kill me?

JUAN ROJO.   Why should they   580
Do that?

COMMANDER. I'm not the kind of man
To kill someone who's innocent.
In any case, if he were guilty,
My men would have put an end to him.
Take him away and lock him up!   585
His father* shall be his judge and so
Pass sentence.

PASCUALA.   But can't you see, my lord,
He's getting married?

COMMANDER.   You think that matters?
There must be someone else to take
His place.

PASCUALA. If he's offended you,   590
You should forgive him, being the man
You are.

COMMANDER. Pascuala, I've no authority
In this. His crime* has been against
Téllez Girón, the Master; against
The Order and its sacred honour.   595
The punishment must serve as an
Example, just in case others in
The future choose to rise against him.
You know already that he aimed
The crossbow at myself, the Grand   600
Commander—proof enough, I think,
Of his true loyalty!

ESTEBAN.   I am
His father-in-law and therefore speak
On his behalf. Are you surprised
That someone so in love should act   605
As he has done? If you attempted to
Abduct his wife, it's natural
That he should want to save her.

COMMANDER. You are
An idiot, magistrate.

ESTEBAN. I appeal
To your virtuous nature,* sir.

COMMANDER. I did 610
Not try to take his wife. She wasn't his wife.

ESTEBAN. Of course you did! There's nothing more
To say. There are new rulers in
Castile who'll introduce such laws
And orders as will put an end 615
To all disorder.* When they have ceased
To be engaged in war, they would
Do well to rid their villages
And towns of men whose power comes
From wearing crosses.* The King alone 620
Should be allowed to wear the cross.

COMMANDER. Seize his rod of office!

ESTEBAN. My lord,
You are most welcome.

COMMANDER. Just the thing
To beat him with, as if he were
Some over-frisky horse!

ESTEBAN. Then beat me! 625
I bow to you as overlord.*

PASCUALA. You'd make an old man suffer?

LAURENCIA. You do
This now because he is my father.
What wrong have I done you that you
Must punish him?

COMMANDER. Take her away! 630
And let ten soldiers guard her!

[*He and his men exit*

ESTEBAN. Let Heaven administer its justice!

[*He exits*

PASCUALA. The wedding's become a wake.

BARRILDO.   Will no
    One here speak out?

MENGO.   Exactly what
    I did. I've got the marks to prove it.   635
    Someone else can test his anger.

JUAN ROJO.   We need
    To talk, all of us.

MENGO.   Much better bite
    Your tongue. My kettle-drums* ache,
    And both as red as salmon steaks.

ACT THREE

Enter ESTEBAN,* ALONSO, *and* BARRILDO.

ESTEBAN. Haven't they come yet?

BARRILDO.   No, not yet.

ESTEBAN. Everything goes from bad to worse.

BARRILDO. Most of them know about the meeting.

ESTEBAN. Frondoso locked up in the tower,
Laurencia in such terrible danger . . .   5
We need God's help in this!

Enter JUAN ROJO *and the* ALDERMAN.*

JUAN ROJO.   Esteban, keep
Your voice down! This meeting must be secret,
For all our sakes!

ESTEBAN.   The wonder is
I do not shout much louder.

Enter MENGO.

MENGO.   Alright,
I'm here. Let the meeting begin.   10

ESTEBAN. Honourable friends, I speak to you
As someone whose grey beard is bathed
In tears, and ask what final rites
We can perform in honour of
This town, so damaged and destroyed.   15
What honourable rites indeed,
If there is not a single one
Of us whose life that criminal
Has not dishonoured? Tell me now if there
Is someone here whose honour is   20
Unscathed. You are as one, I think,

In your complaints. And so I say
To you: if you have common cause,
What are you waiting for? Is not
What has befallen us the greatest of   25
Misfortunes?

JUAN ROJO.   The greatest the world
Has ever seen. But now, we have
Been told, the King and Queen bring peace
To all Castile. Soon they will be
In Córdoba,* so why not send   30
Two aldermen to state our case
And beg them to put right these wrongs?

BARRILDO. But Fernando is still at war
With many enemies. He won't
Have time for our complaints. It's best   35
We think of something else.

ALDERMAN.   If you
Ask me, I think we should evacuate
The town.

JUAN ROJO. There isn't time.

MENGO.   And once
He gets to know our plans, it's going
To cost a good few lives.

ALDERMAN.   The mast   40
Of our ship is broken, all
Of us are overcome by panic.
They violently seize the daughter of
An honourable man, the man
Who justly rules this town of ours, and on   45
His head unjustly break the very rod
Of justice. When was any slave
So vilely treated?

JUAN ROJO.   So what do you think
The town should do?

ALDERMAN.   The town should die,

Or kill these tyrants. We are many, they   50
Are few.

BARRILDO. Take arms against our overlord?*

ESTEBAN. In the eyes of God the King alone
Is our lord, not men like these,
No better than wild animals.
If God is on our side, why should we be   55
Afraid?

MENGO.   Listen to me, my friends.
I beg of you, take care. I speak
For all the common peasants. They
Are the ones who suffer most, and so,
Although I know how fearful   60
They are, I also know that they
Are sensible.

JUAN ROJO.   If all of us
Are made to suffer equally,
What are we waiting for? They burn
Our houses and our vineyards. I say   65
We take revenge!

Enter LAURENCIA, *dishevelled.*

LAURENCIA. Let me in! This meeting is for men,
I know, but if a woman has no vote,
She has a voice! Don't you know me?

ESTEBAN. Are you my daughter?

JUAN ROJO.   Who else is it
But your Laurencia?

LAURENCIA.   You see? I am   70
So changed, you even wonder who I am.

ESTEBAN. My dear daughter!

LAURENCIA.   No, not your daughter!

ESTEBAN. Why not, why not, Laurencia?

LAURENCIA.   For many reasons.
    The first is that you let them take
    Me off and did not seek revenge   75
    For it, did not attempt to make
    Those traitors pay. I'm not Frondoso's wife
    As yet, which means I have no husband to
    Avenge my name. You are responsible*
    For that. Until the marriage-night,   80
    That obligation is a father's, not
    A husband's; it's like a precious stone:*
    I'm not responsible for seeing that
    It's safe from thieves until it's in
    My hands. When Fernán Gómez took   85
    Me off, you let him do it, just
    As shepherds stand and watch the wolf
    Which steals their sheep! They threatened me
    With knives, abused me with their words,
    Did everything they could to force   90
    My chastity to their foul desires!
    You see my hair? You see these marks,
    These cuts and bruises? These stains of blood?
    Do you believe that you are men
    Of honour? Do you believe you are   95
    True fathers? How can you see me here
    And not feel all the pain I feel pierce
    Your very souls? You are like sheep,
    The name of our town* well chosen.
    I'll take up arms, pursue my cause   100
    Myself. You are like stones, unfeeling bronze
    Or jasper . . . tigresses . . . But no,
    Not tigresses!* For when the hunters steal
    Their cubs, they chase and kill them in
    Their rage, then plunge into the sea   105
    Until they drown. But you are more
    Like timid hares. True Spaniards, no!
    Barbarians, yes! Or clucking hens!
    You allow others to carry off
    Your wives! You should bear distaffs!*   110
    Your swords are ornaments that serve

No purpose! I swear to God above
That women alone shall be responsible
For their honour, for their blood,
And make these traitors, these tyrants pay.   115
As for yourselves, you should be stoned
For what you are: housewives, men who are
Not men, effeminate cowards who would
Look better dressed in our skirts
And bonnets, rouge upon your cheeks   120
And lipstick on your lips! No doubt
You know our great Commander plans
To have Frondoso hanged upon
The battlements, without a charge
Or trial. He'll do the same to all   125
Of you. And I'll rejoice in that,
You men who are not men, for then
This town will have more dignity,
And once again we'll see that age
Return when there were women who   130
Were strong, true Amazons,* whose deeds
Amazed the world.

ESTEBAN.   Listen, daughter. I will
Not take these insults lying down!
I'll go alone, no matter who
The enemy.

JUAN ROJO.   Me too, no matter what   135
His strength and number.

ALDERMAN.   All of us
Shall die together.

BARRILDO.   A pole shall bear
Our banner on the wind. We'll put
An end to all these monsters!

JUAN ROJO.   What order shall
We march in?

MENGO.   We'll keep no order. We are   140
As one, a single voice. We're all

Agreed. The tyrants have to die!

ESTEBAN. Take bows, lances, staves, sticks!

MENGO.   Long live
The King and Queen!

ALL.   Long may they live!

MENGO. And all the traitors die!

                                    [*Exit the men*

LAURENCIA.   Go now,   145
And may God guide you! Women of
This town, come quickly! Restore your honour!

          Enter PASCUALA, JACINTA, *and others.*

PASCUALA. What is it? Why this shouting?

LAURENCIA.   See there!

LAURENCIA. They go to kill Fernán Gómez,
Our men, both young and old, as well   150
As boys, all joined in common cause.
But do you think that they alone
Deserve the praise for this, that they
Have suffered more than us?

JACINTA.   So what do you have
In mind?

LAURENCIA. We should arrange ourselves   155
In ordered ranks to undertake
A task which will amaze the world.
Jacinta, the wrong you suffered means
That you should be the corporal in
Our women's regiment.

JACINTA.   But yours   160
Was just as great.

LAURENCIA.   Pascuala, our ensign.

PASCUALA. I'll find a flagpole for our flag.

I'll show you I deserve to be
Our standard-bearer.

LAURENCIA.   No time for that.
Since fortune favours us, our shawls   165
Shall be our flags.

PASCUALA.   Let's choose a captain.

LAURENCIA.   No.

PASCUALA. Why not?

LAURENCIA.   Because no hero from the past,
No Cid or Rodamonte* is
My match in bravery!

> *Exit the women. Enter* FRONDOSO* *with his hands tied;*
> FLORES, ORTUÑO, CIMBRANOS, *and the* COMMANDER.

COMMANDER. The rope you've used to tie his hands . . .   170
There's some left over. Use it to string
Him up. Make him suffer even more.

FRONDOSO. You do your name much good by this,
My lord!

COMMANDER. Hang him from the battlements.

FRONDOSO. But I'd no intention of killing you.   175

> [*Noise off*

FLORES. Listen! That noise!

COMMANDER.   What is it?

FLORES.   They want
To stop the judgement, sir.

> [*Noise*

ORTUÑO.   They try
To break the doors down!

COMMANDER.   The doors of this house,
The residence* of our sacred Order?

FLORES. The entire town is there!

JUAN ROJO [*off*].   Come! Break   180
It down, smash everything! We'll burn
It to the ground!

ORTUÑO.   The people rise against us.
We'll never stop them.

COMMANDER.   Against me?

ORTUÑO. Such is the fury of the crowd,
They've smashed the doors down.

COMMANDER.   Untie him!   185
Frondoso, calm the magistrate.

FRONDOSO. I'll try, my lord. Their love for me
Inspires them.

                                            [*Exits*

MENGO [*off*].   Long live the King
And Queen! The traitors have to die!

FLORES. My lord, they must not find you here.   190

COMMANDER. What they will find is that this room
Is strong and well protected. They'll soon
Turn back.

FLORES.   When people rise against
The wrongs that have been done to them,
They never stop until they've tasted blood   195
Or been avenged.

COMMANDER.   This door will serve
As our portcullis, these swords as our
Defence.

FRONDOSO [*off*]. Long live Fuente Ovejuna!

COMMANDER. Oh, what a leader! Let's meet them face
To face, show them how rash they are!   200

FLORES. My lord, it's you who might be rash.

ESTEBAN [*off*]. We have the tyrant and his vile
   Accomplices. Fuente Ovejuna! They
   Must die!

Enter VILLAGERS.

COMMANDER. Wait, all of you!

VILLAGERS.   Injustice does
   Not wait!

COMMANDER. You have to tell me what   205
   Injustices they are. I'll put them right,
   I swear.

VILLAGERS. Fuente Ovejuna! Long
   Live King Fernando! Death to all
   False Christians and foul traitors!

COMMANDER.   Listen!
   I am your lord and master.

VILLAGERS.   The Catholic Kings   210
   Are our lords and masters!

COMMANDER.   Wait!

[*Exit the* COMMANDER

VILLAGERS. Fuente Ovejuna! Death to Fernán Gómez!

The men of the village leave. The women enter,* armed.

LAURENCIA. Halt! Women—no, brave soldiers! This
   Is where our hopes will be fulfilled.

PASCUALA. He'll see what women are when they   215
   Want vengeance. We'll drink his blood!

JACINTA.   Stick
   His body on our lances!

PASCUALA.   We're all agreed!

ESTEBAN [*off*]. See how the treacherous Commander dies!

COMMANDER [*off*]. Please God, have pity! Help me!

BARRILDO [*off*].   There's Flores!

MENGO [*off*]. Get him! He's the one who flogged me!

FRONDOSO [*off*].   I'm not   220
  Avenged until I've ripped his soul out!

LAURENCIA. We should go in.

PASCUALA.   Don't get so worked up!
  Just watch the door.

BARRILDO [*off*].   I'll not be moved
  By your tears, you puffed-up marquesses!

LAURENCIA. Pascuala, I'm going in. What use   225
  Is any sword still in its scabbard?

                                 [*Exit* LAURENCIA

BARRILDO [*off*]. Why, here's Ortuño.

FRONDOSO [*off*].   Slash his face!*

    FLORES *enters running, pursued by* MENGO.

FLORES. Mengo, spare me! I'm not to blame.

MENGO. It wasn't enough to be a pimp,
  You went and whipped my arse as well!   230

PASCUALA. Hey, give him to us women, Mengo!
  Leave him to us! We'll see to him!

MENGO. He's yours. I know you'll do your best!

PASCUALA. Tit for tat for your flogging.

MENGO.   See
  To it!

JACINTA. Come on, the traitor dies!   235

FLORES. At the hands of women?

JACINTA.   You think
  It's not appropriate?

PASCUALA.   Is that
Why you are crying?

JACINTA.   You organized
His pleasures. Now you die.

PASCUALA.   Let's kill
The traitor.

FLORES.   Please! Have pity!   240

Enter ORTUÑO, *pursued by* LAURENCIA.

ORTUÑO. I swear it wasn't me . . .

LAURENCIA.   I know
It was! Come! Stain your weapons with
The blood of these vile men!

PASCUALA.   I'll kill
Until I have no strength for more!

ALL. Fuente Ovejuna! Long live Fernando,   245
Our King!*

Exit all. Enter KING FERNANDO *and* QUEEN ISABEL,
and DON MANRIQUE, *Master of Santiago.*

MANRIQUE. Our plan worked well and our hopes
Were quickly realized. Our troops
Faced little opposition, and if
They had, I doubt it would have caused   250
Us problems. Cabra holds the town
And will remain there just in case
Our enemies should try to take
It once again.

KING.   A wise decision.
It's best he stays and that his troops   255
Be reinforced so their control
Is even more assured. If we
Do this, Alonso cannot do
Us harm, however many men
He seeks in Portugal. Cabra is well   260

Advised to stay and demonstrate
His bravery. By doing so
He guarantees our safety here,
And like a loyal sentinel
Protects the needs of our kingdom.   265

Enter FLORES,* *wounded.*

FLORES. Oh, noble King Fernando, whom
The heavens have chosen to become
The ruler of Castile:* I beg
You let me speak and tell you of
The foulest deed the world has seen   270
From where the sun begins and ends
Its daily course.

KING.   Control yourself.

FLORES. Oh, sovereign King, my injuries
Are such, my time so short, I must
Inform you of these terrible   275
Events* without delay. I come
From Fuente Ovejuna. The people there
Have mercilessly killed their lord
And master: Fernán Gómez murdered by
His faithless subjects, vassals who,   280
Believing they'd been wronged, rose up
Without good cause. These people called
Him tyrant, and on the strength of that
Committed this foul deed. They broke into
His house, and though he offered, as   285
An honourable man, to see
To their complaints, not only did
They fail to heed his words but rained
Upon the Cross upon his breast
A thousand cruel blows. And then   290
They threw him from the window to
The ground where all the women caught
Him on their pikes and swords.
They dragged his body to a house
And there, in competition with   295

Each other, tore his beard and hair,
And cut his face to shreds. Such was
The fury of the mob, that of
His mutilated flesh his ears
Remained the largest pieces. They smashed   300
His coat of arms with pikes and shouted that
Your coat of arms should take their place,
For his offended them. They then
Ransacked his house, as if he was
Some enemy they'd overcome,   305
And, having triumphed, shared the spoils
Among themselves. I saw all this
From where I chose to hide, for my
Unhappy fate declared that I,
Despite this tragedy, should live.   310
I did not move the whole day long,
But when night came I managed to escape
Unseen and bring you this account
Of what occurred. You are renowned
For being just, your Majesty,   315
And so I ask of you that for
Their evil deeds these criminals
Be made to pay.

KING.   I promise you
They shall be punished. What you describe
Is so incredible, I shall   320
At once dispatch a magistrate
With orders to investigate*
The case and punish those who are
To blame, so everyone may see
Crime does not pay. He'll have a captain for   325
Protection, for wrongs as great as these
Demand a punishment that is
Exemplary. See to this soldier's wounds . . .

Exit all. Enter the PEASANTS, *men and women, with*
FERNÁN GÓMEZ's *head fixed on a lance.**

MUSICIANS. *Long life to King Fernando,**

Long life to Isabel;   330
A cruel death to tyrants,
And let them rot in Hell.

BARRILDO. Let's hear your song, Frondoso.

FRONDOSO.   It goes
Like this. If someone thinks he can
Improve on it, then he can try.   335
Long life to lovely Isabel
And our King Fernando,
They suit each other very well,
Their love is strong, their love is true;
One day Saint Michael* at the gates,   340
Will welcome them and let them in;
Till then long life to both of them,
And punish tyrants for their sins!

LAURENCIA. Barrildo, your turn.

BARRILDO.   Alright,
Here goes. I've put some effort into this.   345

PASCUALA. Just sing it clearly. It'll be fine.

BARRILDO. *Long life to both the Catholic Kings,*
For theirs is the victory;
We welcome them as our Lords
To rule our lands successfully.   350
Whatever battles lie ahead,
We know they'll be triumphant,
Their enemies both great and small,
And down with cruel tyrants!

MUSICIANS. *Long life to King Fernando,*   355
Long life to Isabel;
A cruel death to tyrants,
And let them rot in Hell.

LAURENCIA. Now Mengo!

FRONDOSO.   Yes, come on! Let's hear you!

MENGO. You know I've a gift for poetry.   360

PASCUALA. Let's hear about the other gift,
On the backside of your belly!

MENGO. *One Sunday morning recently,*
He ordered me a whipping;
I promise you it really hurt, 365
My backside's still complaining.
But then we put them on our spit
*And gave them all a roasting.**
Long life to both our Catholic Kings,
An end to the tyrants' boasting. 370

MUSICIANS. *Long life to King Fernando,*
Long life to Isabel;
A cruel death to tyrants,
And let them rot in Hell.

ESTEBAN. Take the head down now.

MENGO.   He looks as if 375
He's just been hanged.

        Enter JUAN ROJO *with the royal coat of arms.*

ALDERMAN.   He's brought the coat
Of arms.

ESTEBAN. Let's see.

JUAN ROJO.   Where shall I put it?

ALDERMAN. Why, there, outside the Council Chamber.*

ESTEBAN. It looks magnificent!

BARRILDO.   A joy
To behold!

FRONDOSO.   As bright as any sun,* 380
It marks the dawn of our new day!

ESTEBAN. Long live León and old Castile,
The bars of Aragón, and death
To tyranny! But listen now,
People of Fuente Ovejuna. 385

I may be old but my advice
Can do no harm. The King and Queen
Will want to know what's happened here,
Not least because our town is on
The route they take. You'd best   390
Agree on what you are to say to them.

FRONDOSO. So what is your advice?

ESTEBAN.   On pain
Of death you all say 'Fuente Ovejuna',
And stick to it.

FRONDOSO.   I think you're right.
Fuente Ovejuna did it!*

ESTEBAN.   Are you all   395
Agreed?

ALL.   Agreed!

ESTEBAN.   Imagine, then, that I'm
The judge. We'd best rehearse what we
Must do. Mengo's to be tortured* first.

MENGO. There must be someone less strong-willed
Than me!

ESTEBAN.   We're only pretending, Mengo!   400

MENGO. All right, get on with it!

ESTEBAN.   Who killed
The Commander?

MENGO.   Fuente Ovejuna!

ESTEBAN. You dog, you shall be tortured!

MENGO.   Ahhhhh!
You can kill me! I'll not confess!

ESTEBAN. Confess, you wretch!

MENGO.   All right, all right!   405

ESTEBAN. Who killed him, then?

MENGO.   Fuente Ovejuna!

ESTEBAN.   Turn
The screw!*

MENGO.   I shan't confess!

ESTEBAN.   To hell
With the trial!

Enter the ALDERMAN.*

ALDERMAN.   What are you doing here?

FRONDOSO. What's happened, Cuadrado?

ALDERMAN.   A judge
Has just arrived.

ESTEBAN.   Let's go! The other way!   410

ALDERMAN. He's brought a captain with him.

ESTEBAN.   Who cares
If he's brought the devil himself!
All of you know what you have to say.

ALDERMAN. They're arresting everyone.

ESTEBAN.   No need
To be afraid. Mengo, who killed   415
The Commander?

MENGO.   Fuente Ovejuna!

All exit. Enter the MASTER OF CALATRAVA *and a* SOLDIER.

MASTER. You mean this really happened? I can't
Believe it. The poor man! For news
Like this you could be put to death!*

SOLDIER. My lord, I'm just the messenger.   420
I didn't mean to make you angry.

MASTER. How can a mere village, though
Incensed, commit this dreadful crime?
I'll take five hundred men and raze

It to the ground. I shall obliterate   425
The memory of their names.

SOLDIER. It's best you calm yourself, my lord.
They now obey the King. It would
Not do to anger him.

MASTER.   How can
They serve the King when they have sworn   430
Allegiance* to the Order?

SOLDIER.   The courts
Would have to settle it.

MASTER.   No court
Will give to me what was initially
Within his power. The King is sovereign,
I must accept it. And if they swear   435
Their loyalty to him, I must
Control my rage* and now submit
To his authority. If I
Have made mistakes, my youth will be
My saviour and salvation. I feel   440
A sense of shame, but even so
My honour is what matters most.
I know full well my obligations.

They leave. Enter LAURENCIA.

LAURENCIA. When we're in love, our fear for
The one we love becomes true anguish,   445
And adds to love a greater care
When it concerns the one we cherish.
Although our love be strong and true,
Our fears affect our sense of trust,
And haunt us with the dreadful thought   450
The one we love may be lost to us.
I worship my beloved husband.
I know my life will be as nothing
If fortune does not favour him.
I only think of his well-being;   455
His presence here adds to my worry,

And yet I die when he's not with me.

Enter FRONDOSO.*

FRONDOSO. Laurencia!

LAURENCIA.   My dearest husband!
It isn't safe. You shouldn't be here!

FRONDOSO. Am I to think my love for you   460
Deserves such coolness?

LAURENCIA.   Your life's at risk.
You must stay hidden.

FRONDOSO.   Heaven forbid
I ever give you cause to grieve.

LAURENCIA. You've seen how cruelly the rest
Are treated, how furiously this judge   465
Proceeds to punish them. You have
To save yourself, avoid the risk,
Not seek it out.

FRONDOSO.   You think I could
Behave like that? Turn my back on all
My friends when they most need me? Leave   470
You here to face the danger? No!
Don't ask me to! It isn't right
For me to save my skin and not
Concern myself with all of you
At such a time.

                                                 [*Cries off-stage*
                        Listen! Someone   475
Is being tortured. Listen!

JUDGE [*off*].   Speak!
Old man, I want the truth!

FRONDOSO.   Laurencia,
They are torturing one of the old men!

LAURENCIA. They show no mercy.

ESTEBAN [*off*].   All right! All right!

JUDGE [*off*]. So let him speak! Who killed Fernando?   480

ESTEBAN [*off*]. Fuente Ovejuna!

LAURENCIA.   Such a noble father!

FRONDOSO. The bravest of men!

JUDGE [*off*].   The boy!
Still tighter! I know you know.
Say who it was. Why won't you speak?
Pull tighter still!

BOY [*off*].   Fuente Ovejuna!   485

JUDGE [*off*]. In the King's name, I'll hang you all
With my own hands. Who killed the Commander?

FRONDOSO. They torture a mere boy and still
He will not tell them!

LAURENCIA.   Such brave people!

FRONDOSO. Each one courageous!

JUDGE [*off*].   Bring the girl! Stretch   490
Her on the rack! Tighten the screw!

LAURENCIA. He's blind with anger!

JUDGE [*off*].   Believe me, the rack
Will see to all of you! Who killed
The Commander?

PASCUALA [*off*].   Fuente Ovejuna!

JUDGE [*off*]. Once more. Tighten!

FRONDOSO.   He's wasting his time.   495

LAURENCIA. Pascuala refuses to tell him.

FRONDOSO. Why be surprised? The children do
So too.

JUDGE [*off*]. You're only tickling them!

Much harder!

PASCUALA [*off*]. Oh, God, have mercy!

JUDGE [*off*].   Again!
Are you deaf?

PASCUALA [*off*]. Fuente Ovejuna!   500

JUDGE [*off*]. The fat one there, the one half-naked.
On the rack with him!

LAURENCIA.   It must be Mengo!

FRONDOSO. I'm afraid he'll tell them!

MENGO [*off*].   No! No!

JUDGE [*off*]. Now tighter!

MENGO [*off*].   No!

JUDGE [*off*].   Do you need assistance?

MENGO [*off*]. No, please!

JUDGE [*off*].   Then tell me, peasant! Who killed   505
The Commander?

MENGO [*off*].   All right, I'll tell you.

JUDGE [*off*]. Ease off a little.

FRONDOSO.   He's going to tell him!

JUDGE. Apply more pressure!

MENGO.   No more, no more!
I'll tell you.

JUDGE.   Who killed the Commander?

MENGO. Fuente Ovejuna! Our little town!*   510

JUDGE. Who ever saw such scoundrels? They mock
Their pain. The very one I thought
Would crack is most defiant. Release them!
This has become most tiresome.

FRONDOSO. God bless you, Mengo! I was scared   515
    Beyond belief, but you have overcome
    My fear!

       Enter MENGO, BARRILDO, *and the* ALDERMAN.

BARRILDO. You were brilliant, Mengo!

ALDERMAN. Oh, very good indeed!

BARRILDO.   A star!

MENGO. Oh, ah!

BARRILDO.   Here, have a drink! Take this!

MENGO. Oh, ah! What is it?

BARRILDO.   Lemon curd.*   520

MENGO. Aaahh!

FRONDOSO.   Get it down you!

BARRILDO.   That's the way.

FRONDOSO. He's drunk it all. Now he'll be fine.

LAURENCIA. Give him some food.

MENGO.   Oh, ah!

BARRILDO.   Have this
    On me!

LAURENCIA. He only wants the wine!

FRONDOSO. A man who's said 'no' should have some, yes?   525

BARRILDO. Do you want another?

MENGO.   Ah, no, yes, yes!

FRONDOSO. And you deserve it, Mengo!

LAURENCIA.   Just look
    At him knocking them back!

FRONDOSO.   Give him
    Some clothes. He must be freezing.

BARRILDO.   Do you want
  Some more?

MENGO.   Three or four? Fine, fine!   530

FRONDOSO. He really means 'wine, wine'!

BARRILDO.   Here, drink
  It down. A man who's said 'no' deserves
  His wine. What's wrong with it?

MENGO.   It's rough,
  That's what. And it's gone to my head.

FRONDOSO. The best place for you is in your bed!   535
  Who was it killed the Commander?

MENGO. Fuente Ovejuna! Our little town!

                    [*Exit all, except* FRONDOSO *and* LAURENCIA

FRONDOSO. They do right to praise him. So tell me,
  My sweet, who killed the Commander?

LAURENCIA. Why, Fuente Ovejuna!

FRONDOSO.   The truth!   540
  Who killed him?

LAURENCIA.   Oh, my sweet, you don't
  Half scare me! Fuente Ovejuna!

FRONDOSO. Then tell me! How did I kill you?

LAURENCIA. By making me love you to death, that's how!

                Exit both. Enter the KING *and* QUEEN.

ISABEL. This is a true surprise, my lord.   545
  I wasn't expecting you.

KING.   And such
  A joy to see you once again!*
  I was on my way to Portugal.
  I couldn't resist breaking my journey.

ISABEL. I trust you will never resist, my lord,   550

Such welcome opportunities.

KING. What news of Castile?

ISABEL. At last it is
At peace. Everything seems calm enough.

KING. I'm not surprised. You are the one
Who fought to bring that peace.   555

Enter MANRIQUE.

MANRIQUE. The Master of Calatrava attends you.
He is outside and seeks an audience.

ISABEL. Then show him in. I wish to speak with him.

MANRIQUE. I would point out that though he's young
In years, he is a valiant soldier.   560

Enter the MASTER OF CALATRAVA.

MASTER. Rodrigo Téllez Girón, Master
Of Calatrava. I come to seek
Forgiveness, knowing that I was
Deceived and ill-advised in causing you
Displeasure. I was misled both by   565
Fernán Gómez and my self-interest.
I humbly beg that you forgive me.
If I am worthy of such favour,
I swear that from this moment on
I am your loyal and obedient servant.   570
The great campaign you plan against
Granada* . . . I promise you you'll see
The valour of my sword. Before
It's even drawn, the Moors shall know
What fear is and see my crimson cross   575
Fly from their battlements.
Five hundred soldiers now in my
Command shall fight on your behalf.
You have my word that I shall not
Offend again.

KING. Rise, Master. You are   580

Most welcome here and always shall be.

MASTER. Your words, your Majesty, provide
  True comfort to the penitent.

ISABEL. Young man, you show true spirit. In that
  Respect, your deeds are equalled by   585
  Your speech.

MASTER.   Your majesties, you are
  The lovely Esther, the mighty Xerxes.*

Enter MANRIQUE.

MANRIQUE. The judge who went to Fuente Ovejuna . . .
  He has returned and wishes to report,
  Your Majesty.

KING.   You shall decide what's to   590
  Be done with these assassins.

MASTER.   If it
  Were up to me, your Majesty,
  They'd get what they deserve. How dare
  They murder the Commander!

KING.   The matter is
  No longer in your hands.

ISABEL.   But soon   595
  Will be in yours, my lord, God willing.

Enter the JUDGE.

JUDGE. I went, as you instructed me,
  To Fuente Ovejuna, and there
  Made every effort to investigate
  The crime. I could not find a scrap   600
  Of proof as to the murder; the evidence
  Is not enough to fill a single page.
  The citizens are all of one accord,
  United in their fortitude,
  For when I asked who was to blame,   605
  They all replied: 'Fuente Ovejuna'.

I tortured them, three hundred on
The rack, including boys of ten
Years old, but none would tell me more.
Whatever method I employed,   610
From force to flattery, had no
Effect. And so, your Majesty, all
Of them must now be pardoned or
Be put to death. They come before you.
They wish to state their case and let   615
You question them.

KING.   Then let them enter.

Enter the two MAGISTRATES, FRONDOSO, *the* WOMEN,
and a group of PEASANTS.

LAURENCIA. Is that the King and Queen?

FRONDOSO.   Rulers
Of all Castile.

LAURENCIA.   I swear they are
The finest couple. Saint Anthony* bless them!

ISABEL. Are these the villains?*

ESTEBAN.   Fuente Ovejuna,   620
Your Majesty: your humble and
Obedient servants. The tyranny,
The cruelty, the insults of
The dead Commander, they were the cause
Of all the trouble. He robbed us of   625
Our own possessions, raped our women,
And showed us not the slightest mercy.

FRONDOSO. This girl . . . Heaven favoured me with her,
So making me the happiest of men . . .
Was seized and carried off by him   630
On our wedding-night, as if
She were his property. What would
Have happened is quite plain if she'd
Not fought him off and showed how virtuous
She is.

MENGO. If I may have my say, now. 635
  I doubt you'll credit what he did
  To me. I tried to save a girl
  His men abused and would have raped.
  For that this wicked Nero* had
  My backside beaten, red as salmon steaks. 640
  I have the marks still plain to see,
  So savagely did three of them
  Complete the task. To tell the truth,
  I've spent more money than my farm
  Would cost on every ointment you 645
  Can think of.

ESTEBAN.   Your Majesty, we wish
  To be your loyal vassals. You are
  Our rightful King, and so we have displayed
  Your coat of arms in our town.
  We pray you will be merciful, 650
  Accepting our innocence as our defence.

KING. There is no written evidence
  As proof of your guilt, and so,
  Although this was a serious crime,*
  You must be pardoned. Since you have sworn 655
  Your loyalty, I shall assume
  Responsibility for your town,
  Until a new Commander can
  Be found.

FRONDOSO. Your Majesty has shown
  Himself to be in this the wisest ruler. 660
  And so, my friends,* we end *Fuente Ovejuna*.

THE KNIGHT FROM OLMEDO

OLMEDO

(*El caballero de Olmedo*)

A Tragicomedy*

THE CHARACTERS OF THE PLAY

Don Alonso
Don Rodrigo
Don Fernando
Don Pedro
The King Don Juan II
The Constable
Doña Inés
Doña Leonor
Ana
Fabia
Tello
Mendo
Laín
Peasant
Shadow
Servants,
Attendants to the King, etc.

ACT ONE

Enter DON ALONSO.

ALONSO. Let no one speak the name of Love
   Who does not eagerly respond to it;
   And yet, who is there on this earth
   Of ours whom it has left untouched?
   Why, Nature itself ensures that   5
   The human race throughout the centuries
   Survives through love, and every animal
   We see owes its existence to
   The joining of two wills, the force
   Of mutual attraction. The brightness of   10
   Those eyes that gazed on me has set
   My soul on fire, ablaze with love.
   I saw in them not harsh disdain
   But more a certain tenderness
   Which made me think that, if there is   15
   A correspondence* which is mutual,
   Then there is hope of love. Perhaps
   My eyes have had the same effect
   On her, in which event love will
   Grow strong, shared by the two of us.   20
   If, on the other hand, blind Cupid* aimed
   His darts quite indiscriminately,
   He cannot claim that victory is his.
   When love is only felt by one,
   It falls far short of true perfection.   25

Enter TELLO, *a servant, and* FABIA.

FABIA. This stranger wants to talk to me?

TELLO. He does.

FABIA.   He must think I'm a dog,
   Obedient to his every call.

TELLO. Of course he doesn't.

FABIA.   So is he sick?

TELLO. He is.

FABIA.   What kind of sickness?

TELLO.   Love.   30

FABIA. Of who?

TELLO.   He's there, Fabia. He'll tell
    You himself, much better than me.

FABIA. God bless you, kind sir.

ALONSO.   Tello, is this
    The woman?

TELLO.   The very same, master.

ALONSO. Oh, Fabia, portrait of the wit   35
    And ingenuity with which
    Mankind has been endowed by Nature!
    Oh, distinguished physician! For those
    Who are sick with love, a second Hippocrates!*
    Oh, let me kiss this hand that so   40
    Becomes this veil, these widow's weeds!

FABIA. I'd best not hear the details of
    Your love. They might embarrass me.
    I see exactly what your sickness is
    From these caresses.*

ALONSO.   Desire is   45
    The master of my will.

FABIA.   A lover's face
    Is but the pulse of passion. Who has
    Bewitched* you?

ALONSO.   An angel!

FABIA.   And so?

ALONSO. Two solutions, both impossible,

Sufficient to deprive me of   50
My senses: the one that I should cease
To love her; the other that she fall
In love with me.

FABIA.   I saw you yesterday.
  You were at the *feria** and only had eyes
  For a young lady whose peasant dress   55
  Concealed her noble origin,
  But not her perfect beauty. I think
  It was Doña Inés, the loveliest flower
  In all Medina.*

ALONSO.   I shan't deny it.
  The peasant girl is the flame which burns   60
  And consumes me.

FABIA.   You aim very high.

ALONSO. My concern is for her honour.

FABIA.   Of course,
  Of course!

ALONSO.   Listen: it was afternoon*
  When Inés appeared, but such
  Was her dazzling beauty, it seemed   65
  The dawn had come once more. Her hair
  Arranged in curls was but a trap
  For unsuspecting lovers. The brightness of
  Her eyes spared many lives, yet they
  Complained that those whose lives she claimed   70
  Were much more fortunate. Her hands
  In all their movements had such grace
  That, like an expert with the sword,
  She seemed to pick the spot where she'd
  Inflict the mortal wound. The ruffles* at   75
  Her neck, extending to her breast,
  Covered at times those hands that were
  Much whiter than the whitest snow.
  The sound of her voice commanded all
  The soldiers more effectively   80

Than any captain of the regiment.
Coral and pearl* she could ignore, for they
Could never match the perfect beauty of
Her teeth and cheeks. Her petticoats
Were French, her overskirt sea-green,   85
As if she felt some foreign tongue
Would keep her secrets better. The slippers*
She wore imprisoned in their ribbons* the eyes
Of all who gazed at her, their laces
The souls. No almond tree in blossom seemed   90
So beautiful, no fragrance sweeter.
Love was her unseen friend, laughing at
The spectacle of all the foolish fish
Which took the bait so willingly.
Some gave her strings of pearls, some earrings   95
Of finest gold, though to a girl as deaf*
As any asp, such gifts are meaningless.
Why decorate her lovely throat
With necklaces of pearl, when she
Is lovelier than any pearl   100
And so despises them? As for
Myself, my eyes became the instrument
Of speech. Her lovely hair enslaved
My soul, her every step my being.
Although she did not look at me,   105
It seemed to me that she was saying:
'Don Alonso, do not leave for Olmedo.*
I want you to stay in Medina.'
And so I had reason to hope, Fabia.
This morning she attended Mass,   110
No longer wearing peasant clothes
But dressed in all her finery.
And as the unicorn,* so it
Is said, makes water holy, so she,
Her finger in the font, transformed it with   115
Her beauty. I looked at her, my love
A basilisk,* and, as I did, her eyes,
Which previously had given out
Such deadly poison, seemed much softer,

As if made gentle by the water.   120
She and her sister both began
To laugh, her beauty such sweet music to
My love and my resolve. And when
They entered a small chapel, I
Went too, my mind obsessed with thoughts   125
Of weddings, such are lovers' fanciful
Imaginings! I saw myself
Condemned to death, my love for her
Informing me: 'Worship* today
And die tomorrow.' My thoughts were so   130
Confused I dropped my glove and then
My rosary. My eyes were only for
Inés, and, truth to tell, I was
Quite soon rewarded. I think she must
Have known of both my love and my   135
Nobility, for only one
Who thinks dares look; and one who looks
And does not think is, Fabia, but
A fool. What's more, no angel like
Inés could ever lack divine intelligence.   140
Believing this, I've written her
This letter. If you would have me favour you,
Then be so bold as to deliver it
And place it in her hands, thereby
Improving all my hopes of marriage,   145
The object of my honest love.
Not only will I be your slave;
A golden chain shall be your prize.
It shall ennoble* these widow's weeds,
And be the envy of unhappy wives!   150

FABIA. An interesting story!

ALONSO.   So what's
   Your opinion?

FABIA.   It's very risky!

TELLO.   Oh, come
   On, Fabia! You won't convince him.

You'll do what expert doctors do,
And end up killing him.*

FABIA.   Tello,   155
I'll use my skill to place this paper in
Her hands, no matter what the risk,
And free of charge. As you well know,
Where such great virtue is concerned,
Who else would be so bold? Show me   160
The note. I need to tart it up
A bit.

ALONSO. Oh, how can I repay you?
You hold my life, my soul in these
Two saintly hands!

TELLO.   Did he say 'saintly'?

ALONSO. So capable of miracles!   165

TELLO. The Devil's own!

FABIA.   For you, kind sir,
I shall employ whatever means
I can. I shan't pretend the chain
Displeases me. I'm a trusting soul,
You see.

TELLO.   You should see her references!   170

ALONSO. Come with me, Fabia. Virtuous,
Respected mother,* I'll show you where
I'm staying.

FABIA.   Tello.

TELLO.   Fabia?

FABIA.   Learn
To hold your tongue! I know a girl,*
Dark hair, nice face, outstanding figure . . .   175

TELLO. Just split the chain with me, I'll hold
My tongue forever and ever!

Exit all, enter DOÑA INÉS *and* DOÑA LEONOR.

INÉS. But everyone says, Leonor, that it's
    Determined by the stars.*

LEONOR.   That means
    That love would not exist if there   180
    Weren't stars.

INÉS.   Explain this, then. For two
    Years now Rodrigo's been my suitor.
    His looks and flattering words turn me
    To ice. And yet, no sooner do I see
    This handsome stranger than my soul   185
    Informs me that I love him, and I
    Reply that, yes, I must agree.
    Who decides that we should love
    One person, not another?

LEONOR.   You know
    That love's completely blind. It shoots   190
    Its darts, some hit the mark, others do not.
    Because Fernando is a friend
    Of your despised Rodrigo, I feel
    I have to plead his cause, and yet
    I must admit the stranger is   195
    Quite handsome.

INÉS.   His eyes met mine and made
    Me look on him with favour. I saw
    In them the passion which I felt
    Within myself and which then drew
    My eyes to his. But now he will   200
    Have left Medina.

LEONOR.   I know from what
    I saw, his life depends on seeing you.

Enter ANA, *a servant.*

ANA. A certain Fabia, or Fabiana,* to see
    You, my lady.

INÉS.   Who is this woman?

ANA. She trades in rouge and face-creams, madam.   205

INÉS. So should we see her, Leonor?

LEONOR. This is a respectable house.
　　How dare she call! A woman of
　　Her reputation! But still, I am
　　Quite curious.

INÉS.   Ana, call her.

ANA.   Fabia,   210
　　My mistress wishes to see you.

Enter FABIA *with a basket.*

FABIA. It never crossed my mind you'd ask
　　Me in! Oh, may God spare for years
　　To come such grace and charm as yours,
　　Such beauty and perfection! Why, every day   215
　　I see you dressed so handsomely,
　　Such pride in every step you take,
　　I bless the two of you. I am
　　Reminded, when I look at you,
　　Of your mother, in every way   220
　　So perfect, the Phoenix of Medina.*
　　She was such a loyal person,
　　So generous and pious too,
　　Never to be forgotten. Oh, how
　　We grieve her loss, and all of us   225
　　The poorer! I doubt there's anyone
　　She did not try to help and succour.

INÉS. What is it you want, woman?

FABIA.   Oh,
　　Her death at such an early age
　　Has left us all abandoned! She was   230
　　As pure as Saint Catalina,*
　　And all my neighbours mourn her still.
　　Such memories! As for myself,

I can't describe the things she did
For me! Oh, cruel death has taken her   235
Before her time, when she was in
The prime of life and scarcely fifty!

INÉS. Good mother, please, come dry your tears.

FABIA. I can't, I can't! I can't console
Myself when death deprives us of   240
Such good and virtuous souls, and I
Am spared! Your father, bless him, is
He at home?

LEONOR.   He went to the country
This afternoon.

FABIA.   Then he'll be late
Returning, I suppose. To tell   245
The truth—you are young and I'm
Experienced in these things—Don Pedro, more
Than once, entrusted me with secrets of
His youth. I never breathed a word,
Respecting her who now lies in   250
Her grave, and knowing where my duty lay.
But out of every ten young women, five
Were never enough for him!

INÉS.   Virtuous father!

FABIA. To be quite frank, he was insatiable.
He longed for every girl he set   255
His eyes on. So if, in that respect,
You, as his daughters, share his disposition,
I'd be surprised if both of you
Are not in love. My dears, don't
You pray for marriage?

INÉS.   No, Fabia, not   260
At our age. That will come soon
Enough.

FABIA.   A father who delays
In this does no one any favours.

Ripe fruit, my dears, tastes so good;
The thing is not to wait too long   265
Until its skin becomes too wrinkled.
Of all the things we know, just two
Are any use when they are old.

LEONOR. So what are they?

FABIA.   A friend, my dear,
And well-matured wine. Just take   270
A look at me. I promise you
There was a time when I was young
And beautiful, the object of
Young men's desires. Who didn't praise
My youthful spirits, who didn't think   275
Himself most fortunate to catch
My eye? You should have seen the silks
I wore, the pots of money I
Went through, the carriages I rode in,
The compliments I revelled in.   280
And as for well-off students, most
Of them would shower me with presents by
The dozen! But now the springtime of
My youth has gone, time marches on.
It puts an end to female beauty;   285
There's no man now will look at me.

INÉS. So what are you selling?

FABIA.   Oh, odds
And ends to make a living. It keeps
Me on the straight and narrow.

LEONOR.   God
Will guide you, mother.

FABIA.   Child, my rosary   290
And missal. Which reminds me, I
Must go.

INÉS.   No, wait! What's that?

FABIA.   Oh, just

Concoctions of camphor and mercury.*
This is for our common sickness.*

LEONOR. And that?

FABIA.   That's not for your eyes,   295
My dear, even though you die
Of curiosity.

LEONOR.   Oh, please, do tell me!

FABIA. Well, there's this girl. She's desperate
To marry, but now has been deceived
By a gentleman from Saragossa.   300
She's put the matter in my hands,
And being such a goodly soul
I plan to help her,* to see if they
Can't live in peace.

INÉS.   What's this?

FABIA.   Tooth-powder,
Hand-soap, pills, unusual and useful things.   305

INÉS. And this?

FABIA.   Just prayers. The souls in heaven
Owe much to me.

INÉS.   And here's a letter!

FABIA. You seized on that as if it was
Addressed to you! I want it back!
It doesn't do to be so curious!   310

INÉS. I want to read it!

FABIA.   A certain gentleman
Lives here. He's handsome and intelligent
And madly loves a certain lady.
He's promised me a chain if I
Deliver this, bearing in mind   315
Her honour and her modesty.
The trouble is that, though he wants
To marry her, I dare not do it.

I wonder if you, most beautiful Inés—
The thought has just occurred to me— 320
Could write me a reply, and I'll
Pretend it comes from her.

INÉS.   No doubt
It will guarantee the chain. Alright,
I'll do it.

FABIA.   God bless you, miss, and may
Your life be long and happy. Read 325
The letter.

INÉS.   I'll go inside and bring
You the reply.

                                        [*Exit* INÉS

LEONOR.   A cunning scheme indeed!

FABIA. Come fires of hell, satanic flames!*
Consume the heart of this young maiden!

            Enter DON RODRIGO *and* DON FERNANDO.

RODRIGO. Until I marry her, must I 330
Endure all these inconveniences?

FERNANDO. A man who is in love is bound
To suffer.*

RODRIGO.   Your lady is at home.

FABIA. These fools and nuisances! What brings
Them here?

RODRIGO.   Instead of mine, this hag! 335

FABIA. The payment would be very welcome.
I'm so very poor!

LEONOR.   I'll see to it
My sister pays you.

FERNANDO.   My dearest
Leonor, if there is something here

You'd like to have, despite the fact   340
That this old lady only seems
To have mere odds and ends, and not
The jewels you deserve, please let
Me pay.

LEONOR.   But we've bought nothing. The lady
Attends to the household laundry.   345

RODRIGO. Is not Don Pedro here?

LEONOR.   He'll be back
From the country soon.

RODRIGO.   And Doña Inés?

LEONOR. Attending to the laundry woman.

RODRIGO. She saw me coming and decided to
Escape! So is my constancy   350
Rewarded by her scant regard!

                    Enter DOÑA INÉS.

LEONOR. She's coming. Inés, Fabia wants
The laundry list.

INÉS.   I have it here.
The boy you spoke of. Make sure that he
Receives it.

FABIA.   Oh, Doña Inés, happy   355
The water that washes linen fine
As this, that not long since has touched
Such perfect skin! Ten towels, six
Chemises, four cloths, two cushion covers,
Six gentleman's shirts, eight bed-sheets . . .   360
I'll get them back to you whiter than
The whites of your eyes.

RODRIGO.   Dear lady, be
So good as to sell me the paper.
I'll pay you well, so I can hold
In these two hands something at least   365

From those ungrateful hands of hers.

FABIA. If I agreed to sell you this,
We'd do some business, sir, for sure!
Goodbye to you, my precious girls.

[*Exit* FABIA

RODRIGO. That paper should have stayed here, not   370
Been taken.

LEONOR.   Retrieve it if you wish.
Perhaps you'd like to check that it's
In order.

INÉS.   Father's arrived. It's best
You leave, or pay him your respects.
He never says a word but, truth   375
To tell, doesn't like you seeing us
Alone.

RODRIGO. I pray that either Love
Or Death provide me with a remedy
For your disdain: Love, by granting me
A favour to reduce the pain   380
Of your harshness; Death, by ending
My life forever. But neither will,
I know, assist me. Caught between
The two of them, I cannot see
The path ahead, for love will not   385
Allow me to enjoy your favour;
And since I am obliged to love,
It forces me to ask that you
Become the agent of my death.*
Ungrateful woman, kill the man   390
Who worships you. If you'll not be
My life, then be my death! All things
That live are born of love, sustained
By love until they die according to
That cruel law which ends all lives.   395
If all my suffering is not
Enough to satisfy love's harsh

Demands, nor great enough to put
An end to me, then I am surely more
Than mortal, for neither life nor death   400
Can do me good or ill.

                    [*Exit* DON RODRIGO *and* DON FERNANDO

INÉS. Whoever saw such foolishness?

LEONOR. I'd say that yours was just as great.

INÉS. You mean the letter, obviously.
    Since when does love behave discreetly?   405

LEONOR. Since when does love oblige you to reply
    To someone you don't even know?

INÉS. I think it's just a ruse, devised
    By our handsome stranger, to see
    If I am interested or not.   410

LEONOR. My thoughts exactly.

INÉS.   Then you'll agree
    He's been discreet. I'll read his poem.

                                        [*Reads*

    'At Medina's fair* my eyes have seen
    The loveliest peasant-girl the sun
    Has gazed upon in journeying   415
    From rosy dawn to where it sets.
    A brightly coloured shoe adorned
    The base of such a beautiful
    And slender pillar,* and drew to it
    The eyes and souls of each admirer.   420
    That any shoe should prove victorious,
    When eyes, as we all know, can be
    The death of love, is quite miraculous.
    And so, surrendering to her, I say:
    "Oh, sweet Inés, if I am now   425
    Destroyed by your feet, what fate
    Awaits me in your lovely eyes?"'*

LEONOR. It seems this suitor wants to dance

With you, Inés.

INÉS.   My feet are just
His starting-point; he'll end by asking for   430
My hand.

LEONOR.   So what was your reply?

INÉS. I told him he should come tonight . . .
To the garden gate.

LEONOR.   Have you gone mad?

INÉS. I don't intend to speak to him.

LEONOR. Then what?

INÉS.   Just come with me and you'll   435
Find out.

LEONOR.   You are a fool and rash
With it.

INÉS.   But when was love not so?

LEONOR. A girl should turn her back on love
As soon as she's aware of it.

INÉS. First love is irresistible.   440
When Nature rules,* how can a girl
Be sensible?

        Exit both. Enter DON ALONSO, TELLO, *and* FABIA.

FABIA.   It must have been
At least four thousand vicious blows!

TELLO. Which goes to show how well you must
Have done the business!

FABIA.   I suppose   445
You think you can do better.

ALONSO.   Such madness to
Aspire to heaven itself!

TELLO.   And Fabia

Condemned to all Hell's torments to raise
You up to Paradise!

FABIA.   Oh, pity Fabia!

TELLO. So who were the wicked sacristans who made   450
A pulpit of your back?*

FABIA.   Two lackeys and
Three pages. I lost my hood. My dress
Was torn to shreds.

ALONSO.   What matters most,
Good mother, is that your blessed face
Is still intact. Oh, what a fool   455
I was to put my faith in those
Two treacherous eyes, those diamonds
Which offered me encouragement
And now have led me to my death!
My punishment is just. Accept   460
This purse, good lady. Tello, saddle up!
Tonight we leave for Olmedo.

TELLO. But why? It's getting dark.

ALONSO.   If I
Stay here, I know I'll die.

FABIA.   My boy,
Don't get excited. Courage! Fabia brings   465
Your remedy.

ALONSO.   A note!

FABIA.   A note indeed!

ALONSO. Is this a trick?

FABIA.   It's from the girl
Herself, replying to your lovely poem.

ALONSO. Tello, kneel before this saint!

TELLO.   I think
You'd better read it first. Who knows?   470

It might contain some savage blows,
Disguised as toothpicks!

ALONSO [*reads*]. 'Eager to know* if you are who I think
you are, and hoping that you prove to be so, I suggest you
come tonight to the garden gate of this house. There   475
you shall find a green ribbon from my shoe. Wear it on
your hat tomorrow, so I may know you.'

FABIA. So what's she say?

ALONSO.   I can't pay you
Enough or say how overjoyed
I am.

TELLO. It's obvious, then. No need   480
To saddle up tonight. Hear that, my beauties?
Calm yourselves! We're staying in
Medina.

ALONSO.   Night falls, advancing coldly where
The day begins to take its leave.
To appear at the garden gate I need   485
To look my best. It could well be
That she, inspired by love, will want
To see who takes the ribbon. I'll go
And change my clothes.

                                        [*Exit* ALONSO

TELLO.   I have to go
As well, Fabia; to get him dressed   490
For these night-watchman's duties.*

FABIA.   No, wait.

TELLO. But he can't dress himself without
My help, not in the state he's in.

FABIA. Just leave him to it. You have to come
With me.

TELLO.   With you?

FABIA.   With me!

TELLO. What, me? 495

FABIA. Yes, you! It has to do with your master.

TELLO. So what d'you want me for?

FABIA. You'll be
My bodyguard. A woman feels
Much safer with a man around.
I need a tooth,* from a highwayman 500
Hanged yesterday.

TELLO. You mean he's not
Been buried?

FABIA. Right.

TELLO. So what's your plan?

FABIA. I need to pull the tooth. And you'll
Accompany me.

TELLO. I think I'd rather stay
At home. Have you gone mad?

FABIA. Don't be 505
A coward! Wherever I go, you have
To follow.

TELLO. But you have dealings with
The Devil!

FABIA. Move yourself!

TELLO. I would
If you instructed me to kill
A dozen men, but messing with 510
The dead . . . !

FABIA. If you don't come,
I'll get the Devil himself to come
And visit you.

TELLO. All right! I'll do it!
Are you a woman or a demon?

FABIA. You'll carry the ladder. You've no
Experience of such matters.

TELLO.   That's true.
And yet I know that he who climbs
Too high may come a cropper!

> *Enter* DON RODRIGO *and* DON FERNANDO,
> *dressed in dark clothing.*

FERNANDO. Why come here merely to see the house?
It seems so pointless.

RODRIGO.   This gate provides   520
At least some consolation. Perhaps
Her lovely hands have touched its bars.
Each day her hands caress them, each night
I offer them my soul. The more
Her cruel disdain attempts to kill   525
My love, the more it burns. Her coldness sets
My heart on fire. See how these bars
Are softened by my sorrow, and yet
That lovely angel is unmoved
By someone who can melt the hardest iron!   530
See there! What is it?

FERNANDO.   A ribbon tied
To the gate.

RODRIGO.   No doubt the souls of those
Who foolishly declared their love
For her are fixed here as their punishment.

FERNANDO. I think it a favour from Leonor.   535
We often meet here.

RODRIGO.   My lack of faith
Persuades me it is not Inés;
And yet the possibility
Remains that those ungrateful hands
Have placed it there. Give me the ribbon.   540

FERNANDO. Impossible. If it belongs

To Leonor, I am obliged to wear it.
If I do not, she will believe
I do not care for her.

RODRIGO.   A suggestion, then.

FERNANDO. Which is?

RODRIGO.   We shall divide it.

FERNANDO.   To what   545
Effect?

RODRIGO. If both of us are seen
Displaying it, the women will
Believe we came together.

FERNANDO.   Listen!
There's someone in the street!

> *Enter* DON ALONSO *and* TELLO, *in dark clothing.*

TELLO.   The gate,
Sir, quickly. Fabia's waiting. We have   550
Important business to attend to.

ALONSO. You have business tonight with Fabia?

TELLO. An elevated matter.

ALONSO.   Really?

TELLO. Hence the ladder, sir.

ALONSO.   And Fabia?

TELLO. A pair of pincers.

ALONSO.   But what do you intend   555
To do?

TELLO.   Extract a little lady from
Her dwelling.

ALONSO.   Be careful, Tello. Don't get
Involved in anything from which
There's no escape.

TELLO.   It's nothing, sir.

ALONSO. You think a lady nothing?

TELLO.   It's just   560
  A tooth, from a highwayman they strung
  Up yesterday.

ALONSO.   Look there. Two men
  Are standing at the gate.

TELLO.   Maybe they're
  On guard.

ALONSO.   So how am I to get
  The ribbon?

TELLO.   She may be teaching you   565
  A lesson, sir.

ALONSO.   If I was over-bold,
  She'd surely find some other way.
  In any case, she is mistaken.
  Little does she know Alonso, praised
  For his courage as the Knight of Olmedo.   570
  I'll teach her to find some other way
  To punish those who serve her!

TELLO.   Don't
  Do anything stupid!

ALONSO.   Gentlemen! No one's
  Allowed to wait outside the gate!

RODRIGO. Who's that?

FERNANDO.   Can't say I recognize   575
  His person or his voice.

RODRIGO.   Who is
  It dares to speak with such effrontery?

ALONSO. Someone, my friend, whose sword will do
  His talking for him.

RODRIGO.   Then he shall find

Someone who'll punish him for arrogance.   580

TELLO. Go to it, master. Much better than
Extracting teeth from corpses!

[RODRIGO *and* FERNANDO *withdraw*

ALONSO.   Let
Them go!

TELLO.   Look! Someone's left his cloak
Behind!

ALONSO. Let's take it over there.
The windows give more light.*   585

[*Exit* DON ALONSO *and* TELLO

Enter DOÑA LEONOR *and* DOÑA INÉS.

INÉS. Leonor, I lay awake all night,
And barely had the dawn begun
To place its feet of ivory
Upon bright April's flowers,* than I
Went out to see the ribbon. I found,   590
With trembling hand, that it had gone.

LEONOR. He must have acted with discretion.

INÉS. Much more than do these thoughts
Which fill my head.

LEONOR.   I can't believe
That someone who was ice itself   595
Has changed so much, and in so short
A time.

INÉS.   It must be punishment
From Heaven, or else Love's sweet revenge.
No sooner do I think of him,
My heart's ablaze. Oh, what am I to do?   600

Enter DON RODRIGO *with a ribbon in his hat.*

RODRIGO. Oh, never did I truly think
My love would be destroyed by fear.

And now I live and hope again!
Ah, here's Inés! I've come to see
Don Pedro.

INÉS.   It's far too early in   605
The morning. He's still asleep.

RODRIGO.   The matter is
Important.

INÉS.   Whoever saw a suitor quite
So foolish?

LEONOR.   The man you love will always seem
Discreet, the man you hate a fool.

RODRIGO. What must I do to pacify   610
This cruel woman, to occupy
In some degree her thoughts?

INÉS.   Leonor,
Rodrigo's here because he thinks
The ribbon was for him. Perhaps
He read my note.

LEONOR.   Fabia's deceived you.   615

INÉS. I shall destroy Alonso's poem, take
Revenge on it for keeping it close
To my heart!

Enter DON PEDRO *and* DON FERNANDO.

FERNANDO.   I come on his behalf.*

PEDRO. Then you and I had best discuss
The matter.

FERNANDO. Ah, here he is! Love is a clock   620
That always runs ahead of time.

PEDRO. So has Inés offered him some hope?

FERNANDO. I'm afraid, the contrary.

PEDRO.   Don Rodrigo!

RODRIGO. At your service.

INÉS.*   It's all a trick
  Of Fabia's.

LEONOR.   What do you mean?   625

INÉS. But don't you see? Fernando wears
  The ribbon too.

LEONOR.   It could well be
  That both of them are now in love
  With you!

INÉS.   That's all I need—you jealous when
  I'm going mad!

LEONOR.   What can they be   630
  Discussing?

INÉS.   Have you forgotten what
  My father said just yesterday
  About me getting married?

LEONOR.   Perhaps
  That means I should forget Fernando.

INÉS. I rather think that both of them   635
  Intend to marry. That's why they share
  The ribbon!

PEDRO.   The matter requires privacy
  And more discussion. Come inside.

RODRIGO. There's little more to say, except
  My hope is to become your son-in-law.   640

PEDRO. I welcome you as husband to Inés,
  But, even so, respect for me
  Demands we speak a little further.

    [*Exit* DON PEDRO, DON RODRIGO, *and* DON FERNANDO

INÉS. My hopes were all in vain, my thoughts
  Quite mad! That Don Rodrigo should   645
  Have read my note, and Don Fernando give

You cause for jealousy! Oh, how
I hate that handsome stranger!

Enter FABIA.
                                How
I curse that treacherous Fabia!

FABIA. Oh, come along, my dear! How can   650
You say such things?

INÉS.   You attempted to
Deceive us!

FABIA.   Oh, no! The cunning trick was yours.
The note you sent the gentleman
Instructed him to turn up at
The garden gate, so he might find   655
The ribbon you had left, but you,
My dear, told two men to wait
For him, no doubt to put an end
To him for good. The fact is, if
They'd not withdrawn, he would have left   660
Them both for dead.

INÉS.   Oh, Fabia! The secrets of
My heart are yours to know, although
It puts at risk my own good name,
My father's reputation.* It seems
The two men took the ribbon for   665
Themselves and now display it as
An indication that I favour them.
Oh, what am I to do! I find
Some consolation only when
I think . . . of him!

FABIA.*   My charms and spells   670
Have worked a treat! The victory
Is mine. My dear, don't lose heart!
I promise you, you'll soon be married to
The noblest gentleman in all
Castile: the one who for his qualities   675
They call the Knight of Olmedo.

Don Alonso saw you at the *feria*,
A peasant-girl as Venus, those
Fair eye-brows Cupid's bow,* your eyes
Themselves his fatal arrows. And so   680
He followed you, for wise men say
That beauty dwells within the eyes
And in the meanings they convey.
As far as he's concerned, his eyes
Became the victims of the ribbons on   685
Your shoes—these days, it seems, it's not
A woman's hair men lose their souls to!
And so, he serves you, you like him;
He worships you, and you destroy him;
He writes to you, you write to him.   690
Who can blame a love that is so honest?
He will inherit, as the only heir,
Ten thousand ducats.* And though he is
So young, his parents are already old.
So love him and be served by one   695
Who is the noblest and most prudent man
In all Castile! And well-proportioned too!
And clever! In Valladolid the King
Has greatly favoured him, for honouring
The royal wedding.* In the bull-ring   700
He was as brave as Hector,* parrying
And thrusting with his sword. He gave
The ladies thirty prizes, including rings,
For all the victories he won. He was
Achilles* in his armour, gazing at   705
The walls of Troy; Adonis* in
His finery . . . though may his fate
Prove better than the two of them!
A prudent husband's something to treasure;
Marry a fool, and it's a disaster.   710

INÉS. Good mother, you are driving me mad!
    Oh, how can I become his wife
    If father offers me to Don Rodrigo?
    Even now he and Fernando discuss

The matter.

FABIA.   You and your young man   715
Will overturn the sentence.

INÉS.   How can
We with Rodrigo here?

FABIA.   But he is just
A witness, not the judge!

INÉS.   Leonor, can't
You advise me?

LEONOR.   You would ignore me if
I did.

INÉS.   Perhaps. Let's not discuss   720
These things in public.

FABIA.   Leave these matters in
My hands. Don Alonso shall be yours!
Happy ever after with the man
Who is in all Castile the jewel of
Medina, the flower of Olmedo!*   725

ACT TWO

Enter TELLO *and* DON ALONSO.

ALONSO. Tello, I think it better that
  I die than live, not seeing her.

TELLO. Master, what bothers me is that
  This secret love will soon be known
  To everyone, what with you travelling   5
  Between Olmedo and Medina.
  Such eagerness could cause us trouble,
  As well as giving food to wagging tongues.

ALONSO. How can I not attempt to see
  Inés if I adore her?

TELLO.   You need   10
  To come and go and speak to her
  With more discretion.* It's only been
  Three days and you're on fire. It must
  Be what they call love's three-day fever!*

ALONSO. My love does not grow cool. It burns!   15
  It does not need encouragement.
  It has a lion's strength, its force
  Is irresistible. And if, on this
  Fourth day, the fever seems much less,
  It is because I am away from her.   20
  If I were where I always saw Inés,
  My soul would be a salamander!*

TELLO. But doesn't this coming and going get
  You down?

ALONSO.   Olmedo to Medina is
  As nothing, Tello. Leander* crossed   25
  An ocean every night, and yet
  That great expanse of water failed

To cool his passion. There is no sea
Between Olmedo and Medina, and so
My sacrifice is insignificant.   30

TELLO. The man who faces danger such
As this sets out upon a different sea
From your Leander. Don Rodrigo knows,
As well as I, of your love.
I didn't know whose cloak it was,   35
You see, and so one day I put
It on . . .

ALONSO.   You fool!

TELLO.   . . . as if it were
My own. Rodrigo spoke to me:
'Tell me, sir, who gave you the cloak?
It's rather familiar.' I said to him: 40
'If I can be of service, sir,
I'll give it to one of your servants.'
At that his colour went. He said:
'It's just that a servant of mine lost it
A few nights back. In any case,   45
It suits you. Keep it!' And off he went,
In angry mood, his hand gripped tight
Upon his sword. He knows I serve you,
And knows as well we found the cloak.
Remember, sir, how dangerous   50
These people are. What's more, we're on
Their patch, and, as you know, each cock
Crows best upon its dunghill.* It scares
Me too to see this love of yours
Begin with witchcraft. I can't believe   55
That magic spells are best if you
Intend to court her honestly.
I tell you, sir, I went with Fabia—
If only I'd said 'no'!—to draw
A tooth from the man they'd hanged.   60
Like Harlequin* I placed the ladder,
Which Fabia climbed while I stood there

Below. And then it was the dead
Man spoke: 'Tello,' he said, 'no need
To be afraid. You come up here, 65
Or else I'll come to you.' Believe
Me, sir, the lights went out, I fell
Down in a faint and hit the ground
So hard, the only wonder is
My senses were restored to me. 70
Fabia reached me just as I came round,
Still terrified and so upset
That, though it hadn't rained at all,
I found that I was soaking wet.*

ALONSO. Tello, a love that's true ignores 75
The greatest danger. It is my fate
That I should have a rival who
Has fallen for Inés and therefore seeks
To marry her. So what am I
To do if, on account of this, 80
I am both desperate and jealous?
I don't believe in spells and witchcraft.
What is the point of it if someone else
Can only be persuaded by
One's merits and affection? Inés 85
Loves me. I worship her, I live
In her, and everything that is
Not her I hate, despise, and scorn.
Inés is my well-being. I am
Her slave,* I cannot live without her. 90
I come and go between Olmedo and
Medina because Inés is mistress of
My soul, regardless of whether I live
Or die.

TELLO. Then you have to say 'I love
You, Inés'. And let's hope some good 95
Will come of it.

ALONSO. Go knock on the door.
It's time.

TELLO.   Right, here we go.

ANA.   Who's there?

TELLO. God, that was quick. It's me. Is
   Melibea* in? Calisto's come to call
   On her.

ANA.   A moment, Sempronio.

TELLO.   Now   100
   All we need is old Celestina!

                    Enter DOÑA INÉS.

INÉS. He's here in person?

ANA.   He is, señora.

INÉS. My dear sir!

ALONSO.   Most lovely Inés!
   This is to be alive at last!

TELLO. Go to it, sir! Strike the iron while   105
   It's hot!

INÉS.   Friend Tello!

TELLO.   My lovely queen!

INÉS. My dearest Alonso. Rodrigo has
   Been here this afternoon. I am
   Annoyed by his insistent claims,
   And so consoled by your presence.   110

ALONSO. Obedience to your father means
   That you might marry him. But I
   Shall not abandon hope until
   That sentence has been passed.
   I knew within my heart—indeed,   115
   I spoke of it to Tello as
   He saddled our horses at
   The break of day—that something new
   And fateful had occurred. And now
   That I am here, you yourself confirm   120

The truth of it. If this is so,
What will become of me?

INÉS.   Do not
  Believe it. I shall say 'no' to everyone
  If I've said 'yes' to you. You alone
  Shall be the master of my life,   125
  My will. And nothing on this earth,
  I promise you, shall stop our marriage.
  I walked in the garden yesterday,
  Alone—the business with Fernando still
  Annoys Leonor—and spoke of love   130
  To the fountains and the flowers.
  I wept because their life is full
  Of joy and, though night comes, they know
  That with each day they'll see
  The sun in their heaven. I swear   135
  A lily spoke to me—such are
  The tricks love plays on us—and said:
  'The sun which you adore, Inés,
  Appears at night, but why complain?
  The other sun has set.'

TELLO.   That's what   140
  A certain Greek once told a man
  Who'd lost his sight. 'Stop moaning, man,'
  He said. 'We always have more fun
  At night, so why complain?'*

INÉS.   And at
  Such hours do I, as if I were   145
  A moth, seek your light. No, not
  A moth!* A phoenix, yes, for in
  That sweet and lovely light I die
  And then am born again.

ALONSO.   God bless
  The coral* of those lips, from whose   150
  Sweet petals tender words of love
  Come forth and seek to comfort me.
  Believe me, when I cannot speak

With Tello, the flowers are a witness to
My love, my fears, my jealousy.   155

TELLO. I've even seen him speak of love
To radishes.* All lovers seem
To want the stones, the wind to be
Their witnesses.

ALONSO.   My thoughts are never alone,
Inés, nor can I keep them to myself.   160
They are with you, they speak of you,
They feel for you. Oh, if I could speak
Those words I speak when I'm alone!
But when I stand before you now,
I even forget that I'm alive.   165
Along the road, Tello hears of all
Your attributes. We celebrate
Your quality of mind. And in
Your name I find such joy, I gave
Employment to a girl who shares   170
Your name, and every day I take
Delight in calling out to her,
Because I think I'm calling you.

TELLO. Believe me, my dear Inés, you have
Such power over both of us.   175
You've given him much greater wit,
And made of me a first-class poet.
Now here's a piece my master wrote:
A very clever working of
A single stanza. It takes each line,   180
Repeats it later, somewhat like
The prayer we say in church for those
Who've died—if such things can be spoken by
A man who's dead but still alive.
'Inés,   185
In the valley, laughing.
If you see her, Andrés,
I beg you to tell her
*I'm dying.'**

INÉS. Did you say Alonso wrote it? 190

TELLO. It's not at all bad for a poet from
  Olmedo.

ALONSO.   But inspired by love!

TELLO. 'Andrés, when Inés's lovely feet*
  Had touched the valley's flowers,
  They grew in such profusion, 195
  The heavens exchanged their stars for them.
  And so the valley is now heaven,
  With everything in springtime bloom,
  And he will see true heaven in this,
  Who sees, for she is heaven, 200
  Inés.

  'With fear and true respect I place
  My feet where hers have left their mark.
  For what greater beauty could we wish
  To make Medina's fields now flourish? 205
  I saw her flee from love
  And everything she gazed on die.
  Her harsh disdain so chilling,
  I left her, while I was weeping,
  In the valley, laughing. 210

  'Tell her, Andrés, I long to see
  Her perfect beauty once again;
  Though by the time you speak to her,
  I think my life may well be over.
  And you, once you've set eyes on her, 215
  Cannot expect a happy future.
  For anyone who sees Inés
  Is doomed to die, as you will be,
  If you see her, Andrés.

  'But should she omit to destroy you 220
  Because she's simply ignored you,
  Then ask her why she murders me,

When I'm the one who loves her dearly.
Tell her I don't deserve to die,
And she'll regret it afterwards.   225
But now this life of mine is over.
What else is there to say, except
I beg you to tell her.

'In matters of love, it's very true,
A lover takes an age to die,   230
For every time you think he's gone,
He sees the girl and is reborn.
But if I live or if I die,
I shan't regret my love for her.
The greatest pleasure lies in knowing   235
That, on account of serving her,
I'm dying.'

INÉS. If that's your work, it doesn't tell
The truth about my love for Don Alonso.

ALONSO. No poem can ever tell   240
The truth about such love as mine.
How can my feelings be expressed
In mere verse?

INÉS.   My father's coming.

ALONSO. What, here?

INÉS.   Quickly, you have to hide!

ALONSO *and* TELLO *exit. Enter* DON PEDRO.

PEDRO. Inés, my dear. I thought you'd be   245
In bed by now. What keeps you up?

INÉS. I was saying my prayers, father.
I haven't forgotten what you told
Me yesterday: that I should pray
That God might help me choose what's best.   250

PEDRO. Whenever I think of what is best
For you, Inés, I cannot think

You'll find a better husband than
Rodrigo.

INÉS.   It seems that everyone
Thinks well of him. I have no doubt   255
That, if I were to marry, no one else
Would be more suitable either in
Medina or in all Castile.

PEDRO. What's this 'if I were to marry'?

INÉS. Father, I wanted to avoid   260
Upsetting you. The truth is, I am
Already married.*

PEDRO.   Married? It's news
To me!

INÉS.   To you, yes! To me my heart's
Desire. And now that I've confessed,
Perhaps you'll have a habit made   265
For me, so I no longer have
To wear these lavish dresses. I think
It best to dress more suitably
While I am learning Latin. You still
Have Leonor, and she, I know,   270
Will give you grandchildren. As far
As I'm concerned, I beg you, for
My mother's sake, do not oppose
This heartfelt wish. Please find a good
And saintly woman who can teach   275
Me everything I need to know;
And a tutor to instruct me in Latin,
As well as singing.

PEDRO.   Can I believe,
Inés, what I am hearing?

INÉS.   My words
Are less important, father, than   280
My will.

PEDRO.   My heart is moved* by what

You say, Inés, but, on the other hand,
Is turned to stone. I'd hoped you'd give
Me grandchildren in my old age.
But if you think that you are called   285
To this, then God forbid that I
Should stand in your way. Do as you
Think fit. Your wishes are not mine,
But, as we know, each individual
May wish for things that Heaven does not.   290
Even so, because we are by nature vain
And prone to change our minds—a fault,
I think, more commonly the case
In women, who are easily persuaded,
And, lacking firmness, rarely do   295
What they have said they'll do—
I beg you do not throw away
These dresses. They will not interfere with
Your singing or your Latin classes,
Or anything you wish to do.   300
Continue, then, to dress with style
And elegance. I would not wish
Medina to be astonished now
By your other-worldliness, and then
To laugh at you should you decide   305
To turn your back on it once more.
I'll find a woman who can teach
You Latin. Why should I complain
If you obey a father much
Superior to myself? So God   310
Be with you, daughter. I'll say goodnight
And let my tears flow where you
Will not be witness to my grief.

Exit DON PEDRO. *Enter* DON ALONSO *and* TELLO.

INÉS. I'm sorry if I've caused you pain.

ALONSO. What pain, Inés, if what you've done   315
Has offered me the certainty of death?
Was there no other remedy

Less painful?

INÉS.   In danger such as this,
   Love is a light which shows true lovers how
   They may escape.

ALONSO.   Is this escape   320
   For us?

INÉS.   In part it is. It puts
   An end to Don Rodrigo's hopes
   Of marriage. Delay is also much
   To our advantage. We live in hope
   If I'm not sentenced for a second time.   325

TELLO. She's quite right, master. While she learns
   To read and sing, the two of you
   Are planning to get to the church yourselves.
   No longer can Rodrigo make
   Don Pedro keep his word to him.*   330
   Nor can he feel affronted by
   Inés rejecting him for who
   She says she wants to marry. What's more,
   It gives me access to this house.
   I can come and go just as I please.   335

ALONSO. I don't quite follow. What do you mean?

TELLO. If she's to study Latin, sir,
   Then I'll become her Latin teacher!
   Believe me, I shall use my skill
   In teaching her to read your letters.   340

ALONSO. A brilliant plan, Tello! I see
   My salvation* close at hand.

TELLO.   I think, too,
   That Fabia could attend her, sir,
   Disguised as a good and holy woman,
   And offer her instruction.

INÉS.   Well said,   345
   Tello. Fabia shall instruct me

In virtue.

TELLO.   She's an expert in
That field, alright!

ALONSO.   My dear Inés,
Love pays no heed to passing time.
The hours fly, and dawn has overtaken us.   350
I fear, as I depart, I might
Be recognized, which makes me think
I ought to stay—oh, if I could!
What sweet imprisonment! But no,
I cannot. Medina celebrates   355
The Festival of the Cross of May.*
I must prepare for it. Not only shall
I do you honour when I fight
The bulls. I am informed the King
Don Juan attends. The Constable's   360
Invited him* to spend some time
With him on his estate outside
Toledo. At his request he also plans
To honour our town, and so
Our noblemen must honour him.   365
God keep you, Inés. I take my leave.

INÉS. Wait, I'll open the door and make
Quite sure it's safe.

ALONSO.   I curse the dawn!
It comes too soon, eager to put
An end to lovers' pleasures.

TELLO.   Let's go   370
Before it's light.

ALONSO.   But why?

TELLO.   Because
It will be day!

ALONSO.   Only if you
Are speaking of Inés. How can
It be day if, when we leave, the sun*

Has set?

TELLO.   It's already rising, sir,   375
But you, it seems, are set to stay.

[*Exit* DON ALONSO *and* TELLO

Enter DON RODRIGO *and* DON FERNANDO.

RODRIGO. I have observed him carefully,
Fernando, prompted by this jealous heart.
He is a handsome fellow, his face
Contains a certain gravity.   380

FERNANDO. You act, my friend, like a true lover.
No sooner do you see a man,
Whom you consider handsome, than
You start to think that, should your lady see
Him too, she might desire him.   385

RODRIGO. The fact is that, although Medina is
Quite small, his fame is great. You will
Recall the youth I saw the other day,
The one who wore the cloak I'd lost,
As if he mocked my name and reputation.   390
I spoke to him and then made some
Enquiries. His master, it seems,
Is Don Alonso of Olmedo, a brave
And noble swordsman, feared by men
And bulls alike. If he now serves   395
Inés, my cause is lost. If she
Loves him, how can I hope that she
Will favour me?

FERNANDO.   But why are you
Convinced that she loves him?

RODRIGO.   I know
She does, and he is worthy of   400
Her love. What can I do if she
Despises me?

FERNANDO.   Jealousy is, my friend,

A kind of monster* conjured up
By envy, wind, and darkness. The things
That we imagine take on solid form,   405
Appear like a phantom in the night,
Become a thought that drives us mad,
A lie that we believe is truth.

RODRIGO. So what explains Alonso's visits to
Medina? He goes there frequently.   410
And why at night so often standing on
Some corner? I want to marry her.
You are a prudent man. Advise
Me now. What can I do, apart
From killing him?

FERNANDO.   I think you ought   415
To ask yourself: if Doña Inés
Does not love you, why now assume
That she loves him?

RODRIGO.   It must be that
He's luckier or better-looking.

FERNANDO. More likely, I think, she has no wish   420
To marry, and you persist in asking her.

RODRIGO. I swear I'll kill a man who makes
Me live dishonoured.* Her cold disdain
Cannot proceed from honest motives.
I lost my cloak and now I lose   425
My reason.

FERNANDO.   No doubt the cloak has spurred
Him on. Arrange the marriage, Rodrigo.
He has the cloak but you achieve
The victory.

RODRIGO.   My love for her
Is overcome by jealousy   430
And rage.

FERNANDO. Be bold. Attend the fiesta.
We'll go together. The presence of

The King demands we take the chestnut and
The bay. Such entertainment makes
Our troubles seem much less.

RODRIGO.   If Don   435
Alonso comes, what chance do you think
Medina has against Olmedo?

FERNANDO. Have you gone mad?

RODRIGO.   Love has made me so!

Exit DON RODRIGO *and* DON FERNANDO.
Enter DON PEDRO, DOÑA INÉS, *and*
DOÑA LEONOR.

PEDRO. But why do you persist?

INÉS.   You will
Not change my mind.

PEDRO.   Daughter, you wish   440
To poison me? There is still time.

INÉS. What difference does it make wearing
The habit now if I intend
To wear it always.

LEONOR.   It's foolish.

INÉS. Be quiet, Leonor!

LEONOR.   The fiesta demands   445
Something much more elegant.

INÉS.   No girl
Who longs for those could possibly
Be pleased by these. As for myself,
These heavenly garments are my one
Ambition.

PEDRO.   Do not my wishes count   450
For anything?

INÉS.   To obey is only right.

Enter FABIA *with a rosary and walking-stick
and wearing spectacles.*

FABIA. God bless this household!

PEDRO.   God bless you, madam.

FABIA. So which of you is Doña Inés,
    About to give herself in marriage to
    Our Lord?* Who is it chooses to be   455
    His bride and offer Him her love
    Throughout eternity?

PEDRO.   Good mother, she stands
    Before you. I am her father.

FABIA.   May
    You be so for many years to come,
    And may she come into the presence of   460
    Her Lord long before you, good sir.
    I pray that you are moved to grant
    Her such a husband, such a noble
    And virtuous bridegroom.

PEDRO.   Indeed He is,
    Mother!

FABIA.   Knowing that Inés has need   465
    Of someone who can guide her youth
    Along the path of moderation, teach her
    The ways of our Lord, help her
    To take the first halting steps that lead
    To love, I prayed. It was revealed   470
    To me that I should come, offer to complete
    This noble task, sinner that I am.

PEDRO. This, Inés, is the woman you need.

INÉS. This is truly the woman I need.
    Embrace me, mother.

FABIA.   Gently, my dear!   475
    The hair-shirt* chafes my skin!

PEDRO.   Whoever saw
  Such humility!

LEONOR. Her virtue is written in
  Her face.

FABIA.   Such grace, such perfect beauty!
  Oh, may your qualities be blessed
  With all that I desire on your behalf!   480
  Is there a chapel here?

INÉS.   Mother,
  I feel more virtuous already.

FABIA. Sinner that I am, I am afraid
  Your father might obstruct our plans.

PEDRO. I'll not oppose a calling as   485
  Divine as this.

FABIA.   In vain, oh Satan, did
  You seek to bring about this girl's
  Destruction! There's to be no marriage in
  Medina; rather a convent in
  Olmedo. *Domine ad juvandum me*   490
  *Festina.**

PEDRO.   The woman is an angel!

            Enter TELLO *wearing a scholar's cap.**

TELLO. If he's at home, he'll be glad to know
  I've come to offer my assistance.
  The teacher you seek is here, Don Pedro.
  For Latin and for other things   495
  Whose benefits will soon become
  Apparent. I understand your daughter is
  Intended for the Church, and so
  You need an expert in religious matters.
  Look no further, sir. I am a stranger, true,   500
  But a student of the things she needs
  To know.

PEDRO.   It seems that everything

Is falling into place miraculously.
The will of God, no doubt. Good mother, you
Shall live with us, and you, young man,   505
Instruct my daughter. I'll leave you to
Arrange things here. Where are you from,
Young man?

TELLO.   Calahorra,* sir.

PEDRO. Your name?

TELLO.   Martín Peláez.*

PEDRO.   Related to
The Cid, no doubt. Where did you study?   510

TELLO. The University of La Coruña,* sir.

PEDRO. And took your holy orders there?

TELLO. I did, sir. Evening classes.

PEDRO.   Excellent!
I'll see you later.

                                    [*Exit* DON PEDRO

TELLO.   Fabia, is that you?

FABIA. Yes, who do you think it is?

LEONOR.   Are you   515
Tello?

INÉS.   My dear friend, Tello!

LEONOR.   Oh, this
Is trickery indeed!

INÉS.   What news
Of Don Alonso?

TELLO.   Can I speak
In front of Leonor?

INÉS.   Of course.

LEONOR. It would offend my love for her   520

If any of her thoughts were not
Revealed to me.

TELLO.   Then you should know
That since the May fiesta is at hand,
Alonso is preparing all the things
He needs: clothes, horses, harnesses,   525
Lances, and spears. The bulls are scared
Already. We've also made a shield,*
In case there is jousting—a product of
My ingenuity. But you shall see
It for yourself, madam.

INÉS.   Has he   530
Not written?

TELLO.   Oh, what a fool
I am! His letter!

INÉS.   I stamp it* with
A kiss!

                Enter DON PEDRO.

PEDRO.   Prepare the carriage if
The chestnut isn't up to it.
What's this?

TELLO.   Your father! Read! I shall   535
Pretend to teach you Latin. *Dominus* . . .

INÉS. *Dominus* . . .

TELLO.   Continue!

INÉS.   Continue how?

TELLO. *Dominus meus* . . .

INÉS.   *Dominus meus* . . .

TELLO. You'll soon be reading perfectly.

PEDRO. Teaching her already?

INÉS.   I long   540

To make progress quickly, father.

PEDRO. Enough for now. The council wants
Me to attend the fiesta.

INÉS.   A wise
Decision. The King himself attends.

PEDRO. I have agreed on one condition: 545
That you and Leonor come too.

INÉS. Then tell me, good mother. Would it be
Considered sinful?

FABIA.   I doubt it would,
My dear. There are religious people who
Are over-scrupulous about such things.   550
They think that everything they do
Offends our Lord. Forgetting they
Are just as human as the rest
Of us, they judge that pleasures which
Distract us from our tasks must be   555
A sin indeed. We must, of course,
Be moderate in what we do,
But you have my permission to
Attend the fiesta. It is, after all,
*Jugatoribus paternus.**

PEDRO.   Let's go   560
At once. I have some money for
This excellent teacher, and some
For our good mother to buy herself
A cloak.

FABIA.   May the blessed cloak of heaven
Protect us all! Leonor, will you   565
Not soon be like your sister?

LEONOR.   No doubt
I shall, good mother. It's only right
That I should follow her example.

Exit all. Enter the KING, DON JUAN, *with*
ATTENDANTS, *and the* CONSTABLE.

KING. Why bring me matters to attend
To at the hour of our leaving?   570

CONSTABLE. A question of your signature,
Your majesty, nothing more.

KING.   Be brief, then.

CONSTABLE. Will you receive no one?

KING.   Not now.

CONSTABLE. His Holiness has granted your request
Concerning the Order of Alcántara.   575

KING. The change of dress will be a great
Improvement.

CONSTABLE.   The old one* was indeed
Quite ugly.

KING.   So now a green cross may
Be worn. I am most grateful to
His Holiness. He favours us greatly.   580
The Infante prospers too, as long
As he is on our side.

CONSTABLE.   Just two
More things. Two stipulations, both
Important.

KING.   Which are?

CONSTABLE.   The first concerns
The kind of dress to be adopted by   585
The Moors and Jews still living in Castile.

KING. This is to meet the wishes of
Our Brother Vicente Ferrer.* He's long
Demanded it.

CONSTABLE.   A holy and learned man.

KING. I saw him yesterday, and we   590
   Agreed that where both Jews and Moors
   Are found together in my kingdom,
   The Jews must wear a tabard with
   A sign on it, the Moors* a cloak
   And hood green in colour. By such   595
   A measure shall all Christians be
   Forewarned and keep that distance which
   Prevents contamination.

CONSTABLE.   This second one
   Concerns the habit* you bestow
   On Don Alonso, the man they call   600
   The Knight of Olmedo.

KING.   A man
   Of singular fame and reputation.
   I saw him here, on the occasion of
   My sister's marriage.*

CONSTABLE.   He comes to
   The fiesta, I believe, intent   605
   On serving you.

KING.   Advise him to
   Gain greater fame in military arts.
   For I intend to honour him
   By making him a Knight Commander.*

[*Exit the* KING *and the* CONSTABLE

Enter DON ALONSO.

ALONSO. Oh, absence, this is hard indeed!*   610
   You are the cruel enemy
   Who splits my soul in two yet does
   Not take away my life! How right
   Are those who have described you as
   A living death, for you give life   615
   To our desires, then put an end
   To us once we have seen what we
   Love most! You would be merciful indeed

If, when I left Medina, you would take
Away my life just as you take   620
Away my soul. Medina, home
To lovely Inés, the glory of
That town, the honour of the Court.
The flowing streams all sing her praises;
The birds all listen to her songs;   625
The flowers imitate her perfect beauty.
She is so lovely she is envious of
Herself, and certain that the sun
Is envious of her. For neither when
It reaches Spain, nor when it winds   630
Its golden ribbon round the far-
Off Indies, does it see a sight
More beautiful than she. I know
That I deserved to love her! Oh,
Fortunate in my audacity!   635
For if I suffer now, it teaches me
To know when I am truly happy.
I long to see, to serve, to worship her.
And yet the need for secrecy
Deprives me of that joy. Such love,   640
It's true, is not as pure or honest* as
It ought to be, but still the pearls
Her eyes produce attempt my death.
She wept as I was leaving, her tears
The proof she meant what she had said.   645
That night confirmed she could be mine.
Oh, cowardly love! Why wait? Why hesitate?
Oh, God! What misery to split
A soul, divide a life in two!

Enter TELLO.

TELLO. So aren't you glad to see me then?   650

ALONSO. I cannot say. You've been away
So long, I've ceased to be myself.

TELLO. But if it's for your benefit,
How can you blame me?

ALONSO.   No one else
Can help me but Inés. Is there   655
No letter?

TELLO.   I've got it here.

ALONSO.   Then you
Can tell me afterwards what you
Achieved.

                                                [*Reads*

'My lord,* when you had gone I ceased to live. You are so
cruel, leaving me lifeless when you depart.'   660

TELLO.   Not reading more?

ALONSO.   No.

TELLO.   Why not?

ALONSO. Because such appetizing food
Is better finished afterwards.
Tell me about Inés.

TELLO.   I wore
My gown and gloves, so I would look   665
Exactly like those students whose
Pretentiousness goes hand in hand
With their collars. I uttered a greeting,
A string of meaningless verbosity,
To make them think that my degree   670
Contained at least a jot of wisdom.
Then I looked around and there was Fabia.

ALONSO. A moment, Tello. I need to read
A little more, such is the strength
Of my desire.   675

                                                [*Reads*

'Everything that you commanded, I have done. One thing I
have not done, which is to live without you, for this is
something you did not command.'

TELLO.   Much food for thought, sir?

ALONSO. So tell me, how did Fabia proceed?   680

TELLO. You should have seen her. She is so wise
　　And cunning, sir, so full of sweet
　　And flattering hypocrisy,
　　I fear for the jobs of those
　　Who spend their lives, heads bowed in prayer.   685
　　In future I'll beware of everything
　　I'm told by fawning women or
　　By clerics who aren't what they seem.
　　You should have seen me, sir. Such piety!
　　The very image of a Moslem.   690
　　And old Don Pedro taken in
　　Completely, even though he seems
　　As wise and sensible as Cato.*

ALONSO. Wait, Tello. The letter calls once more.

　　　　　　　　　　　　　　　　　　　[Reads

　　'Do not be long in coming back, so you may see exactly   695
　　how I am when you depart, and how I am when you return.'

TELLO. Are you stopping again?

ALONSO.　　　　　　　　　　And so
　　You managed to get in and speak
　　To her?

TELLO.　　Her studies were yourself, sir.
　　You were her Latin and her other lessons.   700

ALONSO. And Leonor?

TELLO.　　　　　　　　Oh, full of envy.
　　It's clear she thinks you worthy of
　　Being loved. You see, sir, lots of women love
　　Because they see a person loved,
　　And when a man is passionately loved   705
　　By someone else, they seem to think
　　He has some great big hidden secret.
　　How foolish women are! We all
　　Know love is written in one's star!

ALONSO. Excuse me once again. I have to read   710
    The last line written by those lovely hands.

                                                               [*Reads*

    'They say the King is coming to Medina,
    And quite right too, for you will come,
    And you are my king.'
    The letter ends.

TELLO.   As all things must.   715

ALONSO. How fleeting are our joys!

TELLO.   It seems
    To me a letter in three acts.*

ALONSO. No, wait. A few more words, written in
    The margin.

                                                                 [*Reads*
    'Wear the ribbon* around your neck.   720
    If only I could be that ribbon!'

TELLO.   A fine sight, sir! You in
    The ring and Inés hanging around
    Your neck!

ALONSO.   Where is the ribbon, Tello?

TELLO. They gave me nothing.

ALONSO.   What are you saying?   725

TELLO. I mean, you've given me nothing either, sir.

ALONSO. I see. Then take whatever suit* of mine
    You fancy.

TELLO.   Oh, look, the ribbon!

ALONSO. Quite exquisite!

TELLO.   As are the hands
    Which have embroidered it!

ALONSO.   Inform   730
    The servants that we leave at once.

Oh, Tello!

TELLO.   What now?

ALONSO.   I meant to tell you,
    I had a dream.

TELLO.   You mean you put
    Your faith in dreams?

ALONSO.   I don't believe them,
    And yet they give me cause to be   735
    Afraid.

TELLO.   Stuff and nonsense!

ALONSO.   And some
    Would say they are reflections of
    The soul.

TELLO.   But what could happen, sir,
    If all you have in mind is marriage?

ALONSO. Last night* my sleep was constantly   740
    Disturbed by dreams, and so I rose
    At dawn, opening my window wide.
    I gazed upon the fountains and
    The flowers which there outside were such
    A happy sight, and then I saw   745
    A goldfinch land upon a bush,
    The yellow of its lovely wings
    Like flowers, bright against dark green.
    It stayed there, and from its tiny throat
    There came untrained and beautiful   750
    Complaints of love, when suddenly
    A hawk* appeared from its hiding-place,
    Swooped on the goldfinch from above, and since
    The two were so unequal in their strength,
    The air was quickly filled with feathers,   755
    The flowers stained bright red with blood.
    The poor bird's dying cries were echoed by
    The dawn, and there, not far away,
    A second bird, companion to the first,

Observed, forlorn, that terrible event.   760
As for myself, it seemed a warning which,
Combined with what I dreamed last night,
Filled me with sudden fear. I know
Such things are meaningless, and yet
I lack the will to live, such is   765
My sense of hopelessness.*

TELLO.   Is this
How you repay Inés when she
Has shown such courage in the face
Of fortune's blows? Go to Medina.
Forget these dreams and auguries.   770
Be bold as you are wont to be.
Think just of horses, lances, how you look.
Kill all those men with envy of your deeds.
Slay all the women with your looks.
Doña Inés will soon be yours, no matter what!   775

ALONSO. You make good sense, Tello. She waits
For me. Let's go to Medina. They say
That sorrows thought of in advance
Are doubly sorrowful. Only Inés
Can cause me sorrow, but she is my   780
Eternal joy.

TELLO.   Let's go then, sir.
I'll have those bulls on their knees to her,
Beneath her window.

ACT THREE

The sound of drums. Enter DON RODRIGO *and*
DON FERNANDO, *with* SERVANTS *and lances.*

RODRIGO. No luck at all!

FERNANDO.   It couldn't be worse!

RODRIGO. Such disappointment!

FERNANDO.   What's to be done?

RODRIGO. This sword of mine, quite useless in
   The service of Inés!

FERNANDO.   I feel ashamed.

RODRIGO. And I embarrassed.

FERNANDO.   Let's try once more.   5

RODRIGO. A waste of time for someone out
   Of luck. It seems that fortune smiles
   On this one from Olmedo.

FERNANDO.   He hasn't put
   A foot wrong.

RODRIGO.   I promise you he shall.

FERNANDO. When someone has a run of luck,   10
   Everything he touches turns to gold.

RODRIGO. Love opened its door to him and made
   Quite sure her heart was cold to me.
   Besides, a stranger is always attractive
   To women.

FERNANDO.   Your anger is quite justified.   15
   Although he is a gallant knight,
   What right has he to outshine Medina's best?*

RODRIGO. This town is driving me mad. Just like
    A woman, it despises what it knows,
    And finds appealing what is unfamiliar.   20

FERNANDO. Nothing changes. Such was the case
    In Greek and Roman times.*

                    [*Off-stage, shouting, the jingle of harnesses*

FIRST VOICE. Bravo! Bravo!

SECOND VOICE.   The lance* is broken!
    Bravo!

FERNANDO. Let's wait no longer!

RODRIGO.   Let's go!

FIRST VOICE. Who else can equal him?

FERNANDO.   Listen!   25

RODRIGO. I cannot stand it!

SECOND VOICE.   All hail the Knight
    From Olmedo!

RODRIGO.   Fernando, how
    Can I endure this?

FERNANDO.   The praise
    Of ignoramuses, the common herd!

FIRST VOICE. May God protect you! God protect you!   30

RODRIGO. The King himself would not receive
    Much greater praise. But let them shout,
    Let them lavish praise and do their worst!

FERNANDO. The way of the world, Rodrigo.
    Some novelty always attracts   35
    The easiest acclaim.

RODRIGO.   He's changing horses.*

FERNANDO. But not his fortunes by the look of things.

Enter TELLO *with lance and livery,*
and DON ALONSO.

TELLO. By God, it's going well, sir!

ALONSO.   Give me
  The sorrel,* Tello.

TELLO.   Such praise for both
  Of us!

ALONSO. You think so?

TELLO.   For me on foot,   40
  For you on horseback! Both of us
  Have done our bit.

ALONSO.   Everyone has seen
  How brave you are!

TELLO.   Six bulls I've chopped,*
  As if their legs were home-grown radishes!

FERNANDO. Let's enter the ring* again, Rodrigo.   45
  You may not wish to, but they expect us.

RODRIGO. You, perhaps, not me. Or if they do,
  They merely want to see if I
  Make some mistake, or if I'm gored
  Or killed, so they can laugh as they   50
  Recount it.

                    [*Exit* DON RODRIGO *and* DON FERNANDO

TELLO.   They are watching you.

ALONSO. Indeed they are, both envious of
  The triumphs I enjoy, and jealous too
  Of my good fortune with Inés.

TELLO. You, sir, were the constant object of   55
  Her smiles. They are, you know, the silent words
  That tell us what goes on inside
  A person's heart. Whenever you
  Approached her balcony, I thought

She'd throw herself into your arms.   60

ALONSO. Oh, Inés, if only fortune willed
That I could give my parents such
A precious gift as you!

TELLO.   And so you will,
As soon as Don Rodrigo's sun
Has set. No doubt about it, sir.   65
Inés is all ablaze for you!

ALONSO. Fabia's at the house. I'll take a walk
Towards the ring, and you'll inform
Her that I wish to see Inés
Tonight before I leave. I must   70
Go to Olmedo, or else my parents will
Believe I'm dead. To worry them
Without good cause would be unjust.
It's only fair that they should sleep
At night.

TELLO.   Quite right too, sir. At times   75
Like these they have good cause to worry.
Let them sleep in peace!

ALONSO.   I'll go, then.

TELLO.   God
Be with you, master.

                              [*Exit* DON ALONSO
                    Now I can speak
More freely. I have to see Fabia.
I have a plan to get the chain*   80
From her, in spite of all her cunning.
Medea, Circe, Hecate,* none
Of those famous women could match
Her for her knowledge. The key to her heart,
You'd have to turn it thirty times   85
At least, and yet I think I have
The master-key, which is to say
I love her, which opens every woman's heart,

Especially those her age. They only have
To hear a few sweet words of love,   90
And there you are, they think that they
Are young again and, more than that,
Eternally desirable. So here
We are, I'll call her. Oh, what a fool
I am. She knows I only want the chain,   95
And also I can't stand old women.
I expect Old Nick will have told her that himself.

Enter FABIA.

FABIA. Good God, Tello! What's all this? It's not
   The way to serve good Don Alonso!
   Has something happened?

TELLO.   Remember you're   100
   Supposed to be a holy woman!
   It's because of you I've come. I've brought
   A message from my master.

FABIA.   Was he
   Successful?

TELLO.   Of course he was! He had
   Me with him!

FABIA.   You always were a terrible boaster!   105

TELLO. Just ask the King. He'll tell you which
   Of us was best. Whenever I
   Went past his balcony, he leaned
   Right over, almost fell on top
   Of me to see me all the better.   110

FABIA. A favour indeed!

TELLO.   I'd much prefer yours!

FABIA. Can I believe what I am hearing?

TELLO. Such beauty as I see before me now
   Convinces me I am Orlando!*
   Medina's bulls to me are nothing!   115

You should have seen me, twisting, turning,
Giving them all a real pasting!
Why, in the middle of it all,
This bull is on his knees and begging me
To stop: 'Please, Mr Tello, stop,'   120
He says. 'I've had enough!' 'Enough?'
I said. 'I haven't started yet,'
And gave him such a smack, his leg
Flew off, and landed on a neighbouring rooftop.

FABIA. The roof must be a real mess.   125

TELLO. Ask the owner. I couldn't care less.
Now listen, Fabia. You have to tell
Your mistress that the boy who worships her
Comes here tonight to take his leave.
He has to go back home in case   130
His parents think he's dead. Make sure
She gets the message. I have to go,
Before the King observes my absence.
I am, you see, Master of Bull
Appointed to His Majesty. As such,   135
I'm guaranteed to be the object of
Much praise and adulation. Now,
Before I leave, grant me a favour.

FABIA. What sort of favour?

TELLO.   Reward my love.

FABIA. You mean I am the inspiration* for   140
Your deeds? What is it you like the most
About me?

TELLO.   Those lovely eyes!

FABIA.   Then what
You want is a pair of blinkers.*

TELLO. I am an ass, it's perfectly true.

FABIA. A suitable present, then.

TELLO.   But more   145

Dark-brown than bay.*

FABIA.   Be careful how
You go. A break like this could make
You lose your concentration. Some bull
Could have your trousers off, and everyone
Be treated to a private viewing.   150
Quite funny, that. A bull helps Tello with
Undressing!

TELLO.   I'll fix my braces, protect
My modesty.

FABIA.   I doubt a bull will give
Much thought to your braces.

TELLO.   I tell
You I don't fear them.

FABIA.   Remember that   155
Medina's bulls get quite upset
With servants from Olmedo.*

TELLO.   This arm
Of mine defeats them all.

FABIA.   Let's hope,
Then, Tello, you aren't gored where no
Bull's horn has ever been before.   160

          [*Exit* FABIA *and* TELLO. *Shouting from the bullring*

FIRST VOICE. Don Rodrigo's fallen!

SECOND VOICE.   Don Alonso goes
To help him! Such bravery!

FIRST VOICE.   See how
He now dismounts!

SECOND VOICE.   He draws his sword.

FIRST VOICE. The bull is wounded fatally!

          Enter DON ALONSO, *supporting* DON RODRIGO.

ALONSO.   Take
  This horse. The others have gone wild,   165
  Are running loose inside the ring.
  Are you alright?

RODRIGO.   Yes, thanks to you.
  I fell so heavily.

ALONSO.   Best not enter
  The ring again. Your servants will
  Assist you. I must go back and find   170
  The horse I left there. God be with you!

          Exit DON ALONSO. *Enter* DON FERNANDO.

FERNANDO. Rodrigo, what's happened? Are you hurt?

RODRIGO. Everything goes badly. First, a fall,
  But, more than that, I owe my life*
  To someone I'm so jealous of,   175
  I long to see him dead.

FERNANDO.   The King
  A witness to it all, and now
  Inés has seen her brave young man
  Put down the bull to save your life.

RODRIGO. It drives me mad! Can there be anyone   180
  In this entire world less fortunate
  Than I? I am insulted, offended,
  Rejected, driven mad with jealousy,
  Now dishonoured.* I looked towards
  Inés to see if in her eyes   185
  I could detect the slightest sign
  Of sympathy. Why do I worship her
  When she shows such ingratitude?
  I doubt that Nero showed as much
  Disdain while he observed Rome burn,*   190
  As did Inés when she looked down on me!
  But then, when she observed Alonso,
  Her jasmine cheeks began to blush
  As bright as any pink carnation.

Her rose-red lips revealed those pearls*   195
Which were the sweet reward for his
Success, the joy of seeing me
Prostrate at Don Alonso's feet,
The helpless victim of misfortune.
I swear to God that smile of hers,   200
Before Apollo* ushers in the dawn
And turns the sky to gold, shall be
Transformed to tears if I should meet
This so-called gentleman of hers
Between Medina and Olmedo.   205

FERNANDO. He knows how to defend himself.

RODRIGO. You underestimate my jealousy.

FERNANDO. The greatest monster, so it's said.
But matters of great consequence
Must be approached with common sense.   210

Exit both. Enter the KING, *the* CONSTABLE,
and ATTENDANTS.

KING. The festivities have finished late.
But still, I have not seen better.

CONSTABLE. I have informed them that you leave
Tomorrow. However, they are anxious that
You see the tournament arranged   215
In your honour. Medina begs
Your Majesty to stay just one
More day.

KING.   It would be interesting.

CONSTABLE. And your presence much appreciated.

KING. Then I agree to it. Remember, though,   220
We have to reach Toledo in good time
And meet the Infante* as arranged.

CONSTABLE. The Knight from Olmedo has performed
Superbly.

KING.   He has, indeed, enjoyed
Good fortune.

CONSTABLE.   It's difficult to know   225
Which is the greater: good fortune or
His valour. He is certainly brave.

KING. He seems to excel at everything.

CONSTABLE. Your Majesty is right to favour him.

KING. No more than he deserves, or that,   230
For your part, you favour him too.

Exit both. Enter DON ALONSO *and* TELLO.
*It is night.**

TELLO. Master, we've waited far too long.
It's much too late to start.

ALONSO.   My parents will
Be waiting anxiously. I have
To go, however late it is.   235

TELLO. If you start talking to Inés,
You'll soon forget your parents. You'll still
Be here at daybreak.

ALONSO.   I doubt I shall.
My soul will tell me when it's time
To leave.

TELLO.   I hear voices. Leonor's,   240
I think.

ALONSO. See how the stars shine brighter still
As my Inés approaches.

LEONOR *at the window.*

LEONOR.   Is that Don
Alonso?

ALONSO. It is.

LEONOR.   My sister will soon

Be here. She's with my father, discussing
The fiesta. Tello can come inside.   245
Inés has a present for him.

ALONSO.   Tello, go
Ahead.

TELLO.   If I don't appear again, sir,
Just start without me. I'll catch you up.

                                                    [*Exit* TELLO

ALONSO. Oh, when, Leonor, will I be allowed
To come inside?

LEONOR.   I think quite soon.   250
My father is full of praise for you,
And well disposed. When he's informed
You love Inés and she loves you,
He'll welcome you with open arms.

               INÉS *appears at the window.**

INÉS. Who are you speaking with?

LEONOR.   Why, Don   255
Rodrigo.

INÉS.   You lie, it is my lord.

ALONSO. No, not your lord, Inés. I am
Your slave.

INÉS.   You cannot be if you
Are my true master.

LEONOR.   I'll leave you.
Who would want to disturb lovers   260
Other than someone truly jealous?

                                                  [*Exit* LEONOR

INÉS. So are you well, Alonso?

ALONSO.   It was
As if I had no life, and so,

To live, I come to see you once again.

INÉS. I think the sadness of our parting now   265
    Is meant to temper all the joy
    I felt on seeing you the paragon
    Of knights, the torment of all ladies.
    I am so jealous of each one
    Of them. I wanted them to sing   270
    Your praises, then regretted it
    In case they fell in love with you.
    So many names and titles were
    Conferred on you through envy in
    The men and admiration in   275
    The women. My father longs that you
    Should marry Leonor and so
    Become his son-in-law, a thought
    That gratifies my love for him
    But fills my heart with jealousy.   280
    'You shall be mine,' I tell myself,
    The words contained, my soul proclaiming it
    Quite openly. But how can I
    Be happy if you now depart?

ALONSO. I go only to see my parents.   285

INÉS. And go you should, but that does not
    Prevent my sadness.

ALONSO.   Nor mine, Inés.
    But, going to Olmedo, I leave
    My soul here in Medina. How strange!
    To leave, yet not to leave. Love fears   290
    Such absences, and fear in turn
    Inspires jealousy. And so I go,
    Half dead and yet still half alive.
    What can I say as I prepare to leave,
    *My foot already in the stirrup?** 295

    My lady, all my days are spent
    Amongst such harsh imaginings,
    That sometimes I am happy in

The midst of sadness, yet most sad
When I feel greatest happiness.   300
I am obsessed by darkest thoughts
Of losing you, and when I think
Such thoughts, imagination proves
So strong, no matter how I try,
I am convinced I am to die.   305

I know my rivals envy me,
And fear so much that, though I am
Convinced I can defeat them all,
I spend my anxious days between
Conflicting thoughts of love and fear.   310
I think perhaps we shall not meet
Again, and so I live obsessed
By thoughts that death is close at hand.
I imagine the words I'll put on paper,
And so now write this farewell letter.   315

To be thought of as your husband is
For me the greatest happiness;
And so, for one so loved and favoured as
Myself, it seems but just reward
That I should feel the greatest sadness.   320
To leave is surely to die, to write
Is to describe my death though I still live.
Believe me, Inés, when I return,
I shall be dead when I arrive,
If leaving is to cease to be alive.   325

I know that this is mere sadness,
And yet, Inés, its hold is such,
It speaks to me and tells me this:
'If you are dead when you depart,
How can it be that you'll return?'   330
I go, then, to my death,* although
To die, I know, is not to lose you.
For if you still possess my soul,
How can I then depart and be alive?

How can I not be dead when I arrive? 335

INÉS. My lord, these fears you express
Have saddened me. If they are caused
By jealousy, it means your love
For me lacks faith. In part, I understand,
But you, it seems, have failed to understand 340
My love.

ALONSO.　　I promise you, my fears are
The product not of jealousy,
But of a soul that cannot cast
Aside such dark imaginings.
What I have said is not the fruit 345
Of any doubts I have of you.
But only of my fearful dreams,
Ill-founded fantasies.

LEONOR *appears at the window.*

INÉS.　　　　　　　Leonor
Returns. What is it?

ALONSO.　　　　　　Time for me
To leave, no doubt.

LEONOR.　　　　　　Yes, father is 350
About to go to bed. He wants
To see Inés.

INÉS.　　　Then you must leave,
Alonso. It can't be helped. Goodbye.

[*Exit* INÉS *and* LEONOR

ALONSO. Oh, when, God willing, will we meet
Again? Now that I must depart, 355
My life is at an end. Tello
Has not appeared. Perhaps he too
Finds parting difficult. I'll go
Alone and he can follow later on.

As ALONSO *is about to exit, he is confronted
by a* SHADOWY FIGURE* *wearing a hat and
a black mask. He has his hand placed on the
hilt of his sword.*

What's that? Who's there? He pays me no   360
Attention. Who are you? Speak! That I,
Who fear no one, should now be frightened by
This person! Are you Don Rodrigo?
Tell me who you are!

SHADOW.   I am Don Alonso.

ALONSO. What?

SHADOW.   Don Alonso.   365

ALONSO [*aside*].   Another Don
Alonso, clearly! [*Aloud*] If this
Is some deceit, I challenge you
To draw your sword!

                                        [*Exit* SHADOW
                He's turned away.
It would be madness to pursue him.
Oh, fearful imagination! The man   370
I saw was my own shadow! No,
Not shadow! For it seemed flesh
And blood and said that it was Don
Alonso. These things are fashioned by
My sadness, the product of a restless and   375
Unhappy mind. Oh, why does it
Torment me with this vision of
Myself? Such baseless fears are
The province of more superstitious minds!
Perhaps it is a trick of Fabia's   380
To stop me going to Olmedo.
She's always telling me to be
More prudent, not to journey at night,
And this because she knows, she says,
How others envy me. As for   385
Rodrigo, envy is impossible,

For I have saved his life, and he,
On that account, is in my debt.
For any gentleman of true
Nobility and worth, it is   390
An obligation he must not forget.
Indeed, this is the reason he
And I can now be loyal friends.
Ingratitude does not reside
In noble hearts, only in the hearts   395
Of those who, lacking noble blood,*
Are base and common. In short, it is
The very quintessence of
Ignoble minds and deeds that he
Who has received some benefit,   400
Should in return display ingratitude.

> *Exit* DON ALONSO. *Enter* DON RODRIGO,
> DON FERNANDO, MENDO, *and* LAÍN.

RODRIGO. Today shall see the end of both
   My jealousy and Don Alonso's life.

FERNANDO. Your mind is finally made up.

RODRIGO. Yes, nothing can save him now. Did they   405
   Not break the promise I was given?
   Her wish to be a nun, a cruel trick!
   And all the time his servant, Tello,
   Pretending to teach her Latin,
   While in reality he passed   410
   Her letters from Alonso written in
   Romance!* Don Pedro too, treating Fabia
   As if she were the true embodiment
   Of virtue! Oh, wretched Inés! I do
   Not blame your innocence for falling foul   415
   Of Fabia's evil spells! How could
   You know, as modest as you are,
   What trickery was in the air,
   Or that our honour—yours and mine—
   Was being trampled underfoot?   420
   How many noble families

Have been disgraced by bawds and witchcraft!*
Fabia is capable of moving mountains,
Of stopping rivers in full flood.
She rules the evil ministers   425
Of Acheron,* as does a lord
His servants. Fabia, on whose account
A man can be transported through
The air from here to places far
Away—to burning equatorial lands,   430
To freezing Poles—and she instructs Inés!
Could anything be more ironic!

FERNANDO. The very reason why I would
    Not seek revenge!

RODRIGO.   In God's name,
    Would you have me be a coward too?   435

FERNANDO. Much better if you were indifferent.

RODRIGO. Perhaps you could be that. I cannot.

MENDO. My lord, listen! The echo tells
    Us people come on horseback.

RODRIGO.   If others come
    With him, it means he is afraid.   440

FERNANDO. Do not believe it. He is quite fearless.

RODRIGO. Everyone hide, and not a word!
    You, Mendo, behind the tree, your musket* at
    The ready.

FERNANDO.   How fickle is good fortune!
    How unpredictable success!   445
    Today he dazzled in the presence of
    The King, admired for his deeds
    By all. And now death lies in wait
    For him. We are about to see his fall.

They hide. Enter DON ALONSO.

ALONSO. Never before have I felt fear such   450

As this. And yet I think it caused
By sadness. The sound of running water,
Of leaves that gently rustle in
The wind, increase this sadness, and though
I journey on, I am persuaded to   455
Return. It is no proof of bravery,
But love and loyalty to both
My parents contradict my fears,
And so I am resolved, though I
Admit, to leave Inés so suddenly   460
Was harsh. How dark it is! So full
Of fearful shadows till the dawn
Begins to place its golden feet
On bright and flowered carpets. But now
The sound of someone singing.   465
Who can it be? A shepherd, perhaps,
Who now goes to his flock, the song
Still far away but coming closer.
The instrument he plays is sweet
And sonorous, not rustic. Oh, when   470
One's thoughts are overcome by sadness,
How melancholy music sounds!

[*Singing off, backstage, and coming nearer*

PEASANT. *For at night they killed**
That noble soul,
The jewel of Medina,   475
The flower of Olmedo.

ALONSO. Heavens! Are my ears deceiving me?
If this is how you choose to warn
Me of what lies ahead, it is
Too late. I cannot now turn back.   480
This must be one of Fabia's tricks.
Inés has asked her to devise
Some plan to stop me going to Olmedo.

PEASANT. *A shadow warned*
He should not go,   485
And it advised

He should not go,
The jewel of Medina,
The flower of Olmedo.

ALONSO. You there, you, the singer!

PEASANT.   Who calls   490
To me?

ALONSO. I seem to have lost my way.

PEASANT. I'm coming.

Enter the PEASANT.

PEASANT.   Ask what you will.

ALONSO.   Everything
Now frightens me. Where are you going?

PEASANT. My work beckons.

ALONSO.   Who taught you that song,
So full of sadness?

PEASANT.   I learned it in   495
Medina, sir.

ALONSO.   But I am from
Olmedo, the man the song refers to,
And, as you see, I'm still alive.

PEASANT. I cannot tell you more about
The song than what was told to me   500
By one called Fabia.* You heard its words.
Turn back! Do not go further than
This stream.

ALONSO.   I am of noble birth.
To turn back would be cowardice.

PEASANT. And not to do so would be folly.   505
Go back, go back to Medina!

ALONSO. Accompany me!

PEASANT.   I cannot.

[Exit the PEASANT

ALONSO.   But these
Are phantoms, visions conjured up
By fear. Listen, wait! He's gone,
And yet no sound of footsteps! Wait!   510
The only reply my echoing words!
The songs says I am dead. It must
Refer to something in the past,
When someone from Olmedo* was,
Upon this very road, murdered   515
By others from Medina. I'm half-
Way there. What would be said of me
If I turned back? I hear footsteps.
If these are people going to
Olmedo, I'll gladly join them.   520

Enter DON RODRIGO, DON FERNANDO, *and
their* HENCHMEN.

RODRIGO. Who goes there?

ALONSO.   A man, as you can see.

FERNANDO. Stop at once!

ALONSO.   Gentlemen, if lack
Of money forces you to actions such
As these, my house is close at hand.
I've money there. In fact, it is   525
My custom and my honour to give alms
To those in need.

RODRIGO.   Remove your sword.*

ALONSO. But why?

RODRIGO.   Because I say so.

ALONSO.   You know
Who you are speaking to?

FERNANDO.   That person from
Olmedo, the slayer of bulls, who in   530

His foolish arrogance, offends
The people of Medina,* and who,
By using infamous bawds, insults
Don Pedro.

ALONSO.   If you were truly men
Of noble blood, you would have challenged me   535
Before, not now, when I'm alone.
Why not the time you ran away
And left your cloak behind, instead
Of now, at dead of night, a group
Of you, courageous only in   540
Your arrogance? But even so,
I am indebted, for though you seem
So many, in truth you are but few,
And villains all!

                              [*They fight*

RODRIGO.   I come to kill
You, not to challenge you! If that   545
Were so, this would be single combat!
Shoot him!

                              [*Gunshot off-stage*

ALONSO.   Traitors all! If you did not
Have guns, you'd not have killed me.

FERNANDO.   Well
Done, Mendo!

          [*Exit* DON RODRIGO, DON FERNANDO, *and their* HENCHMEN

ALONSO.   Little did I heed
Heaven's warnings. I have been deceived   550
By my own pride and murdered by
The jealousy of others. Who
Will help me in this solitary place?

                    Enter TELLO.

TELLO. Those riders galloping towards
Medina! I asked them if they'd seen   555

My master. They did not answer me.
The signs are ominous. I can't
Stop shaking!

ALONSO.   Please God, have pity! I'm dying!
You know my sole intention was
To marry her. Oh, Inés!

TELLO.   What voice   560
Is that? Its echo seems so full
Of sadness. It came from over there,
Just off the road. Why, every drop
Of blood has drained from me! My hair
Is stood on end so much, my hat   565
No longer needs my skull to offer it
Support! Sir!

ALONSO.   Who is it?

TELLO.   Oh, God!
Why doubt what I am seeing? My master, Don
Alonso!

ALONSO.   Tello, it's good to see you!

TELLO. Why good if I have come too late?   570
Why good if, now I'm here, I find
You bathed in blood? You traitors, dogs
And villains! Come and kill me too!
You've killed the noblest, bravest, and
Most handsome knight who ever wore   575
A sword in all Castile!

ALONSO.   Tello! Tello!
Such little time remains, think of
My soul. Quickly, help me on to
Your horse! Take me to see my parents!

TELLO. What? To bring them these glad tidings from   580
The fiesta? What will your noble father say,
Your mother, the people of the town?
Oh, merciful Heaven! Vengeance, I beg you!

Exit TELLO *and* DON ALONSO. *Enter* DON
PEDRO, DOÑA INÉS, DOÑA LEONOR, FABIA,
and ANA.

INÉS. So many favours from the King?

PEDRO. Today his Majesty revealed   585
His heart's nobility through all
His generous rewards. Medina thanks
Him, and I, for what I have received,
Now bring you both to kiss his hand.

LEONOR. He's leaving, then?

PEDRO.   He is, Leonor.   590
The Infante awaits him in Toledo.
I cannot thank his Majesty
Enough, both for myself and for
The two of you who later on
Will profit from his kindness.   595
He has made me Warden of Burgos.*
You must kiss his royal hand.

INÉS.   Fabia,
This means I shall be far away
From him.

FABIA.   Fortune, it seems, still does
Not favour you.

INÉS.   Since yesterday   600
I've felt the strangest kind of sadness.

FABIA. Don't be surprised if there's still worse
To come. Who can predict with certainty
What lies in store for us?

INÉS.   What can
Be worse than absence? I think not even death   605
Itself.

PEDRO. Inés, this plan of yours . . .
Nothing would give me greater joy
Than if you now abandoned it.

It's not that I'd oblige you to,
Simply that I'd like to see you married.   610

INÉS. To change my mind would not be just
Because you wish it, father. There'd be
Another reason.

PEDRO.   Well, what is it?

LEONOR. Let me speak on your behalf, Inés.
The marriage you have in mind for her   615
Is one she doesn't want. There, I've said it.

PEDRO. Then, knowing of my love, you should
Have said so. If I had only known,
I'd never have considered it.

LEONOR. She loves a certain gentleman   620
The King has honoured with a cross.*
Her love is honourable, and honest too.

PEDRO. Then if he has such qualities,
And you're in love with him, what can
I say? Marry him, Inés! You have   625
My blessing! Who is this gentleman?

LEONOR. Don Alonso Manrique.

PEDRO.   Why, this
Is excellent news! You mean from Olmedo?

LEONOR. Yes, father.

PEDRO.   A man of worth, quite clearly!
You've chosen wisely. I never thought   630
You suited to a convent! Come
Along, Inés! Speak up!

INÉS.   .   Leonor
Exaggerates. My true intentions aren't . . .

PEDRO. Let's not go into it. It's time
To celebrate the wisdom of   635
Your choice. Consider him your husband as
From now. I shall be honoured by

A son-in-law so rich, so well-
Regarded, so nobly born.

INÉS.　　　　　　　　Thank you, thank
You, father. Fabia, I'm so happy.　　　　　　　　640

FABIA. Let me congratulate you now,
Commiserate afterwards.

LEONOR.　　　　　The King!

PEDRO. Approach, and kiss his royal hand.

INÉS. I do so happily!

　　　　　Enter the KING, *the* CONSTABLE,
　　　　　ATTENDANTS, DON RODRIGO,
　　　　　and DON FERNANDO.

PEDRO.　　　　　Your Majesty.
I offer humble thanks. You honour both　　　　　645
My daughters and myself in making me
Warden of Burgos.

KING.　　　　　I have been pleased,
Don Pedro, both by your valour and
Your loyalty.

PEDRO.　　My one desire is
To be of service.

KING.　　　　Are you married?　　　　　650

INÉS. No, your Majesty.

KING.　　　　　Your name?

INÉS.　　　　　　　　　Inés.

KING. And yours?

LEONOR.　　　Leonor.

CONSTABLE.　　　Your Majesty.
Don Pedro merits sons-in-law
Of worth such as are present here.
On their behalf I now request　　　　　655

That they be married to his daughters.

KING. Who are they?

RODRIGO.   With your permission, sir,
  I seek Inés's hand in marriage.

FERNANDO. And I, sir, offer both my hand
  And will to Leonor.

KING.   In these   660
  Two handsome gentlemen, your daughters will,
  Don Pedro, have most worthy husbands.

PEDRO. Your Majesty, I cannot give
  Inés to Don Rodrigo. She is,
  You see, already promised to Don   665
  Alonso Manrique, the knight
  From Olmedo, whom you saw fit
  To favour.

KING.   I further intend to make
  Him Knight Commander.

RODRIGO.   This is too much!

FERNANDO. Control yourself!

KING.   He is a man   670
  Of many qualities.

Enter TELLO.

TELLO.   Let me in!

KING. What is that noise?

CONSTABLE.   The guard restrains
  A servant who wishes to speak
  With you.

KING.   Leave him!

CONSTABLE.   He comes in tears,
  Demanding justice.

KING.   It is my duty to   675

Dispense it. Such is the meaning of
This sceptre.

TELLO.   Oh, great Don Juan, ruler
Of all Castile, despite the envy of
Your enemies!* I come here to
Medina, accompanied by another, old   680
In years,* to ask that justice be brought
Against two traitors. The old man is
Outside, exhausted if not dead
By such great sorrow, and so, on his
Behalf, I choose to use this violence   685
On both your guards and your ears.
Listen, then, since Heaven above has placed
In your hands the rod of justice,
And given you discretion to reward
Good men and punish those who have   690
Done wrong. Last night, after the fiestas of
The Cross of May, celebrated by
Medina's knights to prove that where
There is a cross, there is true passion,
My master, Don Alonso, the worthy youth   695
Who was deserving of your praise,
Departed from Medina for Olmedo.
He wished to let his aged parents know
That he'd survived the bulls, less fierce,
It proved, than those who were his enemies.   700
Because it was my job to see
To both the horses and the harnesses,
I stayed behind, and by the time
I left, unruly night, half-way
Between both poles,* had offered treachery   705
A sword, ambush assistance, fear
A swift escape. As I passed by
A stream and crossed a bridge that points
The way, I saw six men* riding
Together towards Medina,   710
And clearly disturbed. The moon
Appeared late, blood-red, and though
Its light was pale, it helped me recognize

Two men amongst the group. Perhaps
Heaven's tapers light the darkest and   715
Most silent place in order to reveal
Those who are guilty of true wickedness,
And prove to us there is no secret we
Can hide from God above. I hurried on,
And there I found my master, Don   720
Alonso, covered in blood and on
The point of death. Your Majesty,
The very mention of it makes
Me weep, my grief impedes my speech.
I placed him on my horse, and still   725
There was sufficient life in him
To make his enemies believe
He was not dead, and still enough
To reach Olmedo and receive
The blessing of his aged parents who,   730
Such was their sorrow, bathed his wounds
With tears and kisses. His household and
His lands are deep in mourning. His funeral will,
Your Majesty, remind us of the Phoenix,
For he, though dead, will live again   735
Through his great fame, which, as we know,
Ignores the frailty of men
And time's forgetfulness.

KING.   This is,
Indeed, most strange!

INÉS.   Oh, what am I
To do!

PEDRO.   Restrain your tears, Inés!   740
You'll weep enough when we're at home.

INÉS. Father, the plan I entertained
In jest . . . I now propose it seriously.
As for these evil men, I ask
Your Majesty for justice.*

KING.   You say   745

You saw them. Who, then, are these traitors?
I swear to God I shall not leave
This place until they are my prisoners.

TELLO. They stand before your Majesty.
  The first is Don Rodrigo, the other Don   750
  Fernando.

CONSTABLE. Their guilt is written on
  Their faces.

RODRIGO.   Your Majesty . . .

KING.   Arrest them!
  Tomorrow in a public place
  Cut off their evil heads.
  So ends the tragic history of   755
  *The Knight from Olmedo.**

PUNISHMENT WITHOUT REVENGE

(*El castigo sin venganza*)

A Tragedy*

THE CHARACTERS OF THE PLAY

The Duke of Ferrara
The Count Federico
Albano
Rutilio
Floro
Lucindo
The Marquis of Gonzaga
Casandra
Aurora
Lucrecia
Batín
Cintia
Febo and Ricardo

ACT ONE

Night. The DUKE OF FERRARA. FEBO *and* RICARDO, *servants.*

RICARDO. A splendid trick, my lord!

FEBO.   I think
The lady would be pleased to know
A real duke had just deceived her.

DUKE. Be quiet! No one must know I am
Ferrara.

RICARDO.   Disguise is but a licence   5
For all sins. See how the cloak of night
Conceals the sky, a cape bedecked
With silver stars, the moon above
A brightly jewelled pin on high.

DUKE. Are you gone mad?

FEBO.   You must admit,   10
My lord, the metaphor's appropriate.
No modern poet* would have thought of it.

RICARDO. If I took their liberties,
I expect you'd call it ingenuity.
I read this poet once, would you believe?   15
He called the moon a piece of cottage-cheese!

DUKE. I quite agree. The stuff they write
Today lacks quality. All sleight
Of hand. The poet waves a magic wand
And there, behold, produces from   20
His mouth a string of images.
Oh what a tedious thing this is!
Let's change the subject. The lady seems
Quite interesting.

RICARDO.   The lady is

A jewel, sir, a real gem!   25
But even so, you have to know
The poor girl is sadly burdened.

DUKE. How?

RICARDO.   She has a husband, a man
So mean he keeps her to himself.
Won't let her give herself to someone else.   30

FEBO. My lord, conceal yourself.

DUKE.   Such men
Are by their nature hard of heart.
They lack true generosity.

FEBO. I do agree, my lord. The man
Whose wife receives such welcome gifts   35
As jewels, gold, and clothes, should, as
I see it, feel more sympathy
For him who gives.* I mean to say,
No sooner has the wife passed on,
He gets his hands on half her fortune.   40

RICARDO. It's true. This is the kind of man
Who in the noble art of charity
Is sadly lacking. You see? I turn
The phrase around* to illustrate my skill
In modern poetry.

DUKE.   Such people are   45
The true disciples of the devil.
They tempt us till we sign their pact,
And then they stop us in the act.

RICARDO. We could stop here, my lord. I do,
However, think the going might   50
Be rather hard.

DUKE.   Why so?

RICARDO.   The mother is
A perfect saint, prays all the time.
She does her best to keep her girls

In line. Two lovely creatures, one
Like pearl, the other silver; somewhere   55
Between a sparkling and full-bodied wine.

DUKE. The devil take them. Never judge
A bottle by its label.

RICARDO.   There is
Another girl not far from here,
As sweet as honey; and you should see   60
Her dark complexion.

DUKE.   How about passion?

RICARDO. As much, my lord, as you'd expect
From any fiery dark brunette.*
The bloke who lives with her, a dull,
Suspicious, sullen soul, reminds   65
You of a great, cud-chewing bull.

FEBO. You really mean cud-chewing cow,
My friend. You chose that rhyme to make
The line end like the previous one.

RICARDO. I know another girl. She lives   70
Quite near. Oh, very clever!
She would have made a lovely lawyer.

DUKE. Take me to her.

RICARDO.   She'd never let you in
At this late hour.

DUKE.   Never say 'won't'.
Tell her I'm the duke, and I don't   75
Take no for an answer.

RICARDO.   All right,
It might just work.

DUKE.   Come, knock the door.

RICARDO. She must have been expecting you.
Two hefty kicks and hey presto!

CINTIA *above.* *

CINTIA. Who's there?

RICARDO.   It's me.

CINTIA.   Who's me?

RICARDO.   A friend   80
Of yours, Cintia. Open up. I've got
The Duke down here. I sang your praises
To him, see, and now he wants to see you.

CINTIA. See me? The Duke?

RICARDO.   Don't you believe me?

CINTIA. Oh, I believe he's with you, yes.   85
But as for seeing me, a nobleman
At such a time of night? You must
Think I'm some sort of simpleton.

RICARDO. He comes disguised because he is
A gentleman and wouldn't want   90
A lady's reputation ruined.
I wouldn't tell you lies, now would I?

CINTIA. Ricardo, if you'd told me this
A month ago, I might just have
Believed the Duke would fancy knocking at   95
My door. I mean, the whole world knows
His reputation: he thinks he is
God's gift to women and so has lived
His life devoted to that passion.
To live so freely meant, of course,   100
He never thought of getting married,
Even though, upon his death, his land
And wealth would be inherited,
As some would say, unfairly, by
His only son and heir, the bastard   105
Federico. And so, a month
Ago, I could believe the Duke
Might think of knocking at my door.

But now, they say, he is to change
His ways and has agreed to marry,   110
And for that reason Federico's gone
To Mantua* to fetch Casandra,
The bride-to-be. How, then, can this
Be such a nightly escapade
As he was once accustomed to,   115
When all the wedding-plans are made
And his new bride is almost due?
If this were Federico, it
Would be an impropriety;
In him a sin completely unforgivable.   120
And you, if you had any kind
Of loyalty, would not so openly
Abuse your master's reputation.
I do believe the Duke's at home,
Tucked-up in bed, and what you've said   125
To me is just a pack of lies,
A piece of fiction you've made up
To get me into conversation.
I'll close my window now, so you
Can go. Try your luck again tomorrow.   130

DUKE. What kind of bawdy-house is this
    You've brought me to?

RICARDO.   Don't blame me, master.
    I always try to do my best
    For you.

DUKE [to Febo]. To think tonight's success
    Depended on a fool like him.   135

FEBO. Depend on me, my lord. Just say
    The word, I'll kick the door right in.

DUKE. That I should have to listen to such things!

FEBO. It's true Ricardo is to blame,
    But even so the nobleman   140
    Who really wants to know what kind

Of fame and reputation he
Enjoys, or if he's loved or plain
Despised, should never listen to
A fawning servant's flattery.   145
A better ploy's to sally forth
At night, on foot or in his coach,
And, well-disguised, to ascertain
What shape his reputation's in.
Some famous emperors and kings*   150
Resorted to such subtle cunning.

DUKE. A man who gives himself to listening,
Will only hear the most offensive things
About himself. These kings that seem
So wise to you, to me are fools.   155
The common herd is not concerned
With truth, and any man who puts
His faith in them is bound to get
His fingers burned when everything
They say runs contrary to reason.   160
Some discontented fellow wants
Revenge, and so invents a story which
The common herd then seeks to bend
To satisfy its need for novelty.
And since such people are by rank   165
Forbidden entry to the palaces
Where great men live, they choose instead
To feed the envy that they feel
By means of slanderous attacks.
As for myself, it is a fact   170
That I have lived indulgently,*
Preferring pleasure to the need
To marry anyone: in part
Because I've wanted to be free,
In part because I thought my son,   175
Though illegitimate, should be
My only heir. But now that he
Is on his way to Mantua
To fetch my bride, the fair Casandra,

I am resolved to put my past   180
Behind me.

FEBO.   Marriage is undoubtedly
The remedy, my lord.

RICARDO.   And if
You listen at this door, you'll find
An answer to your melancholy too.

DUKE. You must mean music.

RICARDO.   Can you hear?   185

DUKE. Who is it lives there?

RICARDO.   An actor-manager.*

FEBO. The very best in Italy.

DUKE. They sing extremely well. Does he write
Good plays?

RICARDO.   All plays depend, my lord,
On playing to a friendly audience.*   190
The audience claps, it guarantees
A play's success; the audience boos,
It means the play's a certain miss.

FEBO. I think he means the theatre's
A hit-or-miss affair, my lord.   195

DUKE. For our wedding, Febo, you'll
Prepare the very finest rooms,
And look for plays where wit
And ingenuity exceed
Vulgarity.*

FEBO.   I promise I   200
Shall see to it, my lord. You'll have
Those plays refinement and good taste
Permit.

DUKE.   Are they rehearsing yet?

RICARDO. A woman's speaking.

DUKE.   It might be
   Andrelina,* an actress of   205
   The highest reputation. Such strength,
   Intelligence, such deep emotion!

VOICE [*off*]. Such thoughts will never let me rest,
   Such memories endure and persist,
   And all that once was glory unsurpassed,   210
   Is now a constant agony.
   If I could but forget such memories
   As now remind me of a joy that's lost!
   For though they think they sweeten misery,
   They deepen longing for a pleasure past.   215

DUKE. How well she speaks her lines!

FEBO.   I've always found
   There's nothing finer than a good actress,
   Master!

DUKE.   I would hear more, but find
   Her words depress me so, I'm going home
   To bed.

RICARDO. It's only ten o'clock.   220
   It's far too early.

DUKE.   There's nothing here
   That pleases me.

RICARDO.   Not even her?

DUKE. I am afraid of what she still
   Might say of me.

RICARDO.   Of you? What could
   She say?

DUKE.   A play, Ricardo, is   225
   A mirror to all men,* in which
   The fool, the wise, the young, the old,
   The weak, the strong, the mild, the bold,
   The king, the prince, the governor,
   The girl, the bride, the lover, wife,   230

Can by example learn of honour
And of life. We see our customs there,
Both bold and frivolous. It mixes
Comedy with seriousness and tragedy
With jokes.* But I have heard enough   235
To know her speech informs me of
Myself, and wish to know no more.
The truth is simply the majority of men
Would willingly ignore the truth
About themselves.   240

> *They leave. Enter* FEDERICO, *a handsome*
> *young man. He is dressed in travelling clothes*
> *and accompanied by his servant,* BATÍN.

BATÍN. It beats me what you're up to, Federico.
Why have we stopped amongst these willow-trees?*
Why are their roots a pillow for your head
When there's important business still ahead?

FEDERICO. My mood does not allow me, as I ought,   245
To move with greater speed. I much prefer,
Oppressed by melancholy thoughts,* no other
Company but mine; to lie beneath this canopy
Of trees that listens to the water's sound
And in its silver mirror sees the cool   250
Green image of reflected foliage.
If I could but escape or find
Some refuge from the hideous prospect of
My father's marriage! I am his son and heir,
And now on this account must bear   255
The consequences of this deed.
I must pretend to those I know that I
Am pleased, when in reality my heart
Is heavy with disgust and bleeds
For everything I now consider lost.   260
My father bids me go to Mantua,
Where I shall meet my future stepmother,
And every step I take is one more reason
Why I should regard her as a fatal poison.

BATÍN. The truth is, master, what was once   265
  Your father's scandalous behaviour,
  Condemned by strangers and by friends,
  Has now surrendered at the feet of virtue.
  For anyone who wants to settle down, you see,
  By far the most effective bridle is   270
  To marry. A loyal subject once*
  Presented to the King of France a horse
  Whose two great qualities were liveliness
  Of spirit and outstanding beauty.
  Its name was Swan, such was the snow-   275
  White colour of its coat and mane
  That, when it raised its lovely head,
  Fell to its feet. It was as if,
  Enjoying beauty and disdain,
  It had been blessed by Nature's hand   280
  With attributes that are by men
  Considered feminine, and so,
  If it were mounted by a man,
  At once proclaimed itself unwilling.
  The King, observing that the horse   285
  Was beautiful but obstinate,
  Commanded it be led into a cave
  Where that great primate of the animals,
  A proud and fierce lion, had his den.
  Confronted by the lion's rage,   290
  That mighty horse began to feel
  Its courage quickly fade, and all its mane
  And coat grow stiff as fear made
  Each hair into a bright, sharp spear,
  And what had been a sprightly nag,   295
  Was suddenly a frightened hedgehog.
  From each and every hair it sweated fear,
  And soon became so calm and humble,
  The smallest dwarf was master in the saddle.
  That horse that hated to be ridden did   300
  From that day forth what it was bidden.

FEDERICO. Batín, I know that marriage may well be

The remedy to change my father's ways,
But am I not allowed regret
For having wasted all my hours, all my days   305
In foolish dreams? I know a woman can
Control the proudest and the fiercest man;
She is a lioness before whose gaze he seems
A lamb, his wildness at the very sight
Of his first-born transformed to such extremes   310
Of tenderness as will allow that man
To hold his babbling, gurgling child
And let it pull and tug his beard.
No humble peasant loves his grain
More dearly than a father loves   315
His family. For them he willingly
Abandons evil ways. But should I care
That my own father, having strayed
So far, should now regret the error of
His ways and by his change of heart ensure   320
That only sons who are legitimate
Can, as from now, lay claim to his estate?
I am a mere messenger,
My task to bring to him a lion bent
On my destruction.   325

BATÍN. My lord, the man who's wise and sensible,
And sees himself the object of
Intolerable ills, is best advised
To demonstrate his patience.
He needs to smile, put on a show   330
Of happiness, lest others think
He's envious, or has a mind to vengeance.

FEDERICO. Must I endure a stepmother?

BATÍN. Perhaps you'll learn to love her, sir.
It's true you've had a family   335
Of stepmothers the Duke has introduced
You to. So what's so terrible about
Another one, not least when she's
A lady too?

FEDERICO.   What's that?

BATÍN.   I think
  It's voices on the river-bank.   340

FEDERICO. A woman's cry for help. I'll go and see.

BATÍN. Much safer if you stay with me, my lord.

FEDERICO. Don't be so cowardly, Batín.
  It sounds as if our help is needed.

                                              [*Exit* FEDERICO

BATÍN. A woman's voice, he's gone, as short   345
  On common sense as great on speed.
  I suppose I'd better go. If she
  Needs him, he might need me. If only he
  Had gone as eagerly as this
  To meet his future stepmother.   350

                                              [*Exit* BATÍN

      Enter FEDERICO *with* CASANDRA *in his arms.**

FEDERICO. To carry you to this safe place,
  These arms are more than honoured, madam.

CASANDRA. I am indebted to you, sir,
  For such true courtesy and grace.

FEDERICO. And I to such good fortune as   355
  Has brought me to this wood and led
  Me from the tedious path I followed.

CASANDRA. Who are these people, sir?

FEDERICO.   The servants who
  Go with me. They understand
  Your every wish is their command.   360

      Enter BATÍN *with* LUCRECIA, *a servant, in his arms.**

BATÍN. If women have the common fault
  Of insubstantiality,
  How can it be, my girl, that you

Are so ridiculously weighty?

LUCRECIA. Good sir, where are you taking me?   365

BATÍN. Why, to a place that's free from all
This river mud, where there's no danger
Of you sinking. I think it's all
A devilish conspiracy.
The river, noting your sylph-   370
Like figure, thought you was a water-
Nymph he fancied for himself, and so
He turned your coach right over. Good
Thing I was near, otherwise
You'd be a gonner now, for sure.   375

FEDERICO. Madam, how can I offer such
Respect as is appropriate
To your person, unless I know
Who I am speaking to?

CASANDRA.   There is
No reason, sir, why you should not.   380
I am Casandra, daughter of
The Duke of Mantua, and soon
To be the Duchess of Ferrara.

FEDERICO. My lady! Why are you alone?

CASANDRA. But I am not. To travel on my own   385
Would be too dangerous. Back there
You'll find the Marquis of Gonzaga.
I simply wished to spend the afternoon
Alone and took the path which brought
Me to the river-bank. The trees   390
Seemed thicker there, the air so cool,
But Fortune chose to play a trick
On me; the coach sank deep in mud,
And, unlike Fortune's wheel,* refused
To move. But tell me who you are, sir.   395
I fancy your appearance
Is proof of true nobility,
As well as witness to your bravery.

And such assistance as you've given me
Is worthy of my warmest thanks.   400
I am obliged to you, as are
The Marquis and my father too.

FEDERICO. Before I tell you who I am, madam,
Please let me kiss your hand.

CASANDRA. You kneel to me? Why this is silliness   405
Indeed! I am the one in your debt.

FEDERICO. It is correct and proper, madam.
I am your son.

CASANDRA.   I must confess,
It was extremely foolish of me not
To guess the truth. Who else   410
Would rescue me in my distress?
Let me embrace you!*

FEDERICO.   It honours me
Sufficiently to kiss your hand.

CASANDRA. Not so. Count Federico, my arms
Repay my debt.

FEDERICO.   I bid my soul   415
Sincerely acknowledge it.
I am at your service, madam.

[*They engage in conversation*

BATÍN. Now that by luck we've found her here,
And there's no further need to go
To Mantua, I have to know   420
If you are just plain lady or
Your excellency*—so I can match
The things I say to your quality.

LUCRECIA. The truth is, friend, I've served
The Duchess since I was a child.   425
I help her both to dress and undress.
I cannot properly be called a lady,
More your lady-in-waiting.

BATÍN. Are you in charge?

LUCRECIA.   Oh, no.

BATÍN.   That means
You'll still be waiting, then. I know   430
A good few noblemen with girls
Like you. It's difficult to tell
If they are maids or just old-maids.
So what's your name?

LUCRECIA.   Lucrecia.

BATÍN.   .   What?
Not her from Rome?*

LUCRECIA.   Oh no, from Mantua.   435

BATÍN. Thank God! The thing is, ever since
I read her history, my head's
Been stuffed with thoughts of chastity
And other kinds of painful purgatory.
Ever heard of Tarquin, have you?   440
Now there's a feller greatly fancied*
By Lucrecia.

LUCRECIA.   I fancy you . . .

BATÍN. Oh, good!

LUCRECIA.   . . . have got a wife already.

BATÍN. Hey, steady on! Why would you want
To know?

LUCRECIA.   So I, my friend, can go   445
And ask her if she thinks you trustworthy.

BATÍN. I'd never have believed you'd play
A dirty trick like that on me.
I suppose you know just who I am.

LUCRECIA. I've no idea.

BATÍN.   Do you mean to say   450
Batín's great fame has never spread

As far as Mantua?

LUCRECIA.   What are
You famous for? You must be one
Of those who always boast of big
Accomplishments and great, outstanding   455
Qualities, but when examined close
At hand, are best described as small,
Or even worse, extremely puny.

BATÍN. Come on, I'm never one of those,
Nor would I ever criticize   460
Another man's outstanding virtues.
It was a joke, a bit of fun.
You musn't think I'm someone likes
To boast and brag. I'm just a bloke
Who longs to have his name well known   465
And toasted by celebrities
In all the sciences and arts.
For lesser folk than me, you see, true fame
Is but a harvest reaped by fools
From seeds once sown by silly farts.   470

CASANDRA. I cannot say what meeting you
Like this has meant to me, except
To say that all I've heard of you
Falls short of actual reality.
Your speech and manner are the proof,   475
My son and lord, of noble personage;
Your words and deeds the sign that true
Heroic acts speak of a soul
Whose hallmark is its boundless courage.
I am convinced my straying from   480
My chosen path was luck indeed:
A timely error* so designed
To make us meet with greater speed
Than otherwise seemed possible.
As sometimes happens when a storm   485
Breaks out at sea, and in the dark
Of night St Elmo's fire* burns

And flashes brilliantly, so was
My own predicament the night,
The river sea, my coach a ship,   490
Myself its captain, you the brightest star
In my dark firmament. From this
Day forth I'll be a mother to you,
Federico, and you shall have respect
For me, as any boy must have   495
For his dear mother. You please me so,
You fill my heart with so much joy,
I think I'd rather have you as my son
Than now become the Duchess of Ferrara.

FEDERICO. To have set eyes on you fills me   500
With fear, lovely lady, and so
Much flattery prevents my saying
What I must. I think my father now
Divides in two my very being,
For if I owe my origin to him,   505
Which is to say my flesh and blood,
To you I owe my very soul,
Which is to say that I am born again.
For these two births the victory
Is yours, for if man's soul comes down   510
To him from God, I cannot say
I knew until today where my
Soul was; and so, if I now owe
To you this sudden recognition of
My soul, then you alone can claim   515
You have achieved my resurrection.
Consider too that if, as I
Now claim, you give me life, the Duke
Must see me as his first-born son
When you, my lady, are his wife.   520
And if you think it strange that I,
A full-grown man, can thus be born
Again, I offer you as my excuse
That brilliant star we call the sun,
Which, having lived so many thousand years,   525

Must witness its new birth with every dawn.

Enter the MARQUIS GONZAGA, RUTILIO,
and SERVANTS.

RUTILIO. I can't think where they are, my lord.
I left them here.

MARQUIS.　　　　It would have been
A great misfortune if the man
You speak of had not seen and rescued her.　　　　530

RUTILIO. I swear, she wanted me to leave
Her there. No doubt she thought her feet
Could turn the happy stream to snow,*
Or where the water froths and swirls,
Transform it into gleaming pearls,　　　　535
Such is these modern girls' conception of
Their beauty! And so I couldn't get
To her as quickly as necessity
Would have me do, now could I?
Instead, she suddenly appeared in　　　　540
The arms of the aforsesaid gentleman,
And I, since they were safe and sound,
Rushed here, to give you this account
Of what I saw, exactly as it happened.

MARQUIS. The coach stands there between　　　　545
The water and the sand. Was there
No sign of her?

RUTILIO.　　　　The willow-trees
Were in my way. I couldn't really see
Her properly. Hey, there she is,
His servants as her company.　　　　550

CASANDRA. My people seem to be coming.

MARQUIS. My dear lady!

CASANDRA.　　　　My dear Marquis!

MARQUIS. Concern for your ladyship
Has kept us in a state of deep

And constant anguish. We give our thanks   555
To God we've found you safe and sound
At last.

CASANDRA. After God you'd better thank
This brave young man. His arms
And courtesy were quite enough
To carry me to perfect safety.   560

MARQUIS. My noble Count, who better than
Yourself could give assistance to
A lady who shall soon be justly known
To you as your mother!

FEDERICO.   Marquis,
I'd be like Jupiter* himself   565
And turn into an eagle, king
Of birds, and dare to burn my wings
Close to the sun, in imitation of
Bold Phaethon's pride.* I'd hold her tightly in
These claws, a golden fleece,* and fly   570
With her to where my father waits,
To place her gently at his side.

MARQUIS. My lord, I do believe that Heaven
Abets what we have seen today,
So that Casandra owes to you   575
A debt of constant gratitude,
And never more can people say
That those adversaries of old—
A stepson and his mother—cannot live
As one in perfect love and harmony.   580
This most unusual and rare
Event shall be acclaimed by all of Italy.

[*They speak together.* CASANDRA *and* LUCRECIA *also converse*

CASANDRA. While they are talking, Lucrecia,
What's your opinion of Federico?

LUCRECIA. With your permission, my lady,   585
I'll give you my opinion.

CASANDRA.   In that case,
Reluctantly, you have it.

LUCRECIA.   I think . . .

CASANDRA.   Yes?

LUCRECIA. If he changed places with his father,
You'd be happier.

CASANDRA.   I think you may
Be right, Lucrecia. My fortune goes   590
Against me. But it is settled now.
If I go home to Mantua
And try to fool my father with
Some story, he'll most likely kill me.
My foolishness would soon become   595
A topic for the idle tongues*
Of Italy. Besides, it would
Not mean that I could then expect
To marry Federico; and so
There is no reason to go back   600
To Mantua. I shall go on
To where the Duke awaits me in
Ferrara; though if the stories I
Have heard about his wayward life
Are true, they are for any wife-to-be   605
A source of some anxiety.

MARQUIS. If everyone is now assembled here,
It's best we leave this wood before
Some other accident occurs.
Rutilio, you shall go ahead   610
Of us and let Ferrara know
Of our good news, unless the news
Arrives ahead of you; though it's
More likely only bad news travels fast,
And good news last of all. My lady,   615
Come. See to it a horse is ready for
The Count.

CASANDRA.   I think you'll find, my lord,

My coach provides a smoother ride
By far.

FEDERICO.   Then I agree, so that
It can't be said I ever willingly   620
Refused a lady.

> [*The* MARQUIS *takes* CASANDRA *by the hand.*
> FEDERICO *and* BATÍN *alone*

BATÍN.   I think this Duchess is
Astonishing!

FEDERICO.   So you approve, Batín?

BATÍN. I'd say she is a lily* that,
As gentle dawn arrives, sticks out
Its snow-white stamens, begging it   625
To let it have, in fair exchange
For golden pollen, dewy pearls;
Which means to say I think she is
A pretty girl. On top of that,
My lord—but now she's getting in   630
Her coach, you can't delay her more—
There's something else that I could say
To you.

FEDERICO. In that case, say no more,
Batín. The sharpness of your eyes
Perceives the darkest thoughts within   635
My soul and so awakens and deceives
My appetites.

BATÍN.   But wouldn't it
Be right for you to have her for
Yourself, my lord? This fresh carnation?
This lovely orange-blossom? This piece   640
Of tasty decoration sweet
As sugar? This Venus? This Helen?*
Why should the sodding custom of
The world give her to him?

FEDERICO. Let's go, before suspicion falls   645

On us. I'll be the only stepson
To have claimed a stepmother as beautiful
As this.

BATÍN.   I reckon, master, what
You really need is lots of patience.
If only her outstanding attribute   650
Was good old-fashioned ugliness!

Exit both. Enter the DUKE OF FERRARA
and AURORA, *his niece*

DUKE. If what the servants say is true,
And Federico left no earlier,
He will have met her on the way.

AURORA. I think he was at fault, my lord,   655
If he delayed so long. When we
Received the news, he should have gone
At once and made quite sure that he'd
Escort her all the way from Mantua.

DUKE. I am convinced his sadness was   660
The cause of such discourtesy.
The boy has long believed that one
Day he'll inherit my estates,
And with good cause, for, as you know,
He is my only son. I love   665
Him dearly. But now I am
Embarked upon this marriage, he
Believes I do it of my own accord
And thinks it is some treachery
That I deliberately do   670
To him, when, if the truth be known,
My subjects are the ones to blame
For forcing me to marry and,
In consequence, offending him.
They say they'd have him as their lord—   675
Perhaps for love of him, perhaps
Of me—and yet are overawed
By other members of my family

Who, when I die, consider they
Can rightly press their claims to my   680
Estate, and if they are denied,
Will be prepared to devastate
My lands by fire and by sword.
My subjects are the ones who'd suffer most
By this, and so I gave my word   685
To them that would not be. The only choice
Then left to me was marriage.

AURORA. Then you, my lord, are not the one
To blame. The fault lies clearly
With Fortune. In any case, the Count   690
Has much good sense, which leads me to believe
That if he exercises patience too
He'll find the problem will resolve
Itself. Though I, if I might be
So bold, my lord, would also offer you   695
A remedy that might well ease
The deep concern you feel for him,
As well as his anxiety.
Forgive whatever boldness I
Display. My faith in your love   700
Inspires me to say these things
As honestly as possible.
I am, my lord, the only daughter of
Your brother, who, though still so young,
Was cruelly cut down by death,   705
Just as the budding flower of
The almond-tree is withered by
The north wind's cold and icy breath.
When, not long afterwards, I lost
My mother too, you took me into   710
Your house and ever since have been
To me not just a father but
The precious thread of gold to guide
And help me find my way through this
Most complicated labyrinth*   715
Of adverse fortunes. As well, you gave

Me Federico, your son,
To be my brother, cousins both,
Always together throughout our youth.
I loved him just as truly and   720
As honestly as he loved me,
Our life together one: one law,
One love, one will that joined us both
In such true harmony as now
Our marriage would make permanent   725
By giving him to me and me
To him, thereby ensuring
That only death can ever break
A bond tied so securely.
My poor father's death has also left   730
Me well provided for, which makes
Me think there is not in the rest
Of Italy a better match
For Federico's qualities,
Though it may prove the case that Spain   735
Or Flanders may provide someone
To challenge me. Moreover, if
I marry him, why should some future heir
Cause him anxiety? My fortune is
Enough to free him from such cares.   740
Tell me, my lord, if my advice is good.

DUKE. Let me embrace you, Aurora.*
You are the very light of heaven
That banishes and brightens my
Dark night; the dawn that offers me   745
My remedy; the sun that helps
Me see, as in some clear glass,
The resolution of my deep
Anxiety. You have assured me
Of honour and of life, and so,   750
If your love is equal to
Your eagerness, I now assure you
That I shall be a witness to
This perfect marriage. I have no doubt

He loves you just as honestly   755
As you deserve. If both of you
Are then of one accord, I give
My word that married you shall be.
As soon as he arrives, you'll see
Ferrara come alive with happy   760
Celebration.

AURORA.   My lord, I cannot say
How much today this daughter feels
Her sense of debt and obligation.

Enter BATÍN.

BATÍN. My lord, I cannot say how much
You are today indebted both   765
To me and to the wind, nor if
I am ahead of him or him of me;
Nor if I flew upon his back
Or he more speedily upon
My feet to bring the news I bear: 770
Which is to say the Duchess fair
Will soon be here. Mind you,
There was a scare, as history
Shall one day tell, for Madam's coach
Fell over in a stream, but have   775
No fear, Federico's there,
And there he comes to rescue her
And take her cleanly in his arms!
I tell you, sir, she really warms
To him because of that, as if   780
To prove that stepmothers and step-
Sons* thrown together is not like putting fat
Upon the fire. Just wait, my lord.
The sight of them will bowl you over.
You'd think she was his real mother.   785

DUKE. This is great news, Batín. That they
Should truly like each other! Not only that;
If, as you say, the Count shows signs
Of happiness, the news must also be

Considered novelty. I pray   790
To God that Federico has
The sense to treat Casandra well.
You are quite sure he impressed
Her favourably?

BATÍN.   Oh, yes, my lord.
I think they took each other's fancy.   795

AURORA. And have you news as well for me,
    Batín?

BATÍN. Oh, Miss Aurora, such
A heavenly name! You make the flame
Of poetry dawn in me! What would
You have of me?

AURORA.   I wish to know   800
How beautiful Casandra is.

BATÍN. I think such curiosity
Sits very awkwardly upon
Your ladyship and more befits
The Duke. You know what fame   805
Has so far said of her . . . but why
Repeat what fame has said when she
Is here?

DUKE.   Batín, this golden chain
Proclaims my gratitude.

Enter, with pomp and splendour, RUTILIO,
the MARQUIS OF GONZAGA, FEDERICO,
CASANDRA, *and* LUCRECIA.

FEDERICO. My lady, this pavilion in   810
The garden is reserved for you,
So that the Duke may meet you there
With all the ceremony you deserve.
Meanwhile, Ferrara waits to greet
You with such pomp and majesty   815
As may to you seem miserly or mean,
But is more lavish than the whole

Of Italy has ever seen.

CASANDRA. The lack of welcome did disturb me,
   I admit.

FEDERICO. Then I must hope that I've   820
   Explained the cause of it. Aurora and
   The Duke are here to welcome you.

DUKE. Most beautiful Casandra, mistress of
   My soul and my estate, I bid
   Heaven grant you long and happy life,   825
   That you may bring to this great family
   A greater honour as my wife.

CASANDRA. To serve you well, my lord, is all
   I wish. Your glorious name confers
   Both fame and privilege upon   830
   My family. I only trust
   That any qualities I have
   May prove deserving of your own.

DUKE. My dear Marquis, let me embrace you.
   I am indebted to you for   835
   This loveliest of gifts.

MARQUIS.   Such thanks
   Repay the debt in part, my lord,
   Though you'll agree your wedding-day
   Must add to it substantially.

AURORA. Casandra, let me introduce   840
   Myself. I am Aurora.

CASANDRA.   Amongst
   The many gifts good fortune now
   Confers on me, to have you as
   My friend is easily the best.

AURORA. You may rely on me to serve   845
   You well. Consider everything
   I have at your disposal. Ferrara is
   Most fortunate to have you celebrate

Its future glory.

CASANDRA.   As soon as I
  Arrive, I am the object of   850
  Such favour and such flattery
  As promises my future happiness.

DUKE. I pray, be seated. The members of
  My household pay their homage.

CASANDRA.   Thank
  You, sir. No sooner do you speak   855
  Than I obey.

                          [*The* DUKE, CASANDRA, *the* MARQUIS, *and*
                              AURORA *sit beneath a canopy*

CASANDRA. Federico, you shall sit with us.

DUKE. The boy insists he'll be the first
  To kiss your hand.

CASANDRA.   But this is quite
  Ridiculous. Must I permit   860
  Humility like this?

FEDERICO.   Deny
  It, madam, you insult my love
  And mock my true desire to obey.

CASANDRA. But this . . .

FEDERICO.   Give me your hand.

CASANDRA.   Is foolishness.

FEDERICO. And this the proof that everything   865
  You wish is my command. I kiss
  Your hand three times: the first
  Must be regarded as a sign
  That I, as long as I shall live,
  Intend to be the image of   870
  Unrivalled loyalty; the second is
  The mark of my obedience to
  The Duke, whose wishes I observe

Respectfully; the third is for
Myself, for when both fatherly respect   875
And loyalty are set aside,
My soul speaks for itself and any words
That issue forth, unshaped by other wills,
Must be regarded as the gentle voice
Of true sincerity.

CASANDRA.   Then let   880
These arms become a chain* to bind
The willing neck of one who promises
Such constancy.

DUKE.   The boy shows signs
Of more maturity.

MARQUIS.   Most beautiful
Aurora. Everything that I   885
Had heard of you inspired me
To want to see you for myself.
It falls to my good fortune now
To find myself in such proximity,
And since my deepest wishes have   890
Come true, I swear that beauty such
As you possess obliges me
To put my life at your service.

AURORA. My dear Marquis, flattery
Like this is precious spoken by   895
A man whose name throughout the whole
Of Italy is commonly
Associated with his fame
Upon the battlefield. I had not thought
Of you in terms of gallantry;   900
And yet I should, for are not gallantry
And bravery essential arms
For any man connected with
The military life, not least
In one of such distinguished line   905
And family?

MARQUIS.   The compliment
    Is most appreciated. As from
    Today your wish is my command,
    And I, if you agree, shall pay
    For such festivities Ferrara now   910
    Demands of all its gentlemen.
    I thank you once again, most noble,
    Honourable lady.

DUKE.   The time has come
    For you to rest.* To take more time
    In greeting you repeats the same   915
    Mistake that other husbands in
    The past have made. Let no one say
    This husband is another fool,
    Or love that I abuse this jewel.

        [*Exit all with great ceremony, except* FEDERICO *and* BATÍN

FEDERICO. Oh, foolish, wild imagination!   920

BATÍN. What's foolish, master? What goes on?

FEDERICO. The man who says this life's a dream*
    Is justified. We see such things
    Not merely while we sleep but when
    We are awake that in some sick   925
    Or fevered individual
    Would be dismissed as lies.

BATÍN.   Oh, yes,
    I quite agree. I swear that when
    It comes to seeing things* I always get
    First prize. I do occasionally find   930
    Myself with other gentlemen,
    When I—I don't know why—am seized
    By some mysterious urge to grab
    Their throats and have a go at them.
    And if I do this reckless thing   935
    While standing on some balcony,
    I'll break into a sudden sweat
    And watch my life rush past me.

Or maybe I am sat in church,
And have to hear some boring text,   940
I can't help shouting at the bloke:
'Why can't we have a talk on sex?'
Or maybe it's a feller's funeral,
There am I, one of the crowd,
And seeing how they weep and groan,   945
I feel the urge to laugh out loud.
And if I see a game of cards,
And worry on the player's face,
I'll whisper as I'm going past:
'You'll never win. He's got the ace.'   950
Or maybe it's some lovely piece
I can but fancy in my bed;
You'd think I'd asked her to her face,
The way my pasty face goes red.

FEDERICO. May heaven protect me from such thoughts   955
And dreams that, though I am awake,
Refuse to let me rest! How can
I think these things? How can it be
That longings such as these possess
Me so entirely? I can explain   960
It only as some form of utter madness.

BATÍN. I think you'd better tell me what
It is in that case. Come on, master! Do
Confess!

FEDERICO. It's nothing that I've done,
Batín. It's only something that   965
I've dreamed. And since it never was,
Is not, or shall be, like all dreams,
Is pure fantasy. How can
You, therefore, say that I indulge
In any kind of secrecy?   970

BATÍN. You'd better know, my lord, you can't
Fool me. I know exactly* what
This secret is.

FEDERICO.　　　I think the sky
　Might be ablaze with flowers,* the grass
　Adorned with showers of bright stars　　　　　　975
　Before you guess with any certainty.

BATÍN. You think so, master? Well, let's see
　If I am right. I know you like
　Your stepmother, and if we then
　Put two and two together, that　　　　　　　　980
　Makes . . .

FEDERICO.　　No. Do not say more! But even if
　It's true, am I to blame? Are not
　Our thoughts at least completely free?

BATÍN. So free, my lord, a man can see
　The nature of his thoughts as clearly　　　　　　985
　As in a mirror.

FEDERICO.　　　My father is
　The happiest of men.

BATÍN.　　　　　　Say that again.

FEDERICO. I envy him. He has what is
　For me impossible.

BATÍN.　　　　　That's true.
　And her more suitable* by far　　　　　　　　990
　For you. You do quite right to envy him.

FEDERICO. Then I shall die of love that is
　Impossible and at the same
　Time prove that for a son to be
　So jealous of his father is　　　　　　　　　995
　Quite possible.

ACT TWO

Enter CASANDRA *and* LUCRECIA.

LUCRECIA. Your ladyship. I am amazed
  By this.

CASANDRA. You think nobility
  A guarantee against unhappiness?
  It's even worse when there is vileness such
  As this. What would I give to be   5
  An ordinary peasant-girl;
  To wake and find myself beside
  Some good and honest countryman,*
  Rather than dress in silk and gold and be
  Despised by such a nobleman!   10
  If I were only someone of
  Low birth, I would have found a man
  Who'd cherish me and at the same
  Time recognize my proper worth.
  There is as much contentment to   15
  Be found with someone of low origin
  As with some noble lord, if we
  But realize that love at night
  Is doubly blind,* despises lineage,
  And offers everyone the same reward.   20
  The sun that with each dawn pours through
  The finest window-pane will not
  Find any man and wife embrace
  More happily, or in some palace lie
  More peacefully, than when it peeps   25
  Through cracks in rustic walls, and sees
  In happy couples joined one soul.
  The wife is blessed who does not know
  The nobleman's disdain; who, when
  The morning comes, can rise and know   30
  Her husband's love will never change.

The girl is happy too who washes in
The clear stream, quite free from care,
And, when she dries her face, knows well
She does not wipe away those tears   35
That she would shed if she were told
Her husband favoured someone else's bed.
He held me in his arms one night
In one entire month, since when
He has despised the very sight   40
Of me. But why complain that he
Behaves like this when we are told,
Through history, that men, however much
They try to change,* obey those tendencies
That guide them from their birth? Besides,   45
The man who spends the nights away
From home will not be judged so badly by
The world when freedom to indulge
Himself* is held to be man's privilege.
But that a man should treat a woman of   50
High birth with such contempt, a wife
With scorn, must surely be a sign
He is a total fool who'll soon
Regret the day that he was born.
The Duke is of the school that thinks   55
A wife is something to adorn
His house: an ornament, a piece
Of furniture to call his own,
An item he's gone out and bought
To decorate his drawing-room.   60
I will not willingly accept
Such terms, nor easily believe
That any man who loves his wife
Will use such methods to destroy
Her life and happiness; for if   65
She's genuine, a woman wants
To be a wife and mother, not
Another stick of furniture.
And if her husband proves a thankless man,
That's bad enough, without insulting her   70

As often as he possibly can.
And if he gives her cause to think
These things, much better try to put
Them right than leave them till it's far
Too late.

LUCRECIA.   My lady, everything   75
You tell me fills me both with sadness and
Astonishment. That you should feel
Resentment such as this for what
He's done to you! Who would have thought
The Duke, once wed, would in so short   80
A time neglect his marriage-bed,
Or when he chooses to neglect
You so, would have such scant
Respect for you? If he were just
A young gallant, you'd understand   85
He'd want you to feel jealousy
And try to keep complacency
At bay. He might pretend he wasn't keen
On you, or praise some girl he'd seen
The other day, or maybe crack a joke   90
To show her how amusing he
Could be as she went by. But for a man
To move a wife to jealousy
By treating her like this, it seems
To me, deserves a place in history.   95
You really ought to write and let
Your father know just what the Duke
Has done to you.

CASANDRA.   I can't, Lucrecia.
My eyes shall be the only witness to
My misery.

LUCRECIA.   If I judged this   100
By nature's law and all that's fair,
There's not a scrap of doubt you and
The Count would make a better pair
By far. And if he'd married you,

Your son would guarantee the Duke's   105
Estate. From what I've seen of him,
The Count seems very sad of late.

CASANDRA. I cannot think he's sad because
He's thinking of some future son
That I might bear the Duke. It's far   110
More likely there'll be more to worry him.
If anything has brought about
His melancholy state, it is
The thought that both of us are but
The playthings of our destiny.*   115

                Exit CASANDRA *and* LUCRECIA. *Enter the*
                DUKE, FEDERICO, *and* BATÍN.

DUKE. If I had thought, my son, that sadness such
As this would be the outcome of
My marriage, I'd never have considered it.

FEDERICO. My lord, if that were true, it would
Be madness on my part. I know   120
You do not love me less for it.
If your marriage had distressed
Me, as you now suggest, I would
Have done my very best to hide
Unhappiness. The truth is this: 125
My face proclaims I am unwell.
The cause of it, no one can tell.

DUKE. The doctors of Ferrara have
Consulted with their counterparts
From Mantua, and wondered what   130
The cause of such a malady
Might be. They seem to think—and I
Agree with them—that marriage is
A medicine designed to soothe and ease
Away the ills associated with   135
The deepest melancholy.

FEDERICO. I think that may be so as far
As women are concerned, but as for me,

I doubt it would be any kind
Of remedy.

Enter CASANDRA *and* LUCRECIA.

CASANDRA.   You see? The Duke   140
Ignores me even now. The man
Exceeds the bounds of common decency!

LUCRECIA. How can you blame him, madam? I doubt
That he has even seen you.

CASANDRA.   That's his
Excuse. To add pretence to his   145
Neglect is but a further cruelty.
Unless I am mistaken, I
Shall see to it that one day he
Shall pay for everything he's done to me.

[*Exit* CASANDRA *and* LUCRECIA

DUKE. Unless I am completely wrong,   150
I have in mind a match that you
Might even welcome, given that
You like the girl, and she is of
This kingdom.

FEDERICO.   You mean Aurora?

DUKE.   You read
My thoughts as though they are your own.   155
I have consulted all the wisest men
At Court. They say that marriage ought
To help eradicate the malady.

FEDERICO. Which only goes to prove they do
Not know me, if, as you have said,   160
They think I am aggrieved, and thoughts
Provoked by jealousy now fill
My head. They know I did not say
A single word against the marriage;
Rather, I approved of it, and felt   165
It must be for your good.

DUKE.   I know
　You did, my son. But loyalty
　Like this deserves at least that I
　Should say to you that I regret
　The day I chose to marry.

FEDERICO.   My lord,   170
　If you want proof your marriage does
　Not sadden me, and more than that,
　That you enjoy my love, I'll ask
　Aurora if it is her honest wish
　To marry me. If she says yes,   175
　I shall be happy to obey.
　It would be wrong of me to do
　The opposite of what you say.

DUKE. To judge by what she's said, she eagerly
　Awaits that day.

FEDERICO.   I think she may   180
　Have changed, and that explains why now
　She has the Marquis constantly
　In train.

DUKE.   And why is that of such
　Concern to you?

FEDERICO.   Because the man
　About to marry does not want   185
　To think that some gallant commands
　His lady's thoughts, or when he marries her
　That she's already bought.

DUKE.   If men
　Were constantly concerned about
　The women in their lives, they'd have   190
　To lock them up to keep them safe*
　From prying eyes. Think of a mirror as
　You breathe on it; the image disappears.
　But take a cloth to clean the glass,
　The surface that was soiled appears clear.   195

FEDERICO. I value such advice and wit
   But offer you a different thought
   That surely must counter it.
   A blacksmith working in his forge,
   When suddenly the furnace roars,   200
   And spits its flames—at once he pours
   On water, thinking it will tame
   The blaze, instead of which it is
   Inflamed much more and in the end
   Consumes the water. The same is true   205
   Of any husband who, at first,
   Believes he has contained the lover's fire
   But then observes the flames of love
   Leap higher still. And so I would
   Do well to fear any man   210
   Who loves, and not provide for him
   The water that inflames his love
   And in the process burns my honour.*

DUKE. You speak most foolishly, as though
   Aurora's purity were something you   215
   Consider blackened. I'll not listen
   Any more.

FEDERICO.   My lord.

DUKE.   I said no more.

                                     [*Exit the* DUKE

FEDERICO. Wait, my lord.

BATÍN.   I do admire, master
   The way you try to win your father's favour.

FEDERICO. I welcome his displeasure more,   220
   So I can truly say I have enjoyed
   The fullest measure of unhappiness.
   The depth of my despair* is such,
   I do not really care if I
   Should die; and if I were to die,   225
   I'd want to live a thousand times

Again, so I could die again
As many times as I had lived.
And yet I neither wish to live
Nor die, because to live means I   230
Must suffer anguish in its way
As terrible as death; and if
I do not kill myself, it is
Because death is a lesser evil than
The pain that in this life I am   235
Obliged to bear.

BATÍN.   In that case, if
You neither wish to live or die,
I'd say that you are just like what
They call hermaphrodite,* which is
To say a person who is neither man   240
Or woman really, but a bit
Of both of them, as you yourself
Are split between not knowing if
You are alive or dead. I tell
You truly, sir, the piteous sight   245
Of you upsets me so, you either tell
Me what is wrong with you or I
Shall go and be a servant somewhere else.

FEDERICO. Batín, if I were able to describe
What troubles me, it would be bearable,   250
A malady whose end would then
Seem possible. And yet, the anguish that
I feel is so intense, so terrible,
It cannot be described but only felt.
And if, in order to console   255
Myself, I try to speak, I have
To stop, because the gulf that separates
The spirit from the tongue is just
As great as that which commonly
Divides the earth from heaven. Leave me if   260
You wish, Batín. I'm best alone.
The feelings I now have, no man
Would wish to call his own.

Enter CASANDRA *and* AURORA.

CASANDRA. You weep for that?

AURORA.   You think it strange,
My lady, when the man I love   265
Despises me? He says I love
The Marquis of Gonzaga. Carlos, me!
He cannot tell me why or when,
But just accuses me of that. Oh, I
Know why. This marriage has upset   270
Him so, that even though I was
The very light that shone on him,
He cannot stand the sight of anything
That now reminds him of what was,
And eyes that he once loved are now   275
To be despised. There was a time
When each new dawn saw Federico come
In search of that still brighter dawn*
He'd learned to call his own. Was there
A garden or a fountain then   280
That did not hear sweet words of love?
Could not these lips, this brow compete
With jasmine or some perfect flower?
And when we said goodbye to one
Another, was there a moment he   285
Enjoyed away from me, an instant he'd
Describe as moderately happy?
The truth is that the love we felt
Was purified within the crucible
Of long familiarity,   290
Two souls that God had given us
Made one. But now that love that seemed
To have been born with us is broken by
Deceit, its knot most cruelly undone
By Federico's sense of loss   295
And failed ambition.

CASANDRA.   It grieves me to have been
The cause of it, and yet it may

Not be too late, perhaps, to speak
To him, assuming anyone
Can ever counter jealousy   300
With cool and calculated reason.

AURORA. You really think the Count is jealous?

CASANDRA. The Duke thinks, of the Marquis.

AURORA.   I,
My lady, am convinced the cause
Is neither jealousy nor love,   305
But something else.

                                    [*Exit* AURORA

CASANDRA.   Federico.

FEDERICO. My lady, let me kiss your hand
And always be your humble slave.

CASANDRA. I will not have you kneel to me
Like this. If you persist, I'll have   310
To make you duke to my duchess.*

FEDERICO. If you refuse, you harm my love,
I must insist.

CASANDRA.   Then I shall offer you
My arms and help you up. But what
Is this? Why do you stare at me   315
And tremble so? You know how much
I care for you.

FEDERICO.   The truth is that
My soul dares think you do, informs
My heart, my heart my face,
And thus obliges me to stare   320
At you.

CASANDRA. Batín, I need to be
Alone with him.

BATÍN.   Him in a state
And on his own with her! I think

There's something I can't fathom here.

[*Exit* BATÍN

FEDERICO. If only I could die and not,   325
    In imitation of the Phoenix, be
    Reborn, I could resist the pain
    Of love.

CASANDRA. Aurora tells me you
    Are jealous, Federico, ever since
    The Marquis came, and having promised you   330
    Would marry her, no longer seem
    To have the same intention. Am
    I, then, to think you underestimate
    Your worth when jealousy and envy are
    Both wise, and draw attention to the faults   335
    Of any rival? The Marquis, as
    You know, is bold enough, but more
    The soldier than the dashing courtier.
    On that account I rather think
    The fact your father's married me   340
    The real cause of this dark mood:
    A deep anxiety that our first-
    Born child may rob you of the lands
    You thought your own; that all the hopes
    You had of one day ruling these   345
    Estates have flown. If that is true,
    And I am thus the cause of this
    Unhappiness, regard me too
    As someone who now puts an end
    To all your sadness. Believe me, there   350
    Will be no brothers. The Duke was forced
    To marry me to satisfy
    The will of others. His nightly sports—
    How else can I describe them?—let
    Him spend one night with me,* that seemed   355
    To him a century, before
    Those past delights attracted him
    And seemed more fascinating than

Before. Just as a horse breaks free
When frightened by the sound of some   360
Great drum, and scatters to the wind
Those things—bit, bridle, girth, and rein—
That otherwise would stop its run,
So now the Duke, defiantly
Resisting all the bonds imposed   365
By marriage, shatters them, and seeks
Instead immoral women, tarnishing
My own good name. He rides roughshod
Upon the honour,* valour, worth
And well-earned fame of all his ancestors,   370
And idly spends his days and nights
In pleasure with the women he
Procures. If, then, all this is true,
You can be sure you'll inherit his
Estates. As for myself, I think   375
My father may well help me to escape
When I inform him that the Duke
Is more a tyrant than a husband,
And this is more a prison than
A palace . . . unless my death, of course,   380
Provides an earlier release.

FEDERICO. My lady, first of all you scold
Me like some disobedient child,
And then begin to weep such tears
As would reduce the hardest rock   385
To pure mildness and compassion.
What is the cause of it? No doubt
You see me as the son of someone who
Offends you cruelly. I swear
I'll never be the son of any man   390
Who treats you so unfairly. I am
Amazed, as well, that you should think
My melancholy thoughts are due
To either greed or jealousy.
Who says I need estates to be   395
The man I am? I can quite easily,

By marrying Aurora, gain them.
And if I were to take to arms,
And occupy some wealthy neighbour's lands,
What would it matter to me then   400
If from my father's I were banned?
Oh, no, this sadness does not spring
From any greed or great ambition,
Though you may judge from everything
I say that never was a man   405
More sad or desperate than I
Am now, since love first placed those sharp
And deadly arrows in his bow.
I die and find no remedy.
My life is like a burning candle,   410
Fading slowly. I pray that death
Will not force me to wait until
The wax has dripped away, but like
A gust of wind come suddenly,
Extinguishing the cursed light of day.   415

CASANDRA. Noble Federico, dry these tears.
I cannot think that God intended man
To weep so bitterly; more that he
Display his bravery. The truth
Is Nature planned that women, for   420
The most part, are the ones to weep,
For though they may be brave, they often lack
The courage to defend themselves.
But not so men. There is but one
Occasion when a man may weep: 425
Which is when honour has been lost,
And he is forced to count the cost
Of its recovery. Oh, how,
Aurora, could you so abuse
A man so good, so sweet, so worthy of   430
Your love, and thus reduce him to
This state of utter misery?

FEDERICO. To think Aurora is to blame
Is quite mistaken.

CASANDRA.   Who, then, can
   She be?

FEDERICO. The very sun itself;   435
   For though Aurora is as perfect as
   The dawn, we see such beauty every day,
   But when we gaze upon the sun,
   We know that it is incomparable
   In every way.

CASANDRA.   Then it is not   440
   Aurora?

FEDERICO. My thoughts fly higher still.

CASANDRA. You mean there is a woman you
   Have spoken to, who knows of your love
   For her, and she is still incapable
   Of feeling love for you? I'd say   445
   That such a thing is quite impossible,
   Or else that everything you say
   Is just not true.

FEDERICO.   If only I
   Could tell you how impossible
   It is, you'd say that either I   450
   Am cold and hard as marble, or
   The fact that I am still alive
   Must be regarded as a miracle.
   Consider Phaethon, how he seized
   The golden chariot of the sun;   455
   Or Icarus,* who thought that wax
   And wings would help him overcome
   The challenge of the heavens until,
   His feathers scattered by the wind,
   We saw him plunge straight down into   460
   The sea. Think of Bellerophon,*
   Who rode the winged horse Pegasus,
   And from his vantage-point on high
   Surveyed the world as if it were
   But one more star fixed in the sky.   465

And then the Greek called Sinon,* who,
No sooner did he place the horse
Within the walls of Troy, saw men
Burst forth and in their rage destroy
The city. Again, bold Jason,* he   470
Who from the cloth and giant trees
Of Argos fashioned that great craft
In which to sail the seas and oceans of
The world. They all could boast how great
Was their temerity, but none   475
Of them could claim to be as foolish or
As bold as me.

CASANDRA.   It sounds, then, Count,
As if you are in love with some
Bronze image, nymph, or alabaster goddess.
A woman's soul does not disguise   480
What she in general would willingly
Confess. The contrary is true:
Her thoughts so lightly covered by
A veil that rarely does true love
Assail her soul but she will prove   485
Herself both kind and merciful.
Confess your love to her, whoever she
May be. Consider Venus, how
The Greeks portrayed her in the arms
Of faun and satyr. Consider too   490
The moon, and how Diana from
Above came down so many times
To earth, attracted by Endymion's love.*
Sweet Count, take my advice. The building that
Seems strong is often soonest to   495
Fall down. The passion spoken's far
Less dangerous than that still hidden.

FEDERICO. To catch the Indian pelican,
A hunter thinks the most successful plan's
To start a fire by his nest.   500
The bird, perched in a tree, is forced
To think what it must do to save

Its family, flies down, and in
An effort to safeguard them,* burns
Its wings and so, unable to escape,   505
Becomes the hunter's easy prey.
And so it is, when you encourage me,
I burn and yearn the more; when you
Advise me, I'm confused; when you
Now urge me on, I am disturbed.   510
When you would guide me, I am lost;
When you would free me, I am caught;
When you persuade me, I am trapped;
When you would teach me, I'm distraught.
Such is the danger I now face,   515
I think that, though eventually we
Must die, it is a lesser evil if
I suffer silently what little life
Is left to me.

                                            [*Exit* FEDERICO

CASANDRA. Of all the things heaven's made on earth,   520
Imagination causes in
The minds of men the most confusion.
It has the power to turn the frost
To fire, to give material form
To our desire, and so provoke in us   525
Both war and peace, both storm and calm.
It is, in short, that place within
Men's souls where all our dreams are born,
And yet the pictures it invents
Deceive us more than they inform.   530
At first I saw in Federico's words
A clear statement of intention,
But now what seemed so clear then
Is nothing less than my confusion.
What storm, attracting to itself   535
The winds that rush from all directions, can
Be said to be the equal of
Those storms that, raging uncontrollably
In man's imaginations, are

The greatest storms of all?   540
No sooner do I think I am
The object of Federico's dreams,
Than that same thought advises me
That things aren't always what they seem,
And then reminds me too that I   545
Am married now, and therefore must,
For good or ill, accept my marriage vow.
The truth is we all dream of things
Beyond our grasp, and thus are made
To think achieving them's an easy task.   550
I seem to see so many things
That would, if I could grasp them, make
Me glad, but then the thought I am
The wife of such a husband drives
Me mad. The things I thought impossible   555
Now seem much easier and make
Me start to think of sweet revenge,
But simultaneously I see
My husband's sword stained by my blood,
His precious honour soon avenged.   560
Who can deny the fact the Count
Has many pleasing qualities?
But none of them so great, I think,
That it would match the measure of
My folly if I were to let   565
Myself become too pleased
By them. I'll think of this no more.
Heaven help me banish thoughts that are
So dangerous, yet so enticing.
And yet no harm can come from just   570
Imagining, for if it did,
Then just to think of tarnished honour is
To tarnish it, and this would be
A world from which unblemished honour had
Quite vanished. No one can say   575
Of me that I have so far compromised
My honour when the most I've done
Is paint a picture in my mind,

Dictated by imagination.
They say that God considers it   580
A sin if we on earth are guilty of
Imagining the things we want.
But what is true of God cannot
Be true of honour if, as we
All know, God sees our very thoughts   585
But honour clearly does not.*

Enter AURORA.

AURORA. You've spoken with the Count at length,
My lady. Did he speak of me?

CASANDRA. He says he is most grateful for
Your love. His only wish is that   590
You do not give him cause for jealousy.

[*Exit* CASANDRA

AURORA. Her words do nothing to dispel
My fears. How can the man that I
Adored become so deeply flawed
By rank ambition that my love   595
Means less to him than acquisition of
These lands? But it is also true
That love is powerful, that neither wealth
Nor life nor honour can withstand
Its influence. He loved me once   600
Undoubtedly, and now that love
Has been destroyed because he fears
Casandra's presence here, he thinks
He can pretend the real cause
Is jealousy. But two can play   605
That game, and by pretending love
For someone else I could perhaps
Awaken Federico's love for me
Again. I shall pretend I love
The Marquis of Gonzaga—most   610
Convincingly.

Enter the MARQUIS *and* RUTILIO.

RUTILIO.   How can you hope
To win her heart? You know it is
Already given to another.

MARQUIS. Rutilio, leave me now. Here comes
Aurora.

RUTILIO. My lord, I do not think   615
That you command yourself when you
Are resolute in this and nothing else.

MARQUIS. Aurora, lovely as the dawn;*
No sooner do I set these eyes
On you than I am born again.   620
Aurora, province of the sun,
No sooner do you come than this
Dark burden of my night is banished by
The loveliness of your vision.
Since I arrived from Mantua,   625
My only wish has been to have
You welcome me as your suitor, sworn
To serve you well and sacrifice
Myself as you desire. But now
I know how much I have deceived   630
Myself when that same soul that in
Your worship always proves so bold,
Has in the end awakened not
The warmth of love but only cold
Disdain; discovered not the brightness of   635
Your day but only this my endless night.
The sadness that I feel stems not
From seeing you—who would be sad
To see such brightness?—rather from
The fact it's been the cause of your   640
Forgetfulness. With that in mind,
The only remedy that I
Can find is to depart, and so
Provide this heavy heart with some
Relief from your cruelty.   645
I'll seek my cure in that miracle

Prescribed by absence, now that love
Extracts this cruel vengeance. I kiss
Your hand, my lady, and take my leave
Of you.

AURORA. Before you do, I would   650
Remind you that the lover who
Cannot withstand the first rebuff
Of love, cannot be said to feel
True sorrow when that love has gone.
No honest lady's love is ever won   655
By any man who thinks that in
Such matters he can run before
He walks. I think that if you do
Not love enough, you cannot talk
Of how you suffer. But since you seek   660
My leave to go away, I'll do
The opposite and bid you stay.

MARQUIS. My lady, this most precious favour, though
It may be seen as cruelty,
Obliges me to stay not merely ten   665
Short years, as did the Greeks when they
Laid siege to Troy, nor seven, as did
The shepherd, Jacob,* waiting to enjoy
Laban's most precious jewel. I shall,
I promise, wait for centuries,   670
And be, like wretched Tantalus,*
Devoured constantly by doubt
And certainty. I shall be happy to
Allow my hope to feed my love.

AURORA. Until a man achieves his goal,   675
Suffering improves his soul.

Enter the DUKE, FEDERICO, *and* BATÍN.

DUKE. I have received this letter from
The Pope. He bids me leave for Rome.

FEDERICO. He does not tell you why?

DUKE.   I think
   The best reply is for me now   680
   To leave at once.

FEDERICO.   Then you should go,
   My lord. I shall not try to learn
   What I am not supposed to know.

DUKE. If I knew why, my boy, you too
   Should know. I can but think that, with   685
   The wars in Italy,* the Pope intends
   I should be made commander of
   The great and mighty army of
   The Church. No doubt, to guarantee
   Election, he will want from me   690
   A good supply of money and
   Provisions too.

FEDERICO.   My lord, I would
   Not have you go alone and leave
   Me here. What would they say of me?
   Besides, you would not find a braver or   695
   More loyal soldier.

DUKE.   That cannot be.
   You have to stay behind and, while
   I am away, administer
   My lands and valued property.
   It is my wish. I have no more   700
   To say.

FEDERICO. Nor do I wish, my lord,
   To disobey, but they will think
   Me cowardly in Italy.

DUKE. They will consider we behave
   Most prudently, and realize   705
   The son who guards his father's house
   Cannot expect to keep him company.

FEDERICO. Then my obedience, sir, shall be
   Exemplary.

[*Exit the* DUKE

BATÍN. While you were talking to
    Your father, sir, Aurora had   710
    Your rival's ear. I thought that you
    Might like to know it's not as if
    She's missing you.

FEDERICO.   You mean the Marquis?

BATÍN.   Yes.

FEDERICO. And do you think I could care less?

AURORA. I offer you this ribbon* as   715
    The first amongst my favours.

MARQUIS.   And I,
    My lady, swear I'll never part
    With it, but rather see it as
    A chain around my neck or manacle
    Upon my hand. To let me wear   720
    It now would be quite indescribable.

AURORA [*aside*]. This is a suitable revenge,
    And yet it does offend true love.

                                                  [*Aloud*

    Then wear it, sir, and grant it that
    True greatness it deserves.   725

BATÍN. To make all women treacherous
    Is Nature's way of proving it
    Is marvellous. For if they were
    Not false (I don't mean all, just some),
    The men who fall in love would end   730
    Up on their knees and crawl to them.
    Do you see the ribbon?

FEDERICO.   Ribbon? Where?

BATÍN. Why, there, of course! A ribbon you
    Once said adorned the very sun,
    So perfect was the beauty of   735

The one who always used to wear it.
But now the Marquis has it fixed
Around his neck, I'd say the sun
Has suffered an eclipse, and what
Was light and happiness for you,   740
My lord, has now become your darkness.
There was a time that very ribbon would
Have been the cause of friction, just
Like when the golden apple Paris* gave
To Venus caused a right old rumpus with   745
His women.

FEDERICO.   Times have changed, Batín.
A different time has now begun.

AURORA. I bid you, Marquis, come with me
Into the garden.

                              [*Exit* AURORA *and the* MARQUIS

BATÍN.   Master, look
How eagerly he holds her hand.   750

FEDERICO. It's not surprising if he's fond
Of her.

BATÍN.   You act as if you are
Quite glad.

FEDERICO. What would you have me do?
Go mad?

BATÍN.   A swan, my lord, cannot
Abide another swan come near   755
The one he loves. He'd sooner fly
Away with her to somewhere quieter.
Nor does a cock take kindly to
Some other cock who takes a walk
Amongst his hens. Just see him have   760
A go at him, his cockscomb stood
On end as if he were an angry Turk,
A fierce Barbarossa.* And then
At night he would outdo him too,

His endless crowing boasting of   765
His own superiority.
How, then, can you not feel enraged
When this pathetic Marquis steals
So blatantly the girl you were
Supposed to marry?

FEDERICO.   The proper way   770
To punish female treachery's
To let a woman have the man
She fancies. Let her own capriciousness
Be answered by his fickleness.

BATÍN. I see. You'd better let me have   775
A copy of this 'Teach Yourself
The Art of Courtship', sir, so I
Can learn it all from memory.
Though if I'm honest, there is more
To it than you are telling me,   780
If I'm to judge your mood correctly, sir.
It's my opinion thoughts of love
Are like a waterwheel with all
Its buckets: soon as one is full,
The next one fills with water that   785
Is chucked to it. I think you might
Be like the water, sir, have found
Another love and so chucked her.

FEDERICO. Your mind has great agility,
Batín. It seeks to penetrate   790
My cloak of secrecy. Go now.
Discover when the Duke departs,
So I may go at least part of
The way with him.

BATÍN.   How right you are
To praise my ingenuity.   795
To say that I approve your mood
Would be an insincere form
Of flattery.

                                            [*Exit* BATÍN

FEDERICO.   Oh mad and foolish thought!
   What would you have of me? What would
   You drive me to? Why do you seek   800
   To end my life by forcing me
   To think and do what I dare not?
   I beg you, stop, before you bring
   About my death; before you are
   The fatal end of everything   805
   Once sweet and fresh. There is no thought,
   It's true, that does not feed on hope
   And therefore grow. The lover's thoughts,
   Accordingly, sustained by constant hope,
   Will grow much more than most. But you,   810
   Oh, foolish thought, I know are but
   A fond illusion conjured from
   A hopeless vision.

Enter CASANDRA.

CASANDRA. Love treads a careful path between
   The injuries it has received,   815
   The sweet revenge* it would achieve,
   And in the process sows the seeds
   Of what would be my own dishonour.
   Its object inaccessible,
   It lays foundations that quite soon   820
   Are visible, as if to prove
   You cannot build your happiness
   On ground that is not suitable.
   Because of what the Duke has done
   To me, I feel a wickedness   825
   Within my soul that seeks both pleasure and
   Revenge in what undoubtedly
   Is utter madness. The Count, apart
   From being sweet and handsome, is
   My dear husband's only son,   830
   And thus the very one through whom
   I could be best avenged upon
   That cruel, most ungrateful man.
   I saw how Federico was

Disturbed, and how, when he would speak   835
To me, he could not find the words
To say the things he felt, though men
Can often prove most eloquent
When they are silent. There is, I think,
In Federico's state of mind   840
A confirmation of those things
I dared not think, and since the Duke
Has given me occasion for
Revenge, a voice that whispers here
Inside, convincing me that love   845
Can never be a form of treachery.
What's more, if I now give myself
To him, I cannot be accused
That it is something no one else
Has ever done. Are we not told   850
In history* of fathers who
Have loved their daughters, brothers who
Made love with sisters? Yes, it's true.
If I do such a thing, do I,
Then, pass beyond the bounds of all   855
Normality, become a traitor to
My own integrity? And yet,
To cite the sins that others have
Been tempted to commit in no
Way justifies the things that I   860
Would do if I admit that they
Are wrong. The Count comes here!
What shall I do? I am resolved.
I cast aside both doubt and fear.

FEDERICO. The Duchess comes, this sweet and fatal sword   865
  That, though I die for her, I still adore.
  Ah, Duchess! Beauty such as yours makes
  Heaven glad.

CASANDRA.   I trust, my lord, you are
  No longer sad.

FEDERICO.   You would be more

Correct to call the sadness that 870
I feel eternal.

CASANDRA.   It cannot be.
I rather think it might prove . . . temporary,
An illness of the body, not
The soul.

FEDERICO. My sickness lies in thoughts
That have decided to obsess me so, 875
I know there cannot be a cure.

CASANDRA. And I am sure that I, if you
Will only trust me, can as quickly help
You find the remedy. You know
How much I care for you.

FEDERICO.   And I 880
Trust you, but fear will not allow
My heart to speak.

CASANDRA.   You told me love
Was what had made you sad.

FEDERICO.   Yes, sad.
And glad as well. The reason for
The heaven and hell in which I find 885
Myself.

CASANDRA. Then listen while I tell
A story from the past that deals
With love. Antiochus,* enamoured of
His stepmother, fell ill, and no
One thought he could recover. 890

FEDERICO. Much better if he died of it.
I know that I am sicker still.

CASANDRA. The King, his father, called together all
The doctors of his court. They each
Examined him, but he, of course, 895
Would not admit forbidden love
To be the cause of everything.

But Erasistratus,* wiser than
Galen and even great Hippocrates,*
Soon guessed what really troubled him.   900
He saw the poison lay between
The young man's heart and lip. And so
He took his pulse and ordered that
As many women as then lived
At Court present themselves.

FEDERICO.   So did   905
Some evil spirit speak?

CASANDRA.   He noted how
When he set eyes upon his stepmother
His heart at once beat that much faster.
And so he knew what troubled him.

FEDERICO. How very clever!

CASANDRA.   He came to be   910
Regarded as the finest doctor.

FEDERICO. And did that help the patient to recover?

CASANDRA. You can't deny that what was true
Of him is true of you.

FEDERICO.   Does it
Annoy you?

CASANDRA.   No.

FEDERICO.   It pleases you?   915

CASANDRA. Why, yes.

FEDERICO.   Then know that what is now
Responsible for my distress
Is my impossible and hopeless love
For you, on whose account I've lost
All fear of God, and of my father too.   920
I find myself deprived of self,
Of God, of you; of self because
My soul belongs to you; of God

Because I worship you much more;
Of you because you are still true   925
To someone else.* And if you think
That you are not to blame for this,
Observe the true extent of my distress.
They say that to be dead is worse
Than any other thing we know.   930
If that is so, then I am dead
Because of you, and would be dead
In order not to know myself.
But if I am now dead, I still
Experience equal suffering,   935
And thus, against my will, am forced
To gaze upon myself to know
If I am still what I was then.
As soon as I admit I am
Myself, my wretched state will not   940
Let me acknowledge it, but forces me
To further sufferings, forgetting that
This life is given me by heaven.
The two of us are equally
To blame if I now have no self,   945
For it is on account of you
Alone that I forget myself
And thus have neither God, nor you, nor self.
To have no self is in itself no loss,
Since I can only live in you,   950
But if I am deprived of God,
Who is the very breath of life,
Can such a love as this be true?
And if that love excludes all else,
When God commands that I must not   955
Adore such beauty as I see in you,
Then it is true I have no God,
When all my thoughts are fixed on you.
Oh what a foolish thing it is
For any man to think he can   960
Escape that black abyss when he
Is thus deprived of God, of you,

And of the self that once was his!
What can we do, the two of us,
When I forgot to worship God,   965
And have no other god but you,
Nor self to which I can lay claim,
If I myself must live in you?
The truth is I, for love of you,
Am now condemned to suffer endlessly;   970
That I feel love and you disdain,
And so can properly complain
That you claim me entirely.
If I am thus deprived as much
Of you as of myself, my state   975
Can only be described as one
Of utter helplessness, for I
Can neither you nor self possess.

CASANDRA. When I consider first the Duke,
Then God, I tremble at the thought   980
That punishment both human and divine
Will be for our excess soon brought
To bear on both of us.
And yet, if it is true the world
Considers love excusable,   985
My part in this affair will seem
To most forgivable;
And if my wrong is judged the lesser,
How can my guilt be thought the greater?
I know of others who, because   990
They really wanted to do wrong,
Have sought their inspiration not in those
Who then repented of their sins
But those who most enjoyed wrongdoing.
If there is any remedy   995
For this, it is for you to flee
And never speak to me again,
Thus making sure we shall die,
And never in each other's arms now lie.
I beg you leave me. I prefer   1000

To die than have to turn away
From you.

FEDERICO.   And I, my lady, seek
In death the only favour I
Now wish upon myself. This life
Is meaningless; this body has   1005
No soul; I seek my death, convinced
That it is not a source of fear;
Rather, my one remaining pleasure.
I only ask you let me kiss
This hand, so I may taste the poison that   1010
Now ends my life.

CASANDRA.   To do so is to put
A spark to powder. Leave me now.

FEDERICO. To do so would be treachery.

CASANDRA. If I could only speak more firmly than
I do. I feel this poison spread   1015
From hand to heart.

FEDERICO.   You were the siren* who
Beguiled me on this fatal sea,
And sweetly lured me to my
Own death.

CASANDRA.   As I, if I go on,
Am certain to destroy myself.   1020
Oh, will not name and honour teach
Me greater prudence, greater sense?

FEDERICO. I seem to have no strength.

CASANDRA.   And I
No consciousness of what I think
Or do.

FEDERICO. Such strange infirmity!   1025

CASANDRA. I die for you.

FEDERICO.   I cannot die,

Since I am long since dead.

CASANDRA.   Sweet Count,
You bring about my death.

FEDERICO.   Then I,
Though dead, am happy that my soul
Enjoys such immortality   1030
As will allow me to possess
Your love for all eternity.

ACT THREE

AURORA. I swear that what I say is true.

MARQUIS. I can't believe it possible,
  But if it is, you must take care
  That no one overhears.*

AURORA.   I had
  To tell you what I know so you   5
  Can best advise me what to do.

MARQUIS. First tell me how it was you saw
  The two of them.

AURORA.   As you well know,
  My lord, I loved the Count most dearly,
  And suffered at his hands the kind   10
  Of treachery once practised by
  The cunning Ulysses. The years
  Had nurtured our love, and by
  The time they went to bring Casandra here
  From Italy, our plans were firmly made,   15
  If anyone believes a man
  Will ever keep the word he gave.
  As soon as Federico met
  Casandra, he began to treat
  Me differently, and when the Duke   20
  Proposed we marry soon, said he
  Could not, through jealousy of you.
  That's why, since it is often said
  That love gone cold is best revived
  By favouring someone else, I tried   25
  To make him think that I loved you.
  It had as much effect as if
  I'd tried to make a mark upon

A diamond: for where there is
No love, how can you make a person fond   30
Of you? I could not understand
Why I, who had been loved, should now
Be so despised by him, and so began,
Now driven by my lynx-eyed jealousy,
To watch him carefully. Casandra has   35
A dressing-room containing two
Recesses,* and on the walls not tapestries,
But mirrors, portraits, glasses of
All kinds. It must have been suspicion led
Me there one day, for as I went   40
In quietly, I looked into a mirror
And saw Federico slip as silently
Into the opposite recess,
And straight away begin to pick
The blood-red roses of Casandra's lips.   45
I watched them horrified and then
Could watch no more. I turned and ran,
And when I'd found some quiet place,
Began to weep for my misfortune.
I wept for theirs too, that they   50
Could be so blind as to believe
That, while the Duke was still away,
They could behave so brazenly,
And publicize a love that in
Its infamy was worse than anything   55
We normally attribute to
The lust and savagery of animals.
The mirror, I'm convinced, in order not
To show such hideous love as this,
Assumed a dark and cloudy face,   60
While I, as if transfixed, observed
How they lasciviously indulged
Themselves and took such sweet
Delight in every manner of embrace.
They say the Duke returns triumphantly,   65
And laurel wreaths adorn his brow
To celebrate his victories

Against the Holy Pontiff's enemies.
I beg you, tell me what I am
To do. I am pursued by thoughts   70
That you, in speaking of your love
For me, may not have spoken as
Sincerely as I would like,
And therefore, like the Count, you too
May now be planning to deceive   75
And in the end abandon me.

MARQUIS. Aurora, in this life the only thing
That has no remedy is death.
Though many in the course of time
Are, like the Phoenix, born again   80
And live once more through their fame.
Inform the Duke you wish to marry me.
As soon as he agrees to it,
We'll go to Mantua, and all
The danger that you fear now   85
Will soon be over. The tiger, so
They say, grieves for its poor cubs
That have become the hunter's prey;
Is so distraught it rushes to the sea
And lets itself be swept away   90
Unto its death. If that is so,
What will Ferrara's new Achilles do
In order to avenge his name
And tarnished honour? Who can believe
That such a stain as this can now   95
Be cleansed unless it be by spilling blood,
And thus engraving what they did
Upon our memory, assuming that
The heavens do not seek vengeance first,
And send down bolts to blast their infamy?   100
I give you the advice you asked of me.

AURORA. And I, in my distress, accept
It gratefully.

MARQUIS.   The mirror that

Reflected her will be Medusa's glass
For this new Circe.*   105

Enter FEDERICO *and* BATÍN

FEDERICO. You mean he would not wait until
They went to welcome him?

BATÍN.   He would
Not wait for anything, my lord.
No sooner did he see the frontier,
Than he, more eager than the rest   110
Of them, rode off, not bothering
To give you proper warning of
His coming. Such is his love of you,
He cannot wait to see you once
Again, and though he wants to see   115
The Duchess too, there's nothing else
Can match his love for you. For him
You are the sun itself, and four
Months absence like the moon's eclipse.
He'll be here soon. You'd best prepare   120
A triumph fit to please a king.
The troops he leads will enter here.
The spoils of war all held aloft,
And golden banners greeting him.

FEDERICO. Aurora, why is it I find   125
You always in the Marquis's company?

AURORA. Am I to think you jest with me,
My lord?

FEDERICO. Is that all you can say
To justify such infidelity?

AURORA. I can't believe the Marquis has   130
Awakened your jealousy,
My lord. You seem to be awake
When you have been four months asleep.

MARQUIS. Believe me, Count, I did not know
You felt what you now claim to feel   135

For her. I served Aurora in
Good faith, believing I had no
Competitor, and least of all
Yourself. Such is my loyalty,
Whatever else you'd asked of me   140
I would have given you except
My love for her, for then it was
Not known to me you loved her too
As honestly as I. But since
You say you do and are more worthy of   145
Her love than I can ever be,
I think it proper to withdraw.

[*Exit the* MARQUIS

AURORA. You see what you have done! What kind
Of madness makes you talk like this
When any thought of love has flown?   150
How many times have you set eyes
On me in conversation with
The Marquis since this strange attack
Of melancholy* first began?
You've never looked at me! But now   155
I plan to marry him, why, all
At once, this great display of jealousy!
Believe me, Count, I know full well
What you have planned. If I am not
Allowed to marry him, I'd rather kill   160
Myself than have a hand in it.
I think it best by far if you
Embrace not me but rather that
Sweet melancholy you so obviously
Prefer. Of one thing be quite sure.   165
I'll not forget the pain that you
Cause me. Do not, then, be surprised
If I inflict the same on you.
I only ask that God protect
Me from such lies as yours. I shall   170
Not help you, be quite sure.

[*Exit* AURORA

BATÍN. Whatever have you done to her?

FEDERICO. Who knows, Batín? I've no idea.

BATÍN. If you ask me, my lord, I'd say
    It's really pretty serious this,   175
    And brings to mind the Emperor,
    Tiberius.* He'd had his missus recently
    Snuffed out, no fuss, but then forgets
    That she's a gonner, so shouts out:
    'It's time for dinner.' Then there was   180
    Messala,* just the same, the one
    That constantly forgot his name.

FEDERICO. I have forgotten I'm a man!

BATÍN. And then there was this peasant too,
    Got married, oh, two years ago.   185
    One day he gave his wife a shock
    He realized her eyes were black.

FEDERICO. I do not know, Batín, what I
    Should do.

BATÍN.   I am reminded too,
    My lord, of one peculiar fellow from   190
    Biscay.* He was a fool, you see;
    He'd gone and left the bridle on
    His horse and found it wouldn't eat
    Its hay. You've no idea how dismayed
    He was, and so he thought he'd better call   195
    A horse-doctor to find out what
    Was wrong with her. He saw at once,
    Of course, the problem with the horse
    Was just the bit, so chucked the owner out
    And then removed it. The horse went mad;   200
    He gobbled up the hay, and when
    He'd finished it, the manger too,
    So when his owner saw what he'd
    Chewed through, he was amazed, and poured

Upon the horse-doctor much lavish praise. 205
'By God,' he said, 'you've done the trick.
I'll come to you when I am sick.
You've dealt with him most skilfully.
In future you can see to me.'
I fancy you too, sir, have such 210
A bit that will not let you eat.
I'll be your doctor, if you wish.
Believe me, I'll soon cure it.

FEDERICO. I cannot tell you what is wrong.

BATÍN. Then I can only say to you, 215
You'd better leave the oats alone.

Enter CASANDRA *and* LUCRECIA.

CASANDRA. He's coming then?

LUCRECIA.   He is, madam.

CASANDRA. And not a single word of warning!

LUCRECIA. They say he's left the rest behind
Because he longs to see you once 220
Again.

CASANDRA. And you believe it of
A man like him? As far as I'm
Concerned, I'd rather die. Convince
Me, Count, the story is a lie.

FEDERICO. They say the Duke will soon be here: 225
Proof that his love for you is sure.

CASANDRA. If I see you no more, I know
That I shall die of sorrow.

FEDERICO [*aside*].*   I know
That, now the Duke is here, this love
Shall never see tomorrow.

CASANDRA.   I know 230
I shall go mad.

FEDERICO.   Not I, for I
Am mad already.

CASANDRA.   My soul consumed
With pain.

FEDERICO.   My life as if destroyed
By flames.

CASANDRA. What can we do?

FEDERICO.   What else
Is there to do but die?

CASANDRA.   Is there   235
No other way?

FEDERICO.   If what we do
Means losing you, why should I live
Another day?

CASANDRA.   The remedy
Is not to lose me.

FEDERICO.   It would be best,
I think, if from today I served   240
Aurora once again, invented love,
And asked the Duke to let me marry her.
It is the obvious way to keep
Us clear of suspicion, before
The gossip in the palace harms   245
Our reputation.

CASANDRA.   There is no way
I'll let you marry her. To do so adds
An insult to this injury.

FEDERICO. The danger we now face obliges me.

CASANDRA. I swear that if you contemplate   250
Such treachery when you are most
To blame for this, the world shall hear
Me voice aloud both my own guilt
And your infamy.

FEDERICO.   My lady, please.

CASANDRA. You'll not dissuade me.

FEDERICO.   Everyone   255
Will hear.

CASANDRA.   I do not care. The Duke
Can take away my life, but you,
I swear, will never marry her.

> *Enter* FLORO, FEBO, RICARDO, ALBANO,
> LUCINDO, *and the* DUKE, *handsomely*
> *dressed as a soldier.*

RICARDO. It seems they are not ready yet
To welcome you, my lord.

DUKE.   It is   260
Because my love has brought me here
More swiftly than they thought.

CASANDRA. My dear husband, you have caught
Us unprepared to greet you as
We should.

FEDERICO.   The Duchess is aggrieved   265
Without good cause. The fault is mine
Entirely, my lord.

DUKE.   My son,
A father's love can never cease
To love his flesh and blood. It made
My journey short and guaranteed   270
The longing and the weariness I felt
Should be transformed into this final good.
And you, my lady, are most worthy of
A love that is at least its rival.
Do not, I beg, feel slighted if   275
I speak to both of you as equals.

CASANDRA. Your blood and Federico's goodness, sir,
Demand you favour him; I therefore must
Be pleased you treat me just the same.

DUKE. I know that I am favoured by   280
  You both and truly cannot say
  How much such love as this is worth
  To me. I also know that Federico has
  Administered the state most prudently
  While I have been away, and not   285
  A single vassal disagrees.
  To tell the truth, while I was so
  Preoccupied with lance and sword,
  It gladdened me to know my son was here
  Instead of me, a prudent overlord.   290
  I offer thanks to God that when
  The Church's enemies* observed
  Our might, it was not long before
  They sought escape in cowardly flight.
  The Holy Father greeted me   295
  Triumphantly in Rome, and then
  The city joyously, as if
  I were some conquering Spanish Trajan.*
  On that account I am resolved
  To be a better man than I   300
  Have been and let my virtue, not
  My vices, now be seen by everyone.
  For when a man wins such applause,
  And all in virtue's name, he would
  Be foolish if his vices then   305
  Acquired even greater fame.

RICARDO. Aurora and the Marquis wait
  On you, my lord.

           Enter AURORA *and the* MARQUIS.

AURORA.   I welcome you,
  My lord, as someone truly glad
  To see you home.

MARQUIS.   And I as someone whose   310
  Affection is already known.

DUKE. I thank you and embrace you both.

The consolation for the tedious months
Away is to anticipate
The joy of such a day as this.   315
But now, my dear friends, I need
To rest. I guarantee that when
Day comes, we'll spend the rest
Of it in joyous celebration.

FEDERICO. God bless the Duke and for eternity   320
His glorious life prolong.

[*Exit all, except* RICARDO *and* BATÍN

BATÍN. Ricardo, good to see you!

RICARDO.   Good
To see you too, Batín.

BATÍN.   How was
It then? You know . . . I mean the fighting.

RICARDO. A case of heaven protecting us,   325
So in the end we simply had to be
Victorious. You should see Lombardy.
No, not a pretty sight, and all
The enemy retreating fast
To save their skins in shameful flight.   330
The mighty lion* of the Church
Roared loud—and all of them at once
Just disappeared in a cloud
Of dust. The Duke's a famous man
The length and breadth of Italy.   335
They celebrate his victories
As once upon a time they praised
King Saul and David* for the way
They routed all their enemies.
Not only that; because of what he's done,   340
The Duke's become a different man.
He doesn't chase the women any more;
He doesn't spend his time, as he
Was wont to do, in idle pleasure.
I swear that his entire thoughts   345

Are dedicated to Casandra; and,
Of course, Federico. In short, the Duke's
Become a real saint, I promise you.

BATÍN. A likely story! Do you expect
Me to believe the Duke's so heavenly?   350

RICARDO. There are some men, Batín, who, when
They see that fortune smiles on them,
Grow proud and arrogant, and force
The rest of us to do the things they want.
The Duke, surprisingly, has turned   355
Out different. The thing that marks him out's
Humility, and how he now
Despises all the praise that has
Been lavished on him on account
Of all his famous victories.   360

BATÍN. Let's hope, then, that he'll always stay
Like that, and not be like the cat
They speak of in the well-known story.*
It tells of how a certain Greek
Desired that his cat—I think   365
It was a tabby—be transformed
Into a rather dishy lady.
And so this lady, now arrayed
With hairdo and expensive finery,
Did see one day a tiny creature pass,   370
I mean that paper-eating poet of
The animals—the friendly mouse—
And straight away she jumped on him,
So proving that we cannot change
A thing as far as our natures are   375
Concerned, and pussy will be always pussy,
Doggie, doggie, for eternity, amen.

RICARDO. I don't believe the Duke will be
Again the profligate he was.
Besides, when he has children he   380
Will be transformed. You'll see them run
Their fingers through the lion's mane,

And him lie at their feet, completely tame.

BATÍN. I hope that what you say is true.

RICARDO. I'll say goodbye. I have to go.   385

BATÍN. Where are you going?

RICARDO.   To see a girl.
I can't afford to keep her waiting.

Exit RICARDO. *Enter the* DUKE *with letters.*

DUKE. Is there no servant here?

BATÍN.   There's me,
My lord, a true example of
Servility.

DUKE.   My good Batín.   390

BATÍN. May God protect you, sir. It's good
To have you home with us again.

DUKE. What are you doing here?

BATÍN.   I was,
Until you came, most entertained
By young Ricardo, sir. He told   395
Me of your recent history,
Of how you are regarded as
The Hector* of all Italy.

DUKE. And would you say, Batín, that while
I've been away, the Count has handled my   400
Affairs as properly as I would like?

BATÍN. You could say, sir, his triumphs here
Have been in every way as great
As yours in war.

DUKE.   And what about
Casandra? Did he treat her kindly?   405

BATÍN. I'd put it much more strongly, sir.
I'd say there's never been a stepmother

That favoured any stepson more
Than she has done. It must have been
Her saintliness and virtue, sir,   410
That won him over.

DUKE.   Then I am glad
If, as you say, they get on well
Together. I love the Count above
All else. I know how sad he was
When I was forced to go away   415
To war, and so on that account
Am glad to hear that both of them
Have learned at last to love each other.
How good it is to know that in
This house we celebrate today   420
Two famous victories: my own
In Italy, Casandra's triumph here.
I am indebted to her for
Such warm consideration of
My son, and promise that in future I   425
Shall spurn all other women. What's past
Is past; the life that I propose
To lead now matters most.

BATÍN.   It seems
To me a miracle, my lord, that one
Who couldn't get enough of it   430
Should now come back to us and plan
To live more like a hermit. You ought
To found, if you are really good,
Some new religious brotherhood.*

DUKE. I promise you, Batín, that all   435
Of you shall see how I've reformed.

BATÍN. Of course we shall, my lord. But I
Don't understand why you aren't yet
In bed when half an hour ago
You said you felt half-dead.

DUKE.   And so   440

I do, Batín. But on my way
Upstairs they gave me documents
And letters which reminded me
That I should deal with cares of state
As soon as possible. I plan   445
To solve them first and then sleep easily.
Why let them cause me pointless worry?
Go now. I must attend to them.
The man who rules should feel that everything
Is worthy of his full attention.   450

BATÍN. No doubt heaven will reward you for
The care with which you deal with your
Affairs. You shall enjoy eternal fame,
And centuries to come shall celebrate
Your name.

                                              [*Exit* BATÍN

DUKE [*reads*]. What have we here? 'My lord,   455
I am your palace gardener.
I've cultivated seeds, together with
Six sons, and for the eldest of them now
Request . . .' I know the cheeky fellow.
We'll let his soil lie fallow for a while.   460
What's this? A begging-letter from
A widow called Lucinda. May
The Devil take her! Another from
A fellow called Albano, not
To mention Julio Camilo. To hell   465
With all of them! This from a woman calls
Herself Paula de San Germán.
Describes herself as chaste young maid.
Why write to me unless she thinks
That I can satisfy her need?   470
What's this that comes so tightly sealed?
The fellow gave it to me seemed
So scared, I swear he thought he'd seen
A ghost. So what's it say? [*Reads*] 'My lord,
While you have been away, the Count   475

And Duchess have . . .' I might have known;
I half suspected this, that they
Did not do things as properly
As I would like! [*Reads*] '. . . offended both
Your honour and your bed by means   480
Of their infamy.' How can
I bear such news as this! [*Reads*] 'You shall
Have certain proof of it if you
Observe them carefully.' What can
This letter be that so offends   485
My eyes and asks them to believe
That this is true? I am convinced
That lies like these do not consider how
A father feels when he is told
His wife and son deprive him of   490
His honour! Am I to think Casandra could
Offend me so? Must I believe
Such shameful things of Federico?
And yet, the fact that they are man
And woman leads me to suspect   495
It might be true! There is no sin
Of which man is not capable,
And I am tempted to believe
That heaven, to punish me for all
My sins, has made this possible.   500
It was the punishment inflicted on
King David* by the prophet Nathan,
Which means that Federico has
Become another Absalom.
But this is punishment far worse,   505
For David's women were but concubines,
While here Casandra is my wife.
It is as if the wickedness
Of my own irresponsible
And sinful life has now been sent   510
To punish me, though I have not,
As David did, obtained a wife
By murder and by treachery.
It is my son who is now guilty of

Such treachery! Must I believe   515
That any son is capable
Of infamy as terrible
As this against the very man
Responsible for his own birth?
If this is true, I pray that heaven,   520
When I have killed him once, will grant
Him life again, so I may have
The chance to kill him one time more.
Oh, this is true disloyalty!
Oh, this the very worst offence!   525
A man cannot leave home without
His son abusing what he thought
Was safe, entrusted to his care.
How can I, then, be sure that
I learn the truth and not expect   530
The witnesses I call to draw
Attention* to the full extent
Of my ignoble fall? And yet
It is quite possible that not
A soul will be prepared to speak   535
Of something quite so horrible.
But if they do, it follows that
The revelation of the crime
Is only possible because   540
It's true, and as its consequence
My own disgrace is unavoidable.
To punish him is not to take
Revenge, nor can the man who punishes
Be properly avenged. To force
The truth from him could also be   545
The source of my undoing. Honour lies
Far less in what is done than in
The dreadful things that may be spoken.

Enter FEDERICO.

FEDERICO. My lord, I knew you were not yet
Asleep. I wish to speak with you.   550

DUKE. May God protect you, Federico.

FEDERICO. I come because there is a favour I
  Would ask of you.

DUKE.   There is no need.
  You know my love is such, it favours you
  Before you ask.

FEDERICO.   It was your wish   555
  Not long ago, that I should ask
  Aurora for her hand in marriage.
  Although I shared that wish, I was
  On that occasion most discouraged by
  The Marquis's love of her, and so   560
  Did not pursue my own. But when
  You'd gone to Italy, it was as if
  Aurora, seeing how I really loved
  Her, changed; began to favour me
  Again, and I to hope our marriage could,   565
  Once you came back, soon be arranged.
  I come to ask that you agree
  To our wedding and, of course,
  Confer upon us both your blessing.

DUKE. My son, there's nothing else would give   570
  Me greater pleasure. Even so,
  You must discuss the matter with
  Your mother too, as you have done
  With me. What matters most is that
  We are a happy, caring family.   575

FEDERICO. But she does not have our blood.
  Why should I therefore ask advice
  Of her, my lord?

DUKE.   I would have thought,
  Because the lady is your mother.

FEDERICO. My mother was Laurencia.   580

DUKE. So does that mean you are ashamed
  To call Casandra mother? They tell

Me, while I was away, the two
Of you got on extremely well
Together.

FEDERICO.   My lord, I do not wish   585
To contradict the story others tell.
I know you love her dearly.
But if she was for them the angel they
Describe, she was not so with me.

DUKE.   Then I am sorry if what I   590
Have heard is so untrue. They said
That nothing ever pleased her more
Than seeing you.

FEDERICO.   She favoured me
At times, but also made me feel
As if to be another woman's son   595
Was something of a feckless crime.

DUKE.   I do admit I am inclined
To think there is some truth in it.
I would have been more pleased if she
Had shown you even greater love   600
Than me, for that would surely
Consolidate this kingdom's harmony.
May God go with you.

FEDERICO.   And with you, my lord.

[*Exit* FEDERICO

DUKE.   How could I bear to listen to
Such hideous lies, and see how he   605
Prepares a marriage to Aurora to
Disguise the truth! How eagerly
He blames Casandra, thinking I
Will therefore think the worse of her!
How foolishly are criminals   610
Convinced that they conceal their crimes,
When everything they say and do
Is of their guilt the clearest sign!

He cannot bring himself to call
Her mother—how could he when his father's wife   615
Is now his own devoted lover?
But why am I so easily
Convinced* that such a foul offence
Is true? Is it not possible
Some enemy of mine now plots   620
His own revenge on me by making me
Believe my son's committed such
An act of treachery? That I
Should even think he is to blame
Is both a source of punishment and shame.   625

Enter CASANDRA *and* AURORA.

AURORA. To grant me this, my lady, is
　　To grant me life itself.

CASANDRA.　　　　　　To choose
　　So wisely is to guarantee
　　Yourself both wealth and happiness.

AURORA. The Duke comes here.

CASANDRA.　　　　　　My lord, I had   630
　　Not thought to find you wide-awake.

DUKE. Because I've been away so long,
　　I feel I have to give attention to
　　Affairs of state. And yet this letter here
　　Makes mention of the way you and   635
　　The Count both make most excellent
　　Administrators. Your deeds, it seems,
　　Have made their mark, and won unstinted praise
　　From others.

CASANDRA.　　It is the Count, not me,
　　To whom you owe most gratitude.   640
　　It is not flattery to say
　　He's served you well, displaying both
　　Discretion and nobility,
　　Combining wisdom and true bravery.

He is the image of yourself, my lord.   645

DUKE. You speak as if he copies me
In everything, and you now have
A problem in distinguishing
Between the two of us. For this
I shall reward him as he properly   650
Deserves.

CASANDRA. It is Aurora whom
You now can serve more properly.
The Marquis wants to marry her,
And I have said you'll willingly
Agree to it.

DUKE.   I am afraid that someone else,   655
Whose love and status is by far
Superior, has already asked for her.
The Count has made me promise her
To him.

CASANDRA. The Count?

DUKE.   The Count.

CASANDRA.   Has asked
For her?

DUKE.   I'd say you are surprised,   660
Casandra.

CASANDRA. If someone else had told
Me this, I would have said he lied.

DUKE. To please the Count, the wedding shall
Take place tomorrow.

CASANDRA.   If that is now
Aurora's wish, it shall be so.   665

AURORA. My lord, forgive me. I cannot marry him.

DUKE. What foolishness! The Count is far
Superior to the Marquis in
Good looks, nobility, in anything

You care to name.

AURORA.   But when I loved   670
Him, sir, he would not look at me.
And if he says he loves me now,
I cannot share that sympathy.

DUKE. I ask you do this not so much
For him, Aurora, as for me.   675

AURORA. I do not love him, sir. I swear
To you. I shall not marry him.

[*Exit* AURORA

DUKE. How very strange!

CASANDRA.   She may seem bold,
My lord, but acts most prudently.

DUKE. She'll marry him, I promise you,   680
Or pay the price for her temerity.

CASANDRA. To force her would be pure folly. No
One loves who does not do so freely.

[*Exit the* DUKE

I cannot bear to think the Count
Can contemplate such treachery!   685

Enter FEDERICO.

FEDERICO. Was not my father here?

CASANDRA.   You dare
To speak to me when you have told
The Duke you wish to marry her!
What treachery is this?

FEDERICO.   Casandra, hush!
The danger is too great.

CASANDRA.   There is   690
No danger that can now compare
With all the anger that I feel

For you.

FEDERICO. Casandra, please! Speak quietly,
Or everyone will hear.

Enter the DUKE. *He hides and listens.*

DUKE. I must have proof. I'll listen to   695
Them both from here; far better if
I know the worst than be destroyed
By groundless and imaginary fears.

FEDERICO. Casandra, listen. What matters now
Is your reputation.

CASANDRA.   Who would have said   700
That anyone would do what you
Have done when I have offered you
My love and therefore ask you recognize
Your obligation?

FEDERICO.   My main concern
Was that suspicion should not fall   705
On us. But even so, I think
What happiness we had must end.
The Duke is not so base a man
He will not, once he understands
What we have done, take every step   710
To mend his name and reputation.
Our love consumed us like a fever.
We must regard it now as over.

CASANDRA. You are the greatest coward I
Have ever seen. Those earnest pleas,   715
Those sweet entreaties that you used
To steal my heart and then my honour—
How many women have become,
Like me, men's helpless prisoners?—
Are now the milksop pleadings of   720
A coward racked by fear!

DUKE [*aside*].   How can
I bear to listen any more

And not be made of stone? They have
Confessed their sin without the need
To torture them. But who can say   725
There is no torture here if I
Am forced to listen to this foul
Confession? I need to hear no more.
What I am sure of is honour is
The judge of this offence and is   730
Thus called upon to pass and then
To execute the sentence. But it
Must be in such a way that my
Good name remains unsoiled, and cannot be
By public gossip then destroyed.   735
No living soul shall ever know
I am dishonoured. I shall take steps
To see the crime is quickly buried.*
For it is not enough for any man
To cleanse his honour, when others are   740
Prepared to speak of it forever.

                                        [*Exit the* DUKE

CASANDRA. How women are abused! How false are men!

FEDERICO. I swear, my lady, I shall do
What you demand of me. My word
Bears witness to my loyalty.   745

CASANDRA. You promise me?

FEDERICO.   As I stand here,
You can rely on me.

CASANDRA.   I am
Convinced that love can overcome
All obstacles. I have been and
Shall always now be yours. If it   750
Is true that love can find a way,
I know that I shall see you every day.

FEDERICO. What matters most is that the Duke
Should be convinced of your love.

He must believe that, when he lies 755
With you, you are his gentle, cooing dove.

CASANDRA. I shall convince him I am still
His treasure, though love, when it is feigned,
Does not contain the slightest pleasure.

[*Exit* CASANDRA *and* FEDERICO

Enter AURORA *and* BATÍN.

BATÍN. They tell me, fair Aurora, you 760
Are soon to marry my good friend,
The Marquis of Gonzaga. I've only one
Request: that when you leave, you let
Me come with you to Mantua.

AURORA. But why, Batín? You've always been 765
The Count's most loyal servant.

BATÍN.   That's
The point, my lady. He who serves
Too well can almost guarantee
He'll never prosper. How often do
You hear them say to you: 'No, not 770
Today, you'll have to wait until
Tomorrow.' And when tomorrow comes:
'What cheek! You'll have to wait until
Next week.' There's no reward in what
I do. I know I'd rather go with you. 775
Besides, I don't know if the Count's
Gone mad. He's either happy or
He's sad. He either laughs from ear
To ear, or else his mouth drops down
To here. Then there's the Duchess, just 780
Like him, as if she's in a constant spin.
So what can I expect to get
If all they ever do is fret?
The Duke has conversations with himself;
He wanders round as if he's blind; 785
Pretends he is a perfect saint,
And looks for what he'll never find.

What hope for me if I stay here?
I'll come with you to Mantua.

AURORA. If that is what you really wish,   790
And I am married to the Marquis, so
You shall.

BATÍN.   I kiss your feet a thousand times.
I'm always at your beck and call.

Exit BATÍN. *Enter the* DUKE.

DUKE. How true that we are always bound
By honour's harsh and cruel rule!*   795
What man was it that brought this law
Into the world to prove himself
The most misguided of all fools?
But more than that, to make it all
Depend on woman's fragile nature,   800
When it is evident that man
Himself is easily the stronger!
A man, though he is not to blame,
May by another's guilt or deed,
Be quickly robbed of his good name.*   805
It proves that he who first invented such
A code was equally deceived,
And therefore for revenge made sure
That others also are aggrieved.
Aurora!

AURORA.   Yes, my lord?

DUKE.   It is   810
Casandra's wish that you should give
Your hand in marriage to the Marquis.
I wish to please her rather than
Fulfil the Count's desire.

AURORA.   It makes
Me truly happy, sir.

DUKE.   The Marquis should   815
Inform his family in Mantua.

AURORA. He shall at once, my lord. I'll see
    To it myself he writes the letter.

                                [*Exit* AURORA

DUKE. I swear the punishment that I
    Intend to take is sent from Heaven above.   820
    The justice I now seek comes not
    From any sense of private hurt
    But from God's love. For this is His
    Revenge, not mine, and I am but
    The instrument of punishment divine.   825
    I act not as a husband wronged,
    But as a father called upon to thus
    Avenge a hideous sin and so demand
    A punishment without revenge.*
    It is in any case what each   830
    Of us by honour's law is clearly told:
    Avenge the insult secretly,
    Or else dishonour is twofold.
    The man is doubly shamed who gives
    The punishment publicity;   835
    For having lost his honour once,
    The world then knows his infamy.
    The infamous Casandra I
    Have bound securely, her hands
    And feet both tightly tied,   840
    A cloth across her face, a gag
    Stuffed in her mouth to stop her cries.
    It was quite easily done, for when
    I told her that I knew the truth
    And why I'd come, she fainted at   845
    My feet. To kill her now, despite
    Her pleas, is something pity could
    Ignore, but when I think of killing him . . .
    What heart would not immediately
    Be rent in two? The mere thought   850
    Of it fills me with dread and makes
    My limbs grow weak. My blood runs cold
    Through frozen veins; I cannot find

The strength to speak. I feel as if
My spirit faints; my eyes, despite   855
Myself, now weep. My heart beats hard
Against my breast; I find it difficult
To breathe, just as on some cold winter's night
A flowing stream will start to freeze.
But I must not let love divert   860
Me from the task in hand when, as
The Scriptures tell us, it is God's
Command that sons must be obedient to
Their fathers in the things they do,
And not dishonour them, like Federico.   865
No, I must punish anyone
Who breaks God's law and brings such shame
Upon a father. For it is possible
That such a son is capable
Of murder too. Artaxerxes*   870
Killed fifty men and with less cause;
Torquatus, Brutus, Darius* stained their swords
With blood in order to enforce the laws.
No, love must never stay my swift,
Avenging hand when honour, now   875
Commanding reason, sets out cold,
Implacable demands. For it is truth
That prosecutes, and eyes and ears
That state the evidence of their guilt.
And though both love and blood speak out   880
In their defence, it is their shame
And infamy that now proclaim
Their lack of innocence. It is God's law
That in the end decides the case
When conscience writes man's guilt upon   885
His face. He comes. Why am I so
Afraid? I pray that Heaven now offers me
Its aid.

Enter FEDERICO.

FEDERICO. My lord, am I to think
That you've agreed Aurora's to

Be married to the Marquis of Gonzaga? 890
They tell me that he's soon to take
Her off to Mantua.

DUKE.   I cannot say
That it is true or not. I do
Not know. Other, more important things
Preoccupy me now.

FEDERICO.   No one 895
Who rules can rest, it's true. What is
It that so bothers you?

DUKE.   It seems
A certain nobleman has, with the help
Of others, planned to bring about
My overthrow. He told his secret to 900
A woman who in turn told me,
Thus proving that we always place
Our trust in them most foolishly,
But at the same time flatter them
Most prudently. I summoned him, 905
Pretending there was something we
Must urgently discuss, and when
He came informed him that his little scheme
Had been revealed to us. He went
Quite pale as soon as I referred to it, 910
And then succumbed to what was clearly
A fainting fit. How easy it
Then was to tie him to the chair
And hide his true identity,
So when we put an end to him, 915
His name should not be publicized
Throughout the whole of Italy.
Now you are here, I take you in
My confidence, but no one else
Must know of this. I urge you take 920
Your sword and kill this man for me.
I shall observe from here if you
Have nerve enough to put an end

To my worst enemy.

FEDERICO.   But is
There some conspiracy, or are   925
You merely testing me with this?

DUKE. If any father asks his son
To act on his behalf, does he
Then start to make a fuss and prove
Himself not half the man his father thought?   930

FEDERICO. Give me the sword. Wait here. I swear
That I do not feel fear. You say
The man is tied securely. Why is
It, then, my hands begin to shake
So uncontrollably?

DUKE.   I'll go myself.   935
I'll get the deed done quickly.

FEDERICO.   No.
You ordered me. I'll see it through.
And yet . . .

DUKE.   You lack the nerve to go
And do it now.

FEDERICO.   If it were Caesar, I
Would prove to you that I could run   940
Him through a thousand times!

                    [*He draws his sword and leaves*

DUKE.   I'll watch
From here. He now approaches her.
He drives the sword right through. The man
Who by his actions stained my honour thus
Restores it.* Guards! Come quickly!   945
Servants! Members of my household! Hurry!

            Enter the MARQUIS, AURORA, BATÍN,
                RICARDO, *and others.*

MARQUIS. Why do you summon us? What makes

You call so loudly?

DUKE.   Whoever saw
Such cold and callous treachery?
The Count had learned Casandra was   950
With child. He realized at once
That it would rob him of inheritance
And in his jealousy has murdered her.
I am the Duke. I order you
Take vengeance on the murderer.   955

MARQUIS. Casandra dead?

DUKE.   Yes, there inside.

MARQUIS. I swear I'll not return to Mantua
Until the traitor has been duly tried.

DUKE. He comes. See how his sword is stained
With blood.

Enter FEDERICO.

FEDERICO.   What have I done? I took   960
Away the veil that hid the face
And found the person you had claimed
A traitor was . . .

DUKE.   You dare blame me
For your treachery? Kill him
At once.

MARQUIS. He has admitted guilt   965
And so must die.

FEDERICO.   Why, father, why
Have you done this to me?

[Exit FEDERICO, *pursued by the* MARQUIS

DUKE.   You will
Discover why on Judgement Day.
Aurora, you are free to leave
For Mantua. The Marquis is a good   970
And honest man. Of that be sure.

AURORA. I am confused. I cannot think
Of what to say.

BATÍN.　　　　Say yes. There is
Good cause for what has happened here
Today.

AURORA. Then let me think on it.　　　975
I promise my reply in one more day.

Enter the MARQUIS.

MARQUIS. The deed is done. His treachery
Is over.

DUKE.　　Great is my grief, and yet
I wish to see his body lie beside Casandra.

[The bodies are revealed

MARQUIS. Behold a punishment without revenge.　　　980

DUKE. No man who punishes a sin
Can truly claim he is avenged.
I cannot look. For pity's sake!
My poor heart begins to break!
He thought he could inherit all　　　985
My property; his punishment
This lifeless body.

BATÍN.　　　　And with it ends
This tragedy, a timely lesson for
All Spain,* a wondrous sight for all
Of Italy.　　　990

Praise be to God and the Virgin Mother
In Madrid, First of August 1631.
Fray Lope Félix de Vega Carpio.

EXPLANATORY NOTES

FUENTE OVEJUNA

2 [*The Characters of the Play*] *An Alderman*: there are, in fact, various aldermen, but in the published edition of 1619 there was a good deal of carelessness. Neither is there any mention of Leonelo, a Peasant, and a Soldier.

Act One

3 [*Act One*]: in early editions of Golden Age plays there is no scene division. This practice was introduced by nineteenth-century editors but is no longer regarded as correct.

The Master: the Grand Master of the Order of Calatrava, in this case Rodrigo Téllez Girón, who had succeeded to the position at the age of 8 and who, when the play begins, is 17. The Grand Master was the head of the order, which had been founded in the twelfth century, along with the Order of Alcántara and the Order of Santiago, in order to defend the Christian states of Spain against the Moslems. For the historical situation at the start of the play, see the Introduction, pp. xii–xiii.

Grand | Commander: a position immediately below that of the Grand Master.

4 *cross of Calatrava*: the cloak of the Order of Calatrava was white, with a red cross.

Fernando: the full form of Fernán.

5 *Your brave and famous father*: the father of Rodrigo Téllez Girón was Don Pedro Girón, twenty-eighth Master of Calatrava, who renounced his position in favour of his young son.

Pius: Pope Pius II, who, in 1466, when Rodrigo was only 8, had agreed to the request of the Order that the boy be appointed Master.

Paul: Pope Paul II subsequently appointed Don Juan Pacheco, Marquis of Villena and the boy's uncle, as Coadjutor. Juan Pacheco died when Rodrigo was 16, at which time he became Grand Master on his own.

King Henry the Fourth: King of Castile in the second half of the fifteenth century and who died in 1479.

Juana: in 1462 King Henry married the princess Juana of Portugal, who in the same year produced a child, also called Juana. Her legitimacy was, in fact, doubtful, for many suspected that her real father was Don Beltrán de la Cueva, her mother's favourite at Court, and the child came to be known as Juana la Beltraneja. She later married Alonso V of Portugal.

Fernando: Fernando, heir to the throne of Aragon, became King of Aragon in 1479.

5 *Isabel*: Isabel of Castile was half-sister to King Henry. In 1469 she married Fernando of Aragon and succeeded to the throne of Castile ten years later.

Almagro . . . Ciudad Real: Almagro is a town in the province of Ciudad Real, about 10 miles from the latter. Ciudad Real, in New Castile, is the capital of the province, and at the time in question was an important strategic position.

6 *Urueña*: Don Pedro Girón, Rodrigo's father, had been invested with the title of Count of Urueña in 1464.

Villena's Marquesses: one of these was Juan Pacheco, Rodrigo's uncle. See note on *Paul*, p. 5 above.

7 *Fuente Ovejuna*: the town is situated in the province of Córdoba, some 55 miles to the north-west of that city. At the time of the events dramatized in Lope's play, its population was less than one thousand inhabitants. Until 1468 it owed allegiance to the city of Córdoba, but in that year was seized by Fernán Gómez.

s.d. *They exit . . .*: in a seventeenth-century production there would have been no shifting of scenery. The exit of the Commander and the Master and the entrance of Pascuala and Laurencia, given the differences in costume and speech, would have been sufficient to indicate the change in location from the house of a nobleman to the village.

8 *the stream*: the place where Spanish village-women traditionally washed their clothes. Cf. Federico García Lorca's *Yerma*, Act II, Scene i.

merry, bubbling tune: the musical allusion suggests the harmony which exists in Laurencia's life, soon to be disrupted by the discord which the Commander represents. The description of the meal as a whole evokes the simplicity and wholesomeness of country life, so different from the refinement and artificiality of the nobility and the Court. See the Introduction, pp. xiv–xv.

9 *Twerp, twerp*: in Lope's play the sparrows initially call out *tío, tío* ('mister, mister'), and later on *judío, judío* ('Jew, Jew'). This would have been an insult at the time in question, particularly to Old Christians (see note on *less pure*, p. 31 below), who prided themselves on having pure blood. To translate the joke into English is almost impossible.

sparrows: the sparrow is traditionally associated with lechery.

10 *fiddle*: *rabel*, a small instrument with three strings and a bow. It was a favourite with shepherds.

11 *city talk*: Frondoso's speech (212–39) follows a pattern used earlier by Antonio de Guevara in *Menosprecio de corte y alabanza de aldea* (*Contempt for the Court and Praise of the Village*), written in 1539, in which the euphemisms employed by city flatterers are described.

12 *saltier than water*: the Spanish word *sal* means both 'salt' and 'wit'. Mengo is suggesting that the priest, in christening Laurencia, must have used not only water but wit. In the Roman Catholic baptism the priest

rubs a few grains of salt on the child's lips, but Mengo implies that, in Laurencia's case, he used much more.

12 *blood | Phlegm, melancholy, choler*: blood, phlegm, melancholy (black bile), and choler (bile) constituted the four bodily humours. Good health ensued if they existed in a state of balance, bad health if one were predominant. The doctrine of the humours had initially been set out by the Pythagorean school of Greek physicians and applied by Hippocrates in the fourth century BC. The elements alluded to in 1.282 are the four elements of earth, air, fire, and water, of which the material world was thought to be composed.

13 *perfect harmony*: a Platonic concept according to which the world of man is but an imperfect copy of a higher, perfect world. Thus, the beauty of woman is but the earthly form of a higher, perfect beauty; earthly music and harmony the same; the harmonious love of man and woman the worldly manifestation of an underlying, supreme harmony.

14 *Plato*: the theories on love of the Greek philosopher Plato had been set out in his *Symposium*, and during the Renaissance were taken up again, in particular during the fifteenth-century revival of Neoplatonism in Italy. Marsilio Ficino's commentary on the *Symposium* was the first in a succession of reinterpretations of Plato's ideas on love which extended through the sixteenth century. Since Plato and the Neoplatonists emphasized the spiritual nature of love, it was logical that that aspect of it should be seized upon and emphasized in their sermons by priests, as Barrildo recalls here. Leone Ebreo's *Dialoghi d'amore*, which also expounded Neoplatonic ideas on love, was published in 1535 and twice translated into Spanish in the sixteenth century. The debate conducted by the village characters here is much livelier and down-to-earth than the high-flown discussions on love which formed part of the pastoral novels of the sixteenth century.

15 *falcon*: Flores, the Commander's servant, is a bird of prey in the sense that the village girls are the victims of the predatory instincts of the Commander and his henchmen. But the falcon was also associated with the love chase. So, at the beginning of Fernando de Rojas's *La Celestina* (see Introduction, p. xxiv), Calisto pursues his falcon into Melibea's garden and meets for the first time the young woman whom he will now begin to pursue.

friars: in the Order of Calatrava there were friars who were devoted to the active life, which meant principally the employment of arms against the Moors and other enemies of Catholicism.

Guadalquivir: one of the largest and most important Spanish rivers, though some 60 miles south of Ciudad Real.

16 *Granada*: the action of the play takes place in 1476. By this time Moorish domination of Spain had been virtually ended and only the kingdom of Granada remained in their hands. The city itself surrendered to the Catholic Kings in 1492.

17 *carts*: Esteban clearly indicates the carts. They were either off-stage or in the discovery space.

19 *Whoa now*: because Flores treats the two women as animals, Pascuala responds in kind. The attitude of Flores and the Commander towards the women is in marked contrast to the respect shown by the villagers towards the Commander a few minutes earlier.

22 *Extremadura*: the region between Portugal and Castile and therefore the 'door' whereby Alfonso of Portugal could advance against the Catholic Kings.

Córdoba: Diego de Córdoba, Count of Cabra.

people love to talk: although Laurencia is teasing Frondoso to some extent, her remark has to do with the concept of honour and with the belief that public gossip may damage one's reputation. Although she is only a village girl, Laurencia is a proud and dignified young woman, conscious of her good name. On the honour theme in the play, see the Introduction, pp. xv–xvi.

23 *A single person in the place*: the fact that everyone in the village believes that Laurencia and Frondoso are suited to each other, suggests that between them there is that natural correspondence of which Alonso also speaks in the opening scene of *The Knight from Olmedo*. This natural correspondence and harmony between Laurencia and Frondoso exists too between Fernando and Isabel (3.338), and is something which, in both cases, the Commander threatens to undermine.

This coldness: to some extent Laurencia's coldness brings to mind the traditional disdainful shepherdess of sixteenth-century pastoral novels, while Frondoso is, by the same token, the unhappy, rejected lover. But Lope's characters are, of course, much more human and credible.

an angel's face: a similar example of a young woman who is physically beautiful but emotionally cold occurs in Tirso de Molina's famous play, *The Trickster of Seville* (*El burlador de Sevilla*) in which the fishergirl Tisbea attracts men by means of her good looks but delights in rejecting them. In modern terms Laurencia and Tisbea are interesting psychological studies.

turtle-doves: traditionally associated with Venus and thus with love, doves had the reputation of being always faithful.

24 *frightened deer*: the theme of the love chase hinted at earlier (see note on *falcon*, p. 15 above) is now developed at greater length. This was a common enough literary theme in many countries. A traditional Spanish ballad contains the lines: 'The King went out to hunt ... and met instead a pretty girl ...'.

25 *bow*: the Commander's bow also brings to mind Cupid's bow and further underlines the contrast between the genuine love of Frondoso for Laurencia, and the Commander's lust. When Frondoso aims the bow at

the Commander, making his breast 'the arrow's target' (1.641), the contrast is even clearer.

26 *tying together*: the word *spoliar* meant 'to fasten feet', as of falcons or dead game. Since the Commander is hunting Laurencia, Frondoso's comment has a certain irony.

The rules of chivalry: the Commander means that, according to the code of honour, it would demean him to turn his back on or run away from a peasant. There is, of course, a deep irony in the sense that, morally, his treatment of Laurencia has been the opposite of chivalrous.

Act Two

27 S.D. *First Alderman*: the alderman mentioned here, though not by name, is Cuadrado. A second alderman, Juan Rojo, enters later, see 2.77.

these forecasters: prophecy was a frequent topic in Golden Age drama and was often part of the contemporary debate on the extent to which events and human lives are predestined. Lope made many attacks on astrologers. See F. G. Halstead, 'The Attitude of Lope de Vega toward Astrology and Astronomy', *Hispanic Review*, 7 (1939), 205–19. Lope clearly favoured the down-to-earth practicality exemplified in Esteban.

Transylvania: in Lope's time this part of present-day Romania was regarded as both distant and dangerous.

28 *Hircania*: part of ancient Persia and south-east of the Caspian Sea, famous for its tigers since Antiquity.

Salamanca: the University of Salamanca was established in the thirteenth century and subsequently became one of the most famous in Europe, attracting many students from outside Spain. By 1552 it had 6,328 students—a number which hardly any other university in Europe could match.

Bartolo: Bartolus of Sassoferrato, an Italian jurist of the fourteenth century.

Gutenberg from Mainz: Johann Gutenberg of Mainz is usually regarded as the European inventor of printing from movable types.

29 *publish in the name*: Lope frequently complained about inferior playwrights who, in the highly competitive theatre of his day, passed off their works as his.

30 *do not rise!*: there are clearly benches on an otherwise bare stage. See 'On the Staging of Golden Age Plays', p. xxxii.

the greyhound: this is probably one of the gifts given by the villagers to the Commander, but it also allows Lope to reintroduce and develop the theme of the hunt in which a woman replaces an animal as the object of the chase.

A hare: the hare, apart from being renowned for its speed in escaping from its pursuers, was also a medieval symbol for the vagina.

31 *Aristotle's Politics*: the Commander is probably name-dropping in order to impress both the villagers and his servants, but the importance of Aristotle's writings during the sixteenth and seventeenth centuries cannot be over-emphasized. His *Politics* was a treatise on civil government in the Greek city-state.

honour?: on the theme of honour, see the Introduction, p. xv. The Commander's statement that peasants cannot have honour is based entirely on his belief that it is solely derived from noble birth and social position.

less pure: the presence of many Muslims and Jews in Spain over a long period of time meant inevitably that mixed marriages were common and that even those who claimed to be Christian, such as the knights of Calatrava, could not be sure that they did not have Muslim or Jewish blood in their veins. Pure blood belonged to those who were Old Christians, who were often the peasant class.

33 *Granada and Córdoba*: on Granada see note to p. 16. Córdoba was also a city which for a very long time was dominated by the Moors. Its most famous monument to this day is the great mosque which was completed in the last quarter of the tenth century. The city was finally conquered by the Christians in 1236.

Pascuala: this does not seem to be the Pascuala who is Laurencia's friend, unless, of course, she has fobbed off Flores with a lie.

34 *Aristotle*: on this occasion the reference is to Aristotle's *Physics*, i. 9. Flores's statement is, of course, a distortion of Aristotle's meaning.

35 *The Master of Santiago*: just as Rodrigo Téllez Girón, Grand Master of the Order of Calatrava, supports Alonso of Portugal, so the Grand Master of the Order of Santiago supports the cause of Isabel of Castile. The Order of Santiago, the most powerful of the three orders, was founded in the twelfth century.

the lions | And castles of Castile, the bars | Of Aragon: the coat of arms of León consisted of a red lion rampant on a silver ground, that of Castile of a gold castle on a silver ground. The coat of arms of Aragon, consisting of four vertical bars on a gold ground, was originally that of the Counts of Barcelona and became that of Aragon in 1162 when the region was annexed by the then Count of Barcelona, Ramón Berenguer.

36 *The devil's*: the comparison of the Commander to the devil is strikingly at odds with the Christian obligations required of him as a knight of Calatrava. As the action unfolds, he is also described more and more in terms of predatory beasts and birds.

37 *my sling*: although the image of Mengo as the biblical David is a comic one, the suggestion that the Commander is another Goliath reinforces his evil nature, as well as pointing to his ultimate downfall.

Heliogabalus: Emperor of Rome from AD 218 to 222 (properly 'Elagabalus', a name derived from the Syrian sun-god Elah-Gabal).

40 *baggage*: the Spanish word *bagaje* refers specifically to the equipment, food, and clothing which the army carries with it. The English word, on the other hand, has the added meaning of loose woman, which fits in perfectly here.

s.d. *All exit*: the location changes with the entry of Laurencia and Frondoso to the village of Fuente Ovejuna itself.

41 *I kiss your feet*: the phrase is a formal one most often associated with the nobility and the Court. Used here by a peasant, it points perhaps to the nobility of Frondoso's love for Laurencia, as well as to his adoration of her.

s.d. *Alderman*: the Alderman here is Juan Rojo.

42 *The Catholic Kings*: the title of *los Reyes Católicos* was granted to Fernando and Isabel by Pope Alexander VI in 1494.

rod of office: Esteban carries his staff of office, the symbol of his authority, throughout the play.

44 *always obeys me?*: the relationship between father and daughter and father and prospective son-in-law is shown to be based on the kind of respect and loyalty which is totally absent from the Commander's relationship with his subjects, towards whom he too should show respect. On the theme of love in the play, see the Introduction, p. xvi.

at your age: Esteban's age is not given but he is probably in his forties, and therefore considered quite old at the time of the play's action.

45 *four thousand maravedis*: it is difficult to know which kind of coin is alluded to here. There were in fact 'maravedis' of gold, silver, and bronze, all of different value and also fluctuating in their value from time to time. The word itself is of Arabic origin and yet another example of the profound impact on Spanish life of Muslim influence over eight centuries.

s.d. *Enter the Master*: the following scene takes place away from Fuente Ovejuna. The happiness of Laurencia and Frondoso coincides, significantly, with the triumph of the Catholic Kings, to whom the villagers are loyal, and with the defeat of Rodrigo Téllez Girón and his followers, all of them disloyal to Fernando and Isabel.

the flag of Calatrava: the flag would at this point be on stage.

46 *the highest towers*: at this point in the action the flags or banners of Castile could well have been displayed in the balconies or gallery high above the back of the stage.

s.d. *Magistrate, and Juan Rojo*: the magistrate mentioned here is a second magistrate, the other being Esteban. Juan Rojo is not included in Lope's stage-direction, even though he is involved in this scene. The location is probably the square of Fuente Ovejuna.

47 *pumped*: this would have been done by means of a hollow tube of wood or metal which was attached to a small bag of leather.

47 *Such dreadful poetry*: Mengo is here the literary critic and in this respect
    voices Lope's own opinion on bad poets. Controversies of this kind
    were, of course, quite common at the time, frequently involving those
    who advocated a relatively clear and uncomplicated style and those whose
    preference was for a more ornate and complex kind of poetry.

48 *as one!*: the harmony between Frondoso and Laurencia anticipates that
    between Fernando and Isabel, emphasized in the song in Act Three (see
    3.338). Consequently, it links the main and the sub-plot and also draws
    attention to the disruptive influence of the Commander both in the lives
    of Laurencia and Frondoso and in the political events concerning the
    Catholic Kings.

    The village-girl: in the Spanish original the song is characterized by
    assonance in alternate lines:

> Al val de Fuente Ovejuna
> la niña en cabello b*a*ja;
> el caballero la sigue
> de la Cruz de Calatr*a*va . . .

    In the translation I have opted for rhyme or near rhyme in alternate
    lines.

49 S.D. *Enter the Commander*: a wonderfully dramatic moment. In the song
    the village-girl is not named, nor is the knight who lusts after her. The
    sudden appearance of Fernán Gómez at the very end of the song there-
    fore transforms the words of the song into a pressing and ominous
    reality.

50 *His father*: a rather strange line in the sense that there is no reference
    anywhere in the play to Frondoso's father being a judge (though he
    may, of course, be one).

    His crime: Fernán Gómez attempts to conceal his personal motives in
    taking revenge against Frondoso by pretending that the latter's offence
    has been against him as a representative of the Order of Calatrava, and
    therefore against the Grand Master himself.

51 *virtuous nature*: the implication is that those of noble birth should also
    possess nobility of soul and spirit. There is no sarcasm in Esteban's
    remark. He is simply expressing his genuine expectation of a man in the
    Commander's position of responsibility towards his vassals.

    disorder: one of the first tasks which confronted Isabel when she became
    ruler of Castile was the government of the three Orders of Calatrava,
    Alcántara, and Santiago. By the fifteenth century the orders had become
    immensely powerful and a threat to the monarchy itself, while rivalry
    for the Grand Masterships was a constant source of strife among the
    nobility. By 1499 Fernando, husband of Isabel, had become Grand Master
    of all three orders, and in 1523 they were incorporated into the crown of
    Castile by papal edict.

    crosses: the reference to the cross, which is of course emblazoned on the

Commander's cloak, is another reminder of the Christian virtues which he should embody, and a striking contrast to his subsequent abuse of Esteban's office of magistrate.

51 *overlord*: Esteban recognizes his responsibilities to his overlord in a way which the Commander does not in relation to his vassals. He is therefore prepared to accept the ill-treatment of the Commander in the expectation that God will ultimately see justice done.

52 *kettle-drums*: the kind of drum described here—in Spanish *atabal*—was semi-spherical in shape. Two such drums side by side, therefore, suggest to Mengo the two cheeks of his backside, on which a much harsher rhythm has been played.

Act Three

53 S.D. *Enter Esteban . . .*: the meeting which opens the Act evidently takes place in the village council chamber behind closed doors, hence Juan Rojo's subsequent remark 'This meeting must be secret'.

S.D. *Alderman*: this is the same alderman mentioned at the beginning of Act Two, whose name is Cuadrado.

54 *Córdoba*: some 55 miles from Fuente Ovejuna. See note to 7.

55 *Take arms against our overlord?*: to rebel against the Commander would be to overturn the natural order of things, as is the case in Shakespeare's *Macbeth* when Macbeth murders his overlord, Duncan the King.

56 *You are responsible*: the father, as head of the family, was responsible for its honour and reputation. When a daughter married, that responsibility passed, of course, to her husband. Laurencia's abduction by the Commander was not only an affront to the family name but was also something that would become a source of gossip and speculation as to whether she had been raped and therefore further 'dishonoured'.

precious stone: honour was regarded as precious, something to be guarded with one's life, for without honour life itself became meaningless. In his play *Peribáñez*, 3.2614–65, honour is also presented by Lope as something essentially fragile, comparable to a reed or cane which may be easily broken.

The name of our town: the original name of the town was, in fact, Fuente Abejuna, 'well of the bees', but over a period of time seems to have changed to Fuente Ovejuna, the 'sheep-well'.

Not tigresses!: in Classical literature tigresses had the reputation of pursuing the hunter who had stolen their cubs and of sacrificing their lives in the attempt to rescue them. See also *Punishment Without Revenge*, 3.83.

distaffs: a distaff is a rotating vertical staff which holds the skein of wool in hand-spinning, a task traditionally undertaken by women and therefore symbolic of female activity. Laurencia suggests that the men of the village are more suited to the passive domestic tasks of women.

57 *Amazons*: a legendary race of female warriors in ancient Scythia. The River Amazon is believed to have acquired its name when early Spanish explorers discovered that the women of the tribes who lived on its banks fought with the ferocity of men.

59 *No Cid or Rodamonte*: El Cid (the Arabic *Sayyidi* means 'my lord') was the name given to Rodrigo Díaz de Bivar, who was born in the city of Burgos in 1030 and died in Valencia in 1099. He was, perhaps, the exemplary Christian warrior during the Reconquest, one of his greatest feats being the capture of Valencia from the Moors. The exploits of El Cid are the subject of the anonymous popular epic poem *Poema de mío Cid* (*Poem of my Cid*), which was probably written in the middle of the twelfth century. Rodamonte, King of Sarza, also noted for his bravery, is a character in Ariosto's *Orlando furioso* (1516).

S.D. *Enter Frondoso*: the action moves from the council chamber of Fuente Ovejuna to the house of the Commander, evidently a substantial property, for it has battlements from which Frondoso is to be hanged. The house itself would not have been represented on stage any more than the council chamber, but would have to be imagined by the audience.

the residence: presumably the house is not the personal property of Fernán Gómez but belongs to the Order of Calatrava.

61 S.D. *The women enter*: the location is now outside Fernán Gómez's house as the women arrive.

62 *Slash his face!*: see 2.161–2, where Flores claims to have given Frondoso a present, 'from ear | To ear'. Although there is no other reference in the text to Frondoso's having received such an injury, his anger here points to a desire to inflict a similar injury on Ortuño.

63 *Our King!*: the main and sub-plots are cleverly linked here, for the villagers' victory over their enemy, the Commander, immediately becomes, with the entrance of Fernando and Isabel, an account of their triumph over their foe, the supporters of the King of Portugal.

64 S.D. *Enter Flores*: we have been told earlier (3.29–30) that Fernando and Isabel will be in Córdoba, some 55 miles from Fuente Ovejuna. Flores has therefore travelled that distance in spite of his wounds and, it seems, in the space of a day and a night (see 3.311–12).

The ruler of Castile: Fernando of Aragon married Isabel of Castile in 1469, but she did not succeed to the throne of Castile until 1479, three years after the Fuente Ovejuna uprising.

these terrible | Events: much of the detail of Flores's account corresponds to the description of events set out in Francisco de Rades's *Chrónica . . .* (See the Introduction, p. xiii), though Flores, of course, places the blame entirely on the villagers and presents the Commander as an innocent victim.

65 *orders to investigate*: although he is shocked by Flores's account and anxious to punish wrongdoing, Fernando does not allow his emotions to

rule his head. Lope presents him as an exemplary king, intent on discovering the truth before taking action. In this respect Fernando is reminiscent of King Enrique in *Peribáñez*, who, though initially incensed by the account of the death of a nobleman at the hands of a peasant, in the end makes a fair and just judgement.

65 S.D. *fixed on a lance*: the *Chrónica* makes no reference to this.

Long life to King Fernando: this song in praise of the Catholic Kings echoes the earlier song in celebration of the wedding of Laurencia and Frondoso. To that extent it creates a link between the two couples.

66 *Saint Michael*: the Archangel Michael, who, after death, led righteous souls into the presence of God.

67 *a roasting*: a reference to the practice of smearing hot bacon-fat on the open wounds of individuals who had been flogged, in particular Jews and negroes.

outside the Council Chamber: as the head of Fernán Gómez is taken down, so the royal coat of arms is raised, pointing, as Frondoso observes (3.381), to the 'dawn of our new day!' and the end of the terror inflicted on the villagers by their overlord.

bright as any sun: just as Fernán Gómez's behaviour has been described in images associated with darkness and predatory birds and animals, so the rule of the Catholic Kings is presented in terms of light and illumination. As the monarch occupied the supreme position in the hierarchy of human beings, so the sun was supreme amongst the planets.

68 *Fuente Ovejuna did it!*: in de Rades's *Chrónica* the villagers are said to have called out 'Fuente Ovejuna'. The phrase 'Fuente Ovejuna did it!' ('Fuente Ovejuna lo hizo') is described by Sebastián de Covarrubias Horozco in his *Tesoro de la lengua castellana* of 1611 as having become common usage when the intention was to indicate communal rather than individual guilt in a particular crime.

to be tortured: the implication is clearly that torture was an automatic part of any interrogation by the authorities.

69 *The screw*: either a reference to the rack, on which the prisoner would be stretched out and screws tightened in order to extend further his or her limbs until the pain led to a confession, or to thumbscrews.

S.D. *the Alderman*: see note to 53.

you could be put to death: messengers who are the bringers of bad news traditionally incurred the wrath of those to whom the news was delivered.

70 *Allegiance*: the crown had given Fuente Ovejuna to Rodrigo Téllez Girón's father in 1460, but five years later had placed it under the jurisdiction of Córdoba.

Control my rage: despite the fact that he has been persuaded to attack Ciudad Real, the Master, though young and impetuous, shows signs of growing prudence, in contrast to Fernán Gómez.

71 S.D. *Enter Frondoso*: sufficient time has passed since the arrival of the
    judge—see 3.409—for him to have tortured many of the villagers. Hence
    Laurencia's concern for Frondoso.

73 *Fuente Ovejuna! Our little town*: the name spoken by Mendo in the
    original is 'Fuente Ovejunica', the diminutive form, which cannot be
    translated into English in the same way. The Spanish diminutive form is
    used not only to describe smallness but also as a term of endearment.

74 *Lemon curd*: in Spanish *diacitrón*, a kind of confection made of citrus.

75 *A joy to see you once again!*: the expression of love between Laurencia
    and Frondoso immediately gives way to a display of affection—more
    formal, of course—between Fernando and Isabel, once more creating a
    link between the two couples in terms of the harmony of their relation-
    ship.

76 *Granada*: the events of the play take place in 1476. By 1489 the Chris-
    tians had already captured from the Moors all the important fortresses
    and cities of the kingdom of Granada, until only the city of Granada
    itself remained in their power. It eventually capitulated under siege and
    the Catholic Kings entered it in 1492. By this time Rodrigo Téllez
    Girón was dead, killed near Loja in a campaign against the Moors.

77 *The lovely Esther, the mighty Xerxes*: Xerxes was King of Persia from 485
    to 465 BC, and a noted warrior. Esther was the favourite wife of Ahasuerus,
    King of Persia, in the sixth century BC, noted for her compassion. Her
    story is told in the Book of Esther. Lope's play, *The Beautiful Esther* (*La
    bella Ester*) was written in 1610.

78 *Saint Anthony*: Saint Anthony of Padua is the patron saint of lovers and
    marriage, appropriately invoked by Laurencia.

    villains: Fernando (3.591) has alluded to the villagers as 'assassins'. Al-
    though the reaction of the Catholic Kings can hardly be described as
    regarding the peasants as innocent until proved guilty, Lope is perhaps
    over-emphasizing it in order to show subsequently how they are willing
    to listen to reason.

79 *Nero*: Emperor of Rome from AD 54 to 68, and noted for his cruelty.

    a serious crime: Fernando pardons the villagers because there is insuffi-
    cient evidence to prove their guilt, but he makes them well aware of the
    seriousness of their crime and himself takes temporary control of Fuente
    Ovejuna. The ending of the play represents, therefore, not the triumph
    of the rebels but the restitution of the authority of the crown and up-
    holds the status quo. Certain modern productions, particularly in the
    former Soviet Union, have represented the actions of the villagers as the
    overthrow of tyranny and therefore changed the ending. The great Spanish
    dramatist Lorca, directing the play with his student company 'La Barraca'
    in the 1930s, also emphasized its revolutionary character by presenting
    the uprising of the villagers against the Commander in the context of the
    oppression of twentieth-century Spanish peasants by a tyrannical land-
    owner.

79 *my friends*: Golden Age plays frequently end with one of the characters addressing the audience.

THE KNIGHT FROM OLMEDO

[*A Tragicomedy*]: on this point, see the Introduction.

Act One

83 *correspondence*: as in the case of Laurencia and Frondoso in *Fuente Ovejuna*, there may be, Alonso thinks, a natural correspondence between himself and Inés which is part of the underlying, perfect harmony of creation.

blind Cupid: Cupid was often depicted as blindfolded and equipped with two kinds of arrow: one of gold which awakened love; the other of lead which inspired disdain.

84 *Hippocrates*: (*c*.460–357 BC), Greek physician, generally regarded as the father of medicine.

caresses: in the original *caricias*, though in seventeenth-century Spanish this also had the more general meaning of flattery.

Bewitched: the Spanish word *aojado* suggests someone who is the victim of the evil eye. If Alonso is truly bewitched, it suggests that his life is ruled by forces which he cannot control, though, given Fabia's interest in spells, the word is one which she would use quite commonly and may signify little.

85 *feria*: the 'fair' mentioned here might be the weekly market, but since Inés, a young woman of noble birth, is dressed in peasant costume, the occasion is more likely to be a carnival.

Medina: Medina del Campo is to be found in the province of Valladolid, north-west of Madrid.

it was afternoon: much of the ballad or *romance* which follows appeared in the *Primavera y flor de los mejores romances*, a collection of the best Spanish ballads which was published in Madrid in 1621. This version, intended to be sung, seems to have been taken from Lope's play. The Spanish ballad is characterized by assonance in the final word of alternate lines, which in Lope's original consists of an *i-a* pattern: 'Med*i*na', 'amanec*í*a', 'l*i*ga' ... I have not attempted to reproduce this in the translation.

ruffles: a collar of silk or fine linen which was attached to the dress and which, at the back, fell over the shoulders and, at the front, half-covered the breast.

86 *Coral and pearl*: an elaboration on the kind of imagery to be found in the love poetry of the Italian poet Petrarch (1304–74) and his followers, in which the lady's eyes are brighter than the sun, her skin whiter than snow, her teeth more beautiful than pearls.

The slippers: in Spanish, *chinelas*, which are soft shoes without a heel.

86 *imprisoned in their ribbons*: the ribbons and laces of women's shoes as a trap for men's souls is a common image in Lope's work. It is a variation on the earlier reference to Inés's hair as a trap (see 1.66).

deaf: it was traditionally thought that the asp or adder was deaf, as in, for example, Psalm 58: 4, 'they are like the deaf adder that stoppeth her ear . . .'.

Olmedo: the town is about 10 miles from Medina.

unicorn: according to legend, the inhabitants of the desert regions of Africa feared that their pools of water might be contaminated by snakes and other poisonous creatures. They would therefore wait for the arrival of the unicorn whose horn, they believed, purified the water.

A basilisk: the basilisk was a fabled, serpent-like creature which lived in the African desert and whose gaze was considered fatal. The effect of Alonso's eyes upon Inés is, therefore, fatal in the sense that she immediately falls in love with him.

87 *Worship*: in the double sense, of course, of worshipping in church and worshipping Inés. The mixture of religion and eroticism frequently goes hand in hand in Spanish culture.

It shall ennoble: in the same way that the cross worn on the breast of the master or commander of one of the religious–military orders gave him a special distinction.

88 *killing him*: Golden Age literature is full of attacks on doctors who kill their patients. In Francisco de Quevedo's *Los sueños* (*Dreams*), published in 1627, doctors are condemned to hell for their crimes.

mother: the word was often used when addressing older and respected women.

a girl: in Rojas's *La Celestina* the procuress similarly tempts the servants Pármeno and Sempronio with the promise of two of her girls.

89 *Determined by the stars*: the discussion between Inés and Leonor about the extent to which one's falling in love is determined by the stars is, to an extent, part of the Golden Age debate between free will and predestination.

Fabiana: the form of the name with a suffix was, until fairly recently, preferred in Castilian to the shorter form. Other examples are Juliana and Emiliana.

90 *the Phoenix of Medina*: in comparing the mother of Inés and Leonor with the mythical bird which was reborn from its own ashes, Fabia presumably means that she remains alive in the beauty of her daughters, or indeed in the memory of those who knew her.

Saint Catalina: this refers to the virgin and martyr, Saint Catalina of Alexandria. The phrase used by Fabia was applied to anyone who was pure and good.

93 *camphor and mercury*: camphor was used in ointments and mercury was

an important ingredient in facial make-up.

common sickness: menstruation.

to help her: to apply to the girl some remedy which will give her husband, on their wedding night, the impression that she is still a virgin.

94 *satanic flames*: a suggestion that Fabia, as well as being a go-between, is associated with witchcraft. At the time Lope wrote the play there was a considerable preoccupation in Spain with witches. In Madrid one of the most notorious was a woman known as La Margaritona, who would then have been in her fifties. At the age of 88, in 1656, she was arrested, exhibited publicly, and sentenced to death. As well as being a witch she was a renowned procuress.

To suffer: to a certain extent Don Rodrigo is the typical unrequited lover and Inés the disdainful lady so common in the literature of the time, though the traditional unhappy lover did not usually murder his rival. More often than not, he died himself of a broken heart.

96 *the agent of my death*: because he loves Inés, she is the source of his life, but because she does not love him, he has no life and she is thus the agent of his death. The life–death contrast within the context of love had been a central concept in the poetry of Petrarch and was much imitated and elaborated in the sixteenth and seventeenth centuries. Later in Lope's play it is an important element in Alonso's speeches.

97 *At Medina's fair*: in the original this poem is in the form of a sonnet: two stanzas of four lines each, followed by two stanzas of three lines each, and a rhyming pattern throughout. In the translation I have not attempted to follow the form, but the sense is the same.

slender pillar: a traditional image for the leg of a beautiful young woman, again part of the poetic language of love.

lovely eyes?: the last line of the sonnet contains a sudden twist or surprise, much loved and sought after by those seventeenth-century Spanish poets who delighted in the play of words and ideas.

98 *When Nature rules*: see note to p. 89 above. Inés may, of course, be speaking flippantly, but for the audience of the play her words suggest that not only are she and Alonso destined for each other, but that their destiny is also ruled by forces beyond their control.

99 *A pulpit of your back?*: a reference to the way in which the sacristan beats the pulpit or lectern when leading the congregation in prayer.

100 *Eager to know*: in his plays Lope de Vega used prose only for letters or messages of this kind.

night-watchman's duties: the job of the *sereno* was to walk the streets of a particular area at night in order to safeguard properties and raise the alarm in case of fires.

101 *a tooth*: traditionally witches used for their spells the teeth of criminals who had been hanged. See, for example, the etching 'A caza de dientes' ('Tooth Hunting') from Goya's series of prints, *Los Caprichos* (1797–8).

105 *give more light*: the exterior of Inés's house would not, of course, be
suggested by any set, nor would there be windows giving more light.
Indeed, the performance of the play would have taken place in broad
daylight. As Alonso and Tello exit here and are replaced on stage by
Inés and Leonor, the setting of the action immediately changes from
outside to inside the house and from night to the following morning.
The lines spoken by Inés contain all the information required by an
audience which was accustomed to using its imagination.

bright April's flowers: the comparison of the ground covered with flowers
to a beautiful carpet trodden by lovely feet was common enough in the
poetry of the time. Frequently, contact with a lady's lovely feet ensured
that the flowers flourished in greater abundance.

106 *I come on his behalf*: in matters of courtship and marriage, it was the
custom for an intermediary to act on behalf of the suitor. The fact that
the custom persisted well into the twentieth century is suggested in
Lorca's *The House of Bernarda Alba* (*La casa de Bernarda Alba*), written
in 1936, when, in relation to the forthcoming marriage of Bernarda
Alba's eldest daughter Angustias, it is said that: 'They'll be coming to
make a formal request in the next three days.'

107 *INÉS*: the conversation between Inés and Leonor clearly takes the form
of an aside, though asides are rarely indicated in the text.

108 *My father's reputation*: if it became known publicly that Inés were meeting Alonso secretly when Rodrigo is, as it were, her official suitor, this
would doubtless become a topic of common gossip and therefore a slur
upon the good name of Don Pedro. Secret affairs were much frowned
upon for this reason. Inés is well aware of the danger involved in a secret
relationship, but ignores the dictate of common sense.

FABIA: this is another aside. On the question of spells, Fabia evidently
believes that they work for her.

109 *Cupid's bow*: Inés's arched eyebrows call to mind the shape of a bow,
while the brilliance of her gaze has the effect of Cupid's arrow, fatally
wounding its victim with love.

ducats: the ducat was the most valuable gold coin of the time. The fact
that Don Alonso will inherit ten thousand points to his considerable
potential wealth.

The royal wedding: the King, Juan II of Castile, married Doña María of
Aragon at Medina del Campo in 1418.

Hector: in Homer's *Iliad*, the Trojan hero of the siege of Troy, son of
Priam and Hecuba.

Achilles: the Greek hero of Homer's *Iliad*, son of Peleus and Thetis,
slayer of Hector.

Adonis: the young man adored by Aphrodite, or Venus, for his good
looks. When he was killed by a wild boar, such was the grief of Venus
that the gods allowed him to return to earth for six months each year.

Despite the fact that Fabia suggests that Alonso's fate may be different, the allusions to the three Classical heroes would have been for an audience of Lope's time a pointer to his death.

110 *the jewel of | Medina, the flower of Olmedo!*: Fabia's words here are those of the ominous song sung in Act Three by the peasant prior to Alonso's death. Indeed, after the peasant has sung the song and is questioned about it by Alonso, he observes that it was told to him 'By one called Fabia' (3.501).

Act Two

111 *discretion*: in the sense of prudence. Tello's fears reflect what would have been the opinion of most: that Alonso is putting at risk his own and Inés's good name.

three-day fever!: this refers to a high temperature which, accompanying a fever, appeared every three days. Alonso has known Inés for three days and by the third day, Tello suggests, his passion for her has the character of a burning fever.

salamander: a lizard-like creature which, according to legend, was capable of living in fire. Thus, if Alonso were near Inés, whose passion consumes him, he would be like the salamander.

Leander: in Classical legend Leander swam the Hellespont every night from Abydos to Sestos in order to be with his lover Hero, a priestess of Aphrodite. When he was drowned, Hero threw herself into the sea. Lope seems to have written a play, *Hero y Leandro*, which was subsequently lost.

112 *upon its dunghill*: a well-known Spanish proverb.

Harlequin: the figure of Harlequin, pulling grotesque faces, is often seen in old prints climbing a ladder to one side of the tightrope on which an acrobat is performing.

113 *wet*: Tello has wet himself from sheer terror. The comic character or *gracioso* of Golden Age plays was more often than not portrayed as a coward, concerned only with his own safety and well-being.

Her slave: in many ways Alonso is reminiscent of the traditional courtly lover whose life was totally dedicated to the lady he worshipped.

114 *Melibea*: through the words of Tello, Lope deliberately invites a comparison between the plot of his play and Fernando de Rojas's *La Celestina*, in which Calisto becomes obsessed with Melibea and their meetings are arranged by Celestina, with the assistance of a servant, Sempronio. The comparison reveals Lope's admiration for the earlier work, as well as his confidence in his own ability as a writer, but it also suggests that Alonso's fate will be as tragic as Calisto's. See the Introduction.

115 *why complain?*: the story was a common one, often repeated, and can be traced back to Cicero, *Tusculan Disputations*, v. xxxviii. 112, where the remark is attributed to the Stoic philosopher Antipater.

115 *A moth!*: Inés corrects herself because the moth, seeking a light or flame, is consumed by it, but the Phoenix was not. See note to p. 90.

   The coral: her lips are here compared to a pink rose.

116 *radishes*: it appears that radishes from Olmedo were famous for their quality.

   I'm dying: this poem of five lines—known in Spanish as a *quintilla*—was very well known in Spain before Lope's time. It had appeared as early as 1578 in the *Flor de romances*, a collection of ballads published in Zaragoza. A short poem of this kind frequently served as a basis for elaboration, as is the case here, each of its lines appearing at the end of a new stanza.

117 *Inés's lovely feet*: Lope's original is in stanzas of ten lines, with an elaborate rhyme scheme. In the translation the stanzas are of nine lines, without a regular rhyming pattern. The notion of a lady's lovely feet making the flowers grow has been mentioned earlier. See note on *bright April's flowers*, p. 105.

118 *I'm dying*: the poem is full of traditional poetic clichés, in particular the notion of the beautiful young woman as both the life and death of her admirer. See note p. 96.

119 *Already married*: in intention to Alonso, but, as far as her father is concerned, to Christ.

   My heart is moved: Don Pedro is very much in the tradition of the gullible father who appears in so many Golden Age plays and who is, to a certain extent, a comic figure. He is also, as his speech here suggests, extremely long-winded.

121 *keep his word to him*: if Inés is to enter a convent, Don Rodrigo would now be expected to free her from his promise to marry her.

   salvation: Alonso's references to Inés's being his life and his death have an irony which is now reinforced, following her pretence to want to become a nun, by irony of a religious nature.

122 *The Festival of the Cross of May*: a religious festival which takes place on 3 May.

   The Constable's | Invited him: Don Alvaro de Luna (1390?–1453) was the King's royal favourite and someone on whom he relied greatly. He was much hated by the nobility of Castile for the power he exercised over the King. His ultimate downfall was frequently used by later Spanish writers to illustrate the theme of the fickleness of fortune. Antonio Mira de Amescua (1574?–1644), a contemporary of Lope, was probably the author of *The Good Fortune of Don Álvaro de Luna* (*La próspera fortuna de Don Álvaro de Luna*) and certainly the author of *The Adverse Fortune of Don Álvaro de Luna* (*La adversa fortuna de Don Álvaro de Luna*), both plays serving in part as warnings to kings and their favourites.

   the sun: Inés is the sun in Alonso's heaven. When he is away from her, the sun has, for him, effectively set.

124 *A kind of monster*: jealousy was as much a monster in the Golden Age

theatre as in that of Elizabethan England. Indeed, fear and suspicion regarding the behaviour of a wife, a daughter, or a lover were closely connected with topic of honour in the drama of the time. In certain respects Calderón's *The Greatest Monster in the World* (*El mayor monstruo del mundo*), first published in 1637 in the *Segunda Parte* or second volume of his plays, and whose title he subsequently changed to *Jealousy the Greatest Monster* (*El mayor monstruo los celos*), is a Spanish *Othello*.

dishonoured: if Inés is promised to him in marriage yet persists in seeing Alonso, Rodrigo is, of course, 'dishonoured'. He would not be so if she chose instead to become a nun.

126 *Our Lord?*: only the gullible Don Pedro is unaware of the true meaning of Fabia's words. Lope had observed in his poetic essay, *The New Art of Writing Plays* (see the Introduction, p. x), that 'To deceive with the truth is effective . . .', which is precisely what Fabia is doing here.

hair-shirt: a shirt-like garment made of rough cloth, frequently made from goats' hair, and worn by penitents in order to punish the flesh.

127 *. . . Festina*: the reference is to Psalm 69: 1, and the meaning is 'Lord, hasten to my aid'.

S.D. *scholar's cap*: this would be the cap worn by an impoverished student, in contrast to the more elegant headgear worn by the rich.

128 *Calahorra*: a town in the province of Logroño in northern Spain.

Martín Peláez: a companion of El Cid who, having once been lacking in courage, became one of his bravest men.

La Coruña: this is another example of Don Pedro's gullibility, for there was no university in La Coruña.

129 *a shield*: a shield of leather, used to protect themselves by those who participated in jousting. The jousting alluded to here—in Spanish *juego de cañas*—was introduced into Spain by the Moors and took place on certain special occasions. The jousting involved groups of up to eight men on horseback, four groups at each end of the arena. They proceeded to attack each other either in pairs or in larger numbers, employing both swords and lances.

I stamp it: the stamp was paid for not by the sender but by the recipient of the letter.

130 *Jugatoribus paternus*: strictly speaking, the phrase does not make sense but alludes to the fact that Inés's father is to be present at the games (the jousting).

131 *The old one*: the Grand Master and the Knights of the Order of Alcántara wore a pointed hood. The hood was abandoned in 1411 and the members of the Order were allowed to wear a green cross, just as the members of the Order of Calatrava wore a red cross. This change was not, however, effected by Don Juan II, but by the Infante Don Fernando de Antequera (1379–1416), who in 1412 was elected King of Aragon and who in the previous year had obtained the Pope's permission for the

modification to the dress described above. The reference to the Infante in 581 seems rather strange if, just a few lines earlier, Juan II is given credit for the change of dress.

131 *Brother Vicente Ferrer*: a famous Dominican priest (1350–1419) and celebrated preacher who lived for some time at the Court of Juan II. He supported Fernando de Antequera in his election to the throne of Aragon and had also been confessor to the Pope, Benedict XIII, who gave permission for the change of dress for members of the Order of Alcántara.

132 *Jews . . . Moors*: despite the fact that many Jews and Muslims had sworn to accept and convert to the Catholic faith—*conversos* in Spanish—they often continued to practise their own faith in secret. Because it was feared that Catholics would somehow be contaminated by such people, it was decreed in 1412 that Jews and Moors alike should be restricted to living in certain areas of towns and cities, and that Jews be obliged to wear a tabard or gown with a red sign, and Moors a green hood with a blue moon.

the habit: this was the habit worn by the knights of the three great military-religious orders.

My sister's marriage: Juan II had two sisters, María and Catalina, but neither of them was married in Valladolid, where, it is suggested, this particular scene takes place. Once more, then, Lope is guilty of historical confusion.

Knight Commander: a position in the Order higher than that of a knight and which would allow the individual concerned to collect rents paid by those who lived on the land granted to him by the Order.

Oh, absence, this is hard indeed: the passage which follows also appeared, with certain modifications, in Lope's *La Dorotea*, published in Madrid in 1632. The work is a prose dialogue in five acts and, like *The Knight from Olmedo*, contains many echoes of *La Celestina*. Largely autobiographical too, it reflects Lope's youthful love-affair with Elena Osorio (see the Introduction, p. ix) and tells how the beautiful Dorotea, who is really in love with a poor poet, Fernando, is obliged by her mother and the Celestina-like Gerarda to marry the wealthy Don Bela. His murder means that in the end she loses both her husband and, since widows did not normally remarry, the man she really loves.

133 *honest*: his love for Inés is dishonest in the sense that they meet in secret, not in the sense that they are having improper sexual relations.

134 *My lord . . .*: another example of prose used for a message. See note to p. 100.

135 *Cato*: Marcus Porcius Cato, the Elder (234–149 BC), a Roman statesman noted for his moral seriousness.

136 *three acts*: the traditional length of a play in Lope's time. Just as the letter seems to Tello to be too long, so a play would seem too long and tedious to a notoriously impatient Spanish audience if its plot was not consist-

ently entertaining. The three-act structure of Spanish plays has persisted well into the twentieth century, as many of Lorca's plays suggest.

136 *the ribbon*: worn by the participants in jousting and the like and frequently a gift from their lady.

whatever suit: the servant or squire of a knight was traditionally rewarded with a gift of his clothes.

137 *Last night*: Alonso's account of his dream marks the moment when the play changes from a mood which is often comic to one which is increasingly dark.

A hawk: although the colouring of the hawk is not mentioned here, it is clearly much darker than that of the goldfinch and to that extent a reminder of Rodrigo, who frequently appears in dark clothing and whose passion for Inés and hatred of Alonso is both dark and dangerous.

138 *hopelessness*: it seems quite probable that, at this point in the play, Alonso is suffering from what doctors of the time would have described as unnatural melancholy. This could be caused by extreme heat in the body, which would in turn be the consequence of passion, and whose effect would have been to ignite the four humours of blood, choler, phlegm, and melancholy (natural) and leave behind a poisonous substance known as unnatural melancholy. In this condition the individual would be subject to fearful dreams and visions of future catastrophe. Love-sickness, which is what Alonso is suffering, was therefore a genuine and potentially fatal illness. Another melancholic in Lope's theatre is Federico in *Punishment Without Revenge*, his condition caused by his unspoken passion for his stepmother Casandra.

Act Three

139 *outshine Medina's best?*: the envy, and indeed hatred, felt by Rodrigo—and to a lesser extent by Fernando—towards Alonso are clearly rooted in matters of the heart, but there was also a historical rivalry between Medina and Olmedo which Lope used as the broader context for his play. See the Introduction, pp. xxii–xxiii.

140 *Greek and Roman times*: while the reference is somewhat vague, the topic of a country's ingratitude towards its subjects was a familiar enough one in both Classical and Renaissance literature. One example was Valerius Maximus's *Facta et dicta memorabilia*, iii ('De ingratis romanorum').

The lance: a kind of dart with a wooden shaft and an iron tip which was thrust into the neck of the bull. The breaking of the lance was an indication that the manœuvre was successful.

changing horses: until the eighteenth century the bullfighter was always on horseback.

141 *sorrel*: a horse which is reddish or yellowish-brown in colour.

chopped: when the bullfighter had fatally wounded the bull and withdrawn from the ring, it was the practice of his assistants to cut the tendons of its back legs with a blade in the shape of a half-moon.

141 *enter the ring*: the bullfight in this play clearly takes place off-stage, as the subsequent stage-direction and the earlier shouting suggest. In the theatres of the time there was, nevertheless, an area of the pit which could be roped off and where jousting on horseback could take place.

142 *the chain*: Tello's plan to get the chain from Fabia echoes the resolve of Pármeno and Sempronio in *La Celestina* to make Celestina share with them the reward given her by Calisto.

Medea, Circe, Hecate: in Greek legend Medea was the daughter of Aetes, King of Colchis, who helped Jason to obtain the Golden Fleece. Circe was, in Homer's *Odyssey*, the enchantress who changed the companions of Odysseus into swine by means of a magic potion. Hecate was originally, in Greek mythology, a goddess descended from the Titans who had power over earth, sky, and sea, but she was later regarded as goddess of the underworld and was associated with magic and sorcery. All three are, therefore, examples of supreme cunning and black arts.

143 *Orlando*: the Italian name for Roland, the hero of the Anglo-Norman epic *La Chanson de Roland*, and the protagonist of Ariosto's *Orlando furioso*, which was published in 1516 and which subsequently became a source of inspiration for many Spanish writers. Tello is thinking here of Orlando as a lover rather than a knight, for in Ariosto's poem he falls madly in love with the beautiful but disdainful Angelica.

144 *the inspiration*: this is a parody of the novels of chivalry in which the heroic knight undertook his adventures and achieved great victories in the name and through the inspiration of his lady.

blinkers: the horses which are used in the bullfight are provided with blinkers.

145 *more | Dark-brown than bay*: dark-brown or chestnut horses had the reputation of being more reliable than bays.

With servants from Olmedo: yet another reference to the rivalry between Medina and Olmedo. See the note to p. 139.

146 *I owe my life*: Rodrigo is now indebted to Alonso to the extent that, far from wanting to kill him, he is obliged to protect him. To take away the life of a man to whom one owed one's life was unforgivable.

dishonoured: in the sense that, having been rescued by Alonso, he thinks he has been made to look foolish in public. Witnesses to the incident will therefore talk openly about it in future, praising Alonso at the expense of Rodrigo.

observed Rome burn: in AD 64 Nero watched Rome burn while he stood on the Capitol Hill.

147 *those pearls*: see note on *coral and pearl*, p. 86.

Apollo: the Greek god of youth, masculine beauty, music, song, and prophecy, also identified with the sun-god Helios.

147 *And meet the Infante*: this meeting seems to have no basis in historical fact.

148 S.D. *It is night*: as indicated previously, the performance of the play would have taken place in daylight, in the afternoon. See note to p. 105.

149 *the window*: the window would have bars in the traditional Spanish manner. In such circumstances the suitor would stand outside, usually in the street, and, if the window was on an upper floor, would have to call up to her.

150 *My foot already in the stirrup?*: Alonso's speech here is similar in structure to his poem in Act Two (see note on *I'm dying*, p. 116): a five-line traditional poem which serves as a basis for elaboration, each line becoming the last in five stanzas of ten lines (*décimas*). In the translation I have not attempted to follow the elaborate rhyming pattern of Lope's original but, with the exception of the first stanza, have retained the ten-line format. Lope had previously introduced an elaboration of the same traditional poem in *Knowing Can Be Dangerous* (*El saber puede dañar*).

151 *I go, then, to my death*: the poem is a fine example of the tragic irony which runs throughout the play. The ideas and concepts expressed by Alonso are poetic commonplaces which are entirely to do with death in the sense of absence from the beloved, yet for the audience they have a deeper and darker implication, and even Alonso seems to some extent aware of their relevance to the danger which lies ahead.

153 S.D. *SHADOWY FIGURE*: the appearance of other-worldly figures is no less common in Golden Age than in Elizabethan and Jacobean drama, and Hamlet's famous observation about his father's ghost—'There are more things in Heaven and Earth, Horatio, | Than are dreamt of in our philosophy' (I. v. 174–5)—is equally relevant. Sometimes such figures were prophetic. In the case of Alonso, the figure could be a product of his unnatural melancholy, which previously has been responsible for his dream at the end of the second act. Indeed, a few lines later Alonso himself speaks of the figure as being fashioned by his own sadness, but he also thinks that it might be a vision conjured up by Fabia. Lope allows for various possibilities and therefore makes the episode that much more fascinating.

154 *lacking noble blood*: in expressing the view that honour is to be found only in those of noble birth, Alonso may be compared with Fernán Gómez in *Fuente Ovejuna*, though if he were, as a Knight Commander, to exercise power over lands and their inhabitants, one cannot imagine him behaving in the same way.

Romance!: the word is used here in the sense of the vernacular, or everyday Spanish, as opposed to Latin, which Tello has been pretending to teach Inés.

155 *witchcraft*: see note on *satanic flames*, p. 94. While neither Alonso nor Tello believes in Fabia's magical powers, Rodrigo clearly does.

155 *Acheron*: in Classical mythology, the river of woe, one of the rivers of Hades.

musket: strictly speaking, a harquebus, which was the predecessor of the musket. It was often supported on a tripod or a forked rest.

156 *For at night they killed*: this is the famous song around whose origin so much controversy has raged. For different opinions on this matter, see the Introduction, p. xix.

157 *Fabia*: if the song was told to the peasant by Fabia and warns Alonso to turn back, the implication is that she is concerned with his well-being, not with his downfall. She is not, therefore, an evil woman but a potential saviour. This is yet another example of the ambiguity which makes Lope's play so interesting.

158 *someone from Olmedo*: Alonso—and therefore Lope—may be thinking here, of course, of Don Juan de Vivero, an alderman from Olmedo, who in 1521 was murdered by his enemies on the road between Medina and Olmedo, an incident which, according to some critics, gave rise to the song sung by the peasant in Lope's play. See the Introduction, pp. xviii–xix.

Remove your sword: Rodrigo has claimed earlier to be a man of honour, yet the way in which he disposes of Alonso—a dishonourable act itself because he owes him his life—is made worse by the fact that he strips him of any means of self-defence. The more honourable procedure would have been to challenge Alonso to a duel.

159 *offends | The people of Medina*: see note to p. 139. It is, perhaps, significant here that the hostility towards Olmedo is mentioned not by Rodrigo, whose hatred of Alonso is coloured by jealousy and envy, but by Fernando, whose motives are less personal.

161 *Warden of Burgos*: the Spanish word *alcaide* described in the Golden Age a person who was entrusted by the King with guarding and defending a town, city, or fortress, but it could also mean simply a jailer. Don Pedro has presumably been honoured by the King with the task of defending Burgos, a city in Old Castile and birthplace of El Cid.

162 *a cross*: as a Knight Commander, Alonso will wear the cross which distinguished members of the Order. See note on *the old one*, p. 131.

165 *the envy of | Your enemies*: a reference to the extremely turbulent times in which Castile found itself during the reign of Don Juan II, constantly threatened by enemies both outside and inside its boundaries.

old | In years: Alonso's father.

both poles: the two fixed points on which, it was thought, the heavens turned. The halfway point would have been reached at midnight.

six men: in the earlier stage-direction (3.402) only four are indicated.

166 *justice*: as in *Fuente Ovejuna*, the King, God's representative on earth, is called upon to right wrongs and restore order to a disordered situation.

167 *The Knight from Olmedo*: in the printed text of 1641 the last line of the

play is followed by the words: 'Fin de la Comedia del *Caballero de Olmedo*.'

PUNISHMENT WITHOUT REVENGE

[*subtitle*] *A Tragedy*: on the play as tragedy, see the Introduction.

Act One

171 *No modern poet*: a sarcastic reference to the poet Luis de Góngora and his followers. The so-called *culto* or *culterano* poets of the seventeenth century, of whom Góngora (1561–1627) was the supreme example, developed a style of extreme artificiality, characterized by complex syntax, Classical allusion, and elaborate imagery. Lope was initially much opposed to such a style, scolding Góngora and his imitators for their poetic excesses.

172 *For him who gives*: that is to say, the wife's lover. In the following lines Febo complains that, after the wife's death, the lover's gifts should become the property of the husband.

I turn | The phrase around: as indicated above, syntactical complication, including inversions, was a characteristic of the poet Góngora and his followers.

173 *fiery dark brunette*: the allusion is probably to a girl of gypsy origin. In general they had the reputation of being hot-blooded and passionate.

174 S.D. *Cintia above*: it is quite possible that Cintia would have appeared on one of the balconies of the houses at the back of or to the side of the stage.

175 *Mantua*: a fortified provincial capital in the Italian province of Lombardy. It is situated on the river Mincio, about 40 miles from Ferrara.

176 *famous emperors and kings*: amongst those who used such cunning was the Roman emperor Nero. In Calderón's famous play *The Surgeon of Honour* (*El médico de su honra*), King Peter the Cruel walks the streets of Seville, disguised and at night, in order to keep himself abreast of any scandalous events in the city.

I have lived indulgently: writing this play at the age of 69, Lope was no doubt looking back on his own indulgent life and, not least, on his many love affairs, though he did marry several times. See the Introduction, pp. ix–x.

177 *An actor-manager*: in the Golden Age the actor-manager was called the *autor*, though he was not usually a dramatist but quite often an actor. *Punishment Without Revenge* was first performed, it seems, by the company run by the actor-manager, Manuel Vallejo, who played the part of the Duke.

a friendly audience: as a professional playwright, Lope was only too aware of the importance of the favourable reaction of a theatre audience.

In the Madrid of his day the theatre was an intensely competitive business.

177 *ingenuity exceed | Vulgarity*: in his poetic essay *The New Art of Writing Plays*, Lope gave the impression (tongue-in-cheek) to the stuffy traditionalists of the Madrid Academy that he had lowered his standards in trying to please the public. In reality, of course, his standards were very high and his work distinguished by its intelligence and craftsmanship, as well as by its entertainment value.

178 *Andrelina*: the well-known Italian actress and poetess, Isabel Andreini (1562–1604). The reference is, at all events, anachronistic and fairly typical of Lope in that respect.

A mirror to all men: Lope's definition of a play, like Shakespeare's, has its origin in the saying attributed to Cicero: 'est imitatio vitae, speculum consuetudinis, imago veritas' ('it is an imitation of life, a mirror of customs, the likeness of truth').

179 *Comedy with seriousness and tragedy | With jokes*: Lope sets out here his belief that the new Spanish drama, which he largely helped to fashion, should, in imitation of life itself, mix the serious and the comic in a way which Greek and Roman drama did not. It echoes what he had written more than twenty years earlier in *The New Art of Writing Plays*. See the Introduction, p. x.

willow-trees?: presumably weeping willows and therefore an appropriate setting for Federico's dejection. The change of scene from the streets of Ferrara at night to the countryside in the daytime is suggested largely by the dialogue, which locates the action quite precisely.

melancholy thoughts: Federico appears to be dejected here rather than truly melancholic. The kind of melancholy experienced by Alonso in *The Knight from Olmedo*, and which was often the result of excessive passion, affects Federico in Act Two. On the topic of melancholy, see note to p. 138 above.

180 *A loyal subject once*: this is a good example of the stories often told by servants to their masters in Golden Age plays, which are both amusing and relevant to the master's particular predicament. Although, as in Batín's case, the servant is a comic character, he is usually wiser and more observant than his master. The source of this particular story is unknown.

182 S.D. *with Casandra in his arms*: this is, of course, a quite brilliant foreshadowing of the events which lie ahead, when Casandra will lie in Federico's arms in quite a different context. The important point here concerns the physical contact between two young people who are immediately attracted to each other before they become aware of their respective identities.

S.D. *Batín with Lucrecia, a servant, in his arms*: in many Golden Age plays the activities of servants act as a comic counterpoint to the events concerning their masters. Here, for example, the beautiful and sylph-like Casandra, borne effortlessly to the river-bank by Federico, provides a delightful contrast to the overweight Lucrecia, carried with some effort by a breathless Batín.

183 *Fortune's wheel*: the image of Fortune's wheel, constantly turning, was an extremely common one in literature of the medieval and Renaissance periods. As it turned, a man might find himself at one moment at the very peak of good fortune only to be plunged at the next moment to the depths of misfortune.

184 *Let me embrace you!*: a pointer, perhaps, to Casandra's youthful impetuosity and imprudence, as well as an ironic anticipation of her subsequent relationship with Federico.

Your excellency: Lope frequently made fun of the rules governing the different forms of address.

185 *Not her from Rome?*: the wife of Collatinus, Lucretia, was raped by Sextus Tarquinius and, in consequence, committed suicide in 510 BC. She thus became a symbol of female chastity.

greatly fancied: Batín distorts the traditional story, assuming, of course, that he knows it, in order to persuade the 'chaste' modern Lucrecia to succumb to him, just as, he suggests, the Roman epitome of chastity yielded to Tarquin.

186 *A timely error*: Lope seems to be using the word *errar* ('to err') here not in a moral sense but in the Aristotelian sense of error or accident, whereby the paths of individuals may accidentally cross, and that coincidence leads subsequently to tragedy.

St Elmo's fire: after violent storms an unusual light, of an electrical nature, which appears in the masts and rigging of ships.

188 *turn the happy stream to snow*: the effect upon the water of the whiteness of her feet and the perfection of her skin. This is a variant of the notion of a beautiful woman's feet making the grass grow more abundantly as she walks on it. See note to p. 105 above.

189 *Jupiter*: in Greek mythology Zeus—the Roman Jupiter— transformed himself into an eagle and carried the handsome boy, Ganymede, up to Olympus so that he could succeed Hebe as cupbearer to the Gods.

Phaethon's pride: in Greek mythology Phaethon, son of Helios and Clymene, was allowed to guide the chariot of the sun for one day. Unable to control the horses, he would have set the heavens and the earth on fire had not Zeus destroyed him with a thunderbolt.

a golden fleece: in Greek mythology the fleece of gold owned by Aetes, King of Colchis, guarded by a dragon and taken by Jason.

190 *A topic for the idle tongues*: and thus a source of dishonour. See note to p. 108.

191 *she is a lily*: Batín, as is the custom of the comic character, the *gracioso*, in Golden Age plays, is here mocking the flowery language of lovers of noble origin.

191 *This Helen?*: Helen of Troy, according to legend the most beautiful woman in the world.

193 *labyrinth*: in Greek mythology the maze built by Daedalus for King Minos of Crete. It contained the Minotaur to which human sacrifice was made. Theseus, having killed the Minotaur, found his way out of the labyrinth by means of a thread of gold.

194 *Aurora*: her name is, of course, suggestive of the dawn and, inasmuch as the dawn brings light, Aurora is also the light of reason. In Calderón's famous play, *La vida es sueño* (*Life is a Dream*), the name Rosaura has a similar symbolic function.

195 *stepmothers and step-|Sons*: echoing the earlier comment on this notoriously difficult relationship in ll. 577–80, but with a possible reference to Phaedra who, in Greek mythology, fell in love with her stepson Hippolytus, bringing about his death and her own suicide.

199 *These arms become a chain*: a moment of supreme irony in the sense that Casandra's growing attraction to Federico will indeed prove to be inescapable. Her embracing of him is also a pointer to her youthful, unthinking indiscretion.

200 *For you to rest*: the Duke's remark is to Casandra. The 'mistake' which other husbands make, to which he refers in the following lines, is the mistake of prolonging the welcome to the newly arrived wife-to-be instead of letting her rest after a long journey.

life's a dream: see note to p. 194 above. Calderón's *Life is a Dream* was probably written a few years after *Punishment Without Revenge*, but the theme of life as a dream was, of course, a commonplace. At the same time, there are in Lope's play a number of allusions—to the labyrinth, for example—which are typically Calderonian and which may point to the influence of the younger dramatist on Lope's later theatre.

to seeing things: the speech which follows describes those things which Batín imagines doing but never has the courage to do. In one way the comic character in Golden Age plays is often his master in a lower key. The difference between Federico and Batín is, of course, that Federico realizes his imaginings.

201 *I know exactly*: see note to p. 180. Since the comic characters in Golden Age literature in general are constantly concerned with material things— food, money, sex—they are generally more down-to-earth than their masters and quick to see to the heart of things, as is the case with Batín here.

202 *ablaze with flowers*: Federico points to the unlikelihood of Batín's being able to guess the nature of his secret thoughts, but the concepts alluded to here—the sky ablaze with flowers, the grass covered with stars—were also characteristic of poets such as Luis de Góngora, to whom Lope was initially opposed. See note to p. 171.

more suitable: there is between Casandra and Federico the natural correspondence of youth which we have seen in *The Knight from Olmedo* in the mutual attraction of Inés and Alonso.

Act Two

203 *honest countryman*: Casandra praises the simplicity and honesty of country life much as does Laurencia in *Fuente Ovejuna*: see the Introduction, pp. xiv–xv.

doubly blind: if love is traditionally blind, it is logically doubly blind in the dark.

204 *however much | They try to change*: the notion of the extent to which a man's life is predestined or not was much discussed in the Golden Age. In relation to the Duke, the question arises of whether his conversion in Act Three to a new, Christian way of life is genuine or whether, beneath that appearance, he is still the old Duke.

freedom to indulge | Himself: in this context it is worth bearing in mind Lope's many affairs, including his extra-marital relationship with the actress Micaela de Luján. See the Introduction, pp. ix–x.

206 *playthings of our destiny*: although Casandra's conclusion here is coloured by her unhappiness, there are throughout the text references to the role of fate in the lives of these characters which contradicts A. A. Parker's argument that in Golden Age plays the characters are in control of their decisions and thus their lives. See A. A. Parker, *The Approach to the Spanish Drama of the Golden Age* (London, 1957).

208 *to keep them safe*: in the theatre of the Golden Age, and to a degree in real life, husbands and fathers lived in constant fear of their wives or daughters attracting the attention of some unscrupulous male who would seek to seduce them and thus bring about the dishonour of the family. Consequently, women were closely guarded. The most extreme example of this occurs in Cervantes's short story, *The Jealous Extremaduran* (*El celoso extremeño*), in which the old husband, Carrizales, seeks to hide his wife from the world at large by blocking up the windows of his house.

209 *burns my honour*: Federico's argument is that, if his father obliges him to marry Aurora, this will merely inflame her passion for the Marquis, just as water, instead of putting out a fire, makes it blaze even more fiercely. The consequences of her attraction to the Marquis might then be the cause of Federico's dishonour.

The depth of my despair: as the action of Act Two unfolds, Federico is overtaken more and more by unnatural melancholy. See note to p. 138.

210 *hermaphrodite*: originally the name of the son of Hermes and Aphrodite, who, according to myth, grew together with the nymph Salmacis. By extension, the word came to mean a human being or animal in which parts characteristic of both sexes are combined.

211 *that still brighter dawn*: Aurora herself.

212 *duke to my duchess*: the meaning here is that if Federico were granted such a title, he would not then be able to kneel before her.

213 *one night with me*: the point here is that the marriage has been consummated, which in turn means that any sexual relationship between Casandra and Federico would be adulterous.

214 *the honour*: in spite of Casandra's opinion, it is doubtful that in the society of the time the Duke would be regarded as staining the honour of his family as a result of his activities. While such behaviour in men was accepted, a man could be considered as dishonoured if his wife or daughter was seduced or raped. Thus, the Duke's honour is endangered much more by Casandra's attraction to Federico than by his own affairs.

216 *Phaethon*: see note to p. 189.

Icarus: in Greek mythology the son of Daedalus, who made him wings fastened on with wax. Icarus flew too near the sun, which melted the wax and caused him to fall to his death in the sea.

Bellerophon: in Greek mythology he slew the Chimera with the aid of the winged horse Pegasus, but subsequently died in his attempt to scale the heavens.

217 *Sinon*: the Greek who induced the Trojans to drag the wooden horse into Troy. See Virgil, *Aeneid*, ii. 57 ff.

Jason: in Greek mythology leader of the Argonauts, sent by his uncle Pelias to fetch the Golden Fleece from Colchis.

Endymion's love: in Greek legend a handsome hunter whom the moon goddess Selene—Roman Diana—visited every night in a mountain grotto. He was the subject of John Keats's poem, *Endymion*.

218 *safeguard them*: the origin of this story may lie in the fact that the pelican, according to legend, sacrificed itself for its young, allowing them to feed on blood from her breast.

220 *honour clearly does not*: a man's honour could only be tarnished if the offence done to him became public knowledge. Private thoughts could therefore dishonour no one.

221 *lovely as the dawn*: see note to p. 194. The Marquis may, in Casandra's opinion, be 'more | The soldier than the dashing courtier' (2.337–8), but his words here certainly contradict this, rivalling Federico's earlier in the act (2.435–40).

222 *Jacob*: see Genesis, 29: 18. The 'precious jewel' alluded to here was Rachel. Jacob was obliged to wait for seven years before her father, Laban, gave him permission to marry her.

Tantalus: in Greek legend he was the son of Zeus. As a punishment for revealing his father's secrets, he was placed in water up to his chin and immediately beneath delicious fruits, unable to taste either.

223 *The wars in Italy*: it is difficult to know which wars are being alluded to here. One possibility is that the Pope in question is Pope Martin V (1417–31), who was much concerned with making the Papacy a power-

ful force, but there were other Popes too who were involved in military struggles in Italy, such as Pope Clement VII, at different times an ally and an enemy of the Spanish King, Charles V (1516–56).

224 *this ribbon*: the ribbon as a token of love also plays an important part in *The Knight from Olmedo* (1.472 ff.), when, intended by Inés for Alonso, it is taken and worn the following day by Rodrigo and Fernando.

225 *Paris*: in Greek legend, the son of King Priam of Troy and Hecuba. Called upon by the three goddesses, Hera, Aphrodite, and Athena, to decide who was the most beautiful, he chose Aphrodite, awarding her the golden apple because she had promised him the most beautiful woman in the world for his wife. With Aphrodite's help, he abducted Helen, wife of Menelaus, thereby causing the Trojan War.

Barbarossa: the name given by Christians to a family of sixteenth-century Turkish admirals and pirates, possibly on account of the fact that they had red beards—in Spanish 'red beard' is *barba roja*. The reference here is, of course, to the cockerel's red comb.

227 *The sweet revenge*: Casandra sees an affair with Federico as an appropriate revenge against her husband for the affairs in which he has been involved since their marriage.

228 *In history*: Lope possibly has in mind Genesis 19, relating the story of Lot, who fled with his daughters during the destruction of Sodom and Gomorrah and who subsequently lay with them and made them pregnant, and 2 Samuel 13, which recounts the incestuous relationship between Amnon, son of David, and his half-sister, Tamar.

229 *Antiochus*: the story is told in Valerius Maximus.

230 *Erasistratus*: Lope made an error in the spelling of the name, writing it as 'Eróstrato'. He was a Greek physician, grandson of Aristotle, and believed to be the doctor to have introduced dissection.

Galen and even great Hippocrates: Galen (AD 131–210) was a Greek physician whose importance remained undiminished until the seventeenth century. His fame equalled that of his predecessor, Hippocrates (460–357 BC), usually regarded as the father of medicine.

231 *of self,* | *Of God, of you . . . someone else*: these lines represent a traditional theme in Spanish poetry from the fifteenth century which had been elaborated upon before Lope's time by poets such as Garcilaso de la Vega (1501–36). Lope proceeds to develop the short poem through the whole of Federico's speech much as he had done in *The Knight from Olmedo* in the case of Alonso's farewell to Inés (see note to p. 150). The speech is notable for the way in which Lope plays with ideas, a characteristic of the seventeenth-century Spanish literary movement known as *conceptismo*, whose exponents aimed to appeal to the intellect, in contrast to *culteranismo*, whose practitioners emphasized style and imagery. See note to p. 171.

233 *the siren*: in Greek legend the Sirens were nymphs who lived on an island and lured sailors to their death with the beauty of their singing.

298 EXPLANATORY NOTES

Act Three

235 *no one overhears*: the point here is that, if Casandra's illicit relationship
with Federico becomes the subject of common gossip and therefore
public knowledge, the honour and reputation of the Duke will be destroyed. In Calderón's *The Surgeon of Honour* the characters are constantly afraid of speaking their thoughts for fear of being overheard.

236 *Recesses*: the reference is to two small rooms off the dressing-room in
which Casandra would keep her jewels, jars of cream, and suchlike.

237 *The tiger*: see note on *Not tigresses!*, p. 56.

238 *Medusa's glass . . . Circe*: in Greek mythology Medusa was the Gorgon
whose head had the power of turning to stone those who looked at her
directly. When Perseus killed her, he used his shield as a mirror in
order to avoid her fatal gaze. Circe was the enchantress who could turn
men into beasts. The meaning here is that Aurora, having seen such a
terrible thing in the mirror, has avoided the even worse fate of being
married to Federico, who has fallen under the spell of another Circe,
i.e. Casandra.

239 *melancholy*: see note to p. 209. Aurora has just stated that Federico has
paid no attention to her for four months. His melancholic state is therefore one which is deeply ingrained.

240 *Tiberius*: the Roman emperor in question was in fact Claudius, who had
his wife Messalina put to death for adultery. The incident is related by
Suetonius in his *Lives of the Caesars* (v. 39).

Messala: Messala Corvinus, described in Pliny's *Natural History* (vii.
90), is said to have forgotten his own name in consequence of a fall.

Biscay: one of the four areas of the Basque country, of which the capital
is Bilbao and to the north of which is the Bay of Biscay itself. The
Basques, having a language of their own which was quite different from
any other, frequently had problems with the grammar and pronuncia-
tion of Spanish and were mocked on that account. In Lope's original the
Biscayan is such a person, using the second person of the verb for the
first.

241 *[aside]*: this is not an indication that Federico is speaking to himself or to
the audience, unheard by Casandra, but that Federico and Casandra are
speaking to each other well away—apart—from the servants.

244 *The Church's enemies*: see note to p. 223.

Trajan: Marcus Ulpius Trajanus, Roman Emperor from AD 98 to 117,
was born in Spain. He was responsible for many notable foreign con-
quests.

245 *The mighty lion*: some critics seem to think that the reference is to the
Pope, but it is surely to the Duke, in whose service Ricardo has fought.

King Saul and David: the events concerning Saul and David are re-
counted in 1 Samuel, 18. Saul had made David captain of his troops,

and after his victories the women of Israel sang his praises, claiming that Saul had killed thousands, but David tens of thousands.

246 *well-known story*: the story told by Batín is one of Aesop's fables. It was familiar in Spain in both Latin and Spanish from the end of the fifteenth century.

247 *Hector*: see note to p. 109.

248 *religious brotherhood*: the original refers to Camándula, which was a religious order founded by Saint Romualdo at the beginning of the eleventh century in Camaldoli, near Florence.

250 *King David*: the events referred to here are described in the second book of Samuel. In order to possess Bathsheba, David arranged the death of her husband, Uriah. Thereupon the prophet Nathan predicted that punishment for David's sins would be brought upon him through the members of his own family. The prophecy was subsequently realized when David's daughter, Tamar, was raped by her half-brother Amnon and he in turn was murdered by her brother Absalom, who then rebelled against David.

251 *draw|Attention*: if the Duke calls witnesses, he will virtually ensure that the offence committed against him will become public knowledge, thereby guaranteeing his public disgrace.

254 *easily | Convinced*: the answer to his question is, of course, that he himself has had long experience of treachery and deception in matters of love.

258 *the crime is quickly buried*: the predicament of the Duke is similar to that of Don Gutierre Solís in Calderón's *The Surgeon of Honour*. Gutierre believes—mistakenly—that his wife Mencía is having an affair with Prince Enrique. Determined that the matter should not become public knowledge, which would inevitably mean dishonour, Gutierre arranges that she be bled to death by a doctor and that the death be reported as an accident. In this way Gutierre buries the offence against his honour along with Mencía's body.

260 *harsh and cruel rule*: the complaints against the harsh and ruthless demands of honour are frequent in Golden Age plays. In Calderón's *The Painter of Dishonour* the dishonoured husband, Don Juan Roca, similarly curses the inventor of such a merciless and tyrannical code. A similar attack on honour occurs in Lope's *The Dog in the Manger*.

robbed of his good name: dishonour very often stemmed not from the actions of an individual but from an offence done to that individual. See note to p. 214.

261 *A punishment without revenge*: if the Duke is simply the instrument through which God punishes the wrongdoers, there can be no element of personal revenge in his actions. The fact that his honour will be avenged in the process is less important, he suggests, than God's vengeance.

262 *Artaxerxes*: the reference is probably to Artaxerxes III, King of Persia

from 359 to 338 BC, who, in order to obtain the throne for himself, murdered his brothers and most of his relatives.

262 *Torquatus, Brutus, Darius*: Manlius Torquatus had his son executed when he took part in single combat, strictly forbidden by his father. Lucius Junius Brutus, founder of the Roman Republic, had his sons put to death when they conspired against him. Darius II, King of Persia, killed his own brother when the latter attempted to seize the throne.

264 *Restores it*: the Duke's honour is restored only in part by the spilling of Casandra's blood. It will be restored in full only with the death of Federico. Even so, it is possible that, since others know of their affair, it will still become public knowledge and that the Duke's attempt to conceal his dishonour will be in vain.

266 *a timely lesson for all Spain*: the lesson to be learned by the Spanish audiences at Lope's play was as much to do with the lustful, sinful nature of the Duke's life as with the behaviour of Casandra and Federico. They are punished with death, but the Duke's life will be darkened by the knowledge that he is responsible in more ways than one for the death of his only son.

The Oxford World's Classics Website

www.worldsclassics.co.uk

- Information about new titles
- Explore the full range of Oxford World's Classics
- Links to other literary sites and the main OUP webpage
- Imaginative competitions, with bookish prizes
- Peruse *Compass*, the Oxford World's Classics magazine
- Articles by editors
- Extracts from Introductions
- A forum for discussion and feedback on the series
- Special information for teachers and lecturers

www.worldsclassics.co.uk

American Literature

British and Irish Literature

Children's Literature

Classics and Ancient Literature

Colonial Literature

Eastern Literature

European Literature

History

Medieval Literature

Oxford English Drama

Poetry

Philosophy

Politics

Religion

The Oxford Shakespeare

A complete list of Oxford Paperbacks, including Oxford World's Classics, OPUS, Past Masters, Oxford Authors, Oxford Shakespeare, Oxford Drama, and Oxford Paperback Reference, is available in the UK from the Academic Division Publicity Department, Oxford University Press, Great Clarendon Street, Oxford OX2 6DP.

In the USA, complete lists are available from the Paperbacks Marketing Manager, Oxford University Press, 198 Madison Avenue, New York, NY 10016.

Oxford Paperbacks are available from all good bookshops. In case of difficulty, customers in the UK can order direct from Oxford University Press Bookshop, Freepost, 116 High Street, Oxford OX1 4BR, enclosing full payment. Please add 10 per cent of published price for postage and packing.